THE PASTOR
AS PUBLIC
THEOLOGIAN

THE PASTOR AS PUBLIC THEOLOGIAN

Reclaiming a Lost Vision

KEVIN J. VANHOOZER
AND OWEN STRACHAN

Baker Academic
a division of Baker Publishing Group
Grand Rapids, Michigan

© 2015 by Kevin J. Vanhoozer and Owen Strachan

Published by Baker Academic
a division of Baker Publishing Group
PO Box 6287, Grand Rapids, MI 49516-6287
www.bakeracademic.com

Paperback edition published 2020
ISBN 978-1-5409-6189-1

Printed in the United States of America

The Library of Congress has cataloged the hardcover edition as follows:
Vanhoozer, Kevin J.
    The pastor as public theologian : reclaiming a lost vision / Kevin J. Vanhoozer and Owen Strachan.
        pages cm
    Includes bibliographical references and index.
    ISBN 978-0-8010-9771-3 (cloth)
    1. Pastoral theology. 2. Christianity and culture. I. Strachan, Owen.
BV4211.3.V37 2015
253—dc23   2015001680

20   21   22   23   24   25   26   7   6   5   4   3   2   1

Contents

Preface

The idea for this book began with a shock (in a cemetery) and a scandal (in a seminary). Kevin was teaching in the University of Edinburgh when he happened to overhear two American tourists visiting Greyfriars Kirk (most come to see the statue of Greyfriars Bobby). The couple were looking at headstones when the wife suddenly blurted out, "Look, honey: they buried two people in one grave!" "What makes you think that?" asked her husband. The woman replied: "It says so right here: 'Here lies a pastor and a theologian.'"

It is not comic but tragic that we instantly understand what's funny about the anecdote, namely, the source of the woman's confusion. The average American is simply not used to thinking of pastors as theologians or theologians as pastors. However, for much of church history, the distinction we today take for granted would have been viewed as an aberration. What happened? The reasons are complex, and though we will mention some of them, the primary focus of our book lies not in understanding how we got here, but rather in proposing how best to move forward.

As to the seminary scandal, it happened during Kevin's office hours. A bright student came to ask advice about his future. Jordan (not his real name) was struggling between wanting to pursue further theological studies, which in his case meant applying for a PhD, and working in a church. He was not sure his grades were good enough (which was code for "Am I intelligent enough?") to get into a doctoral program. "Please don't tell me I'm only smart enough to be a pastor," he pleaded. I found the implication that pastors were somehow second-class intellects wrong-headed. It took me a few moments to rightly order my righteous indignation and collect my thoughts. Then I replied: "I regret to inform you that you may not have the right stuff. It takes wisdom and joyful enthusiasm to be a pastor. To get a doctorate, you need only have a modicum of intelligence and the ability to grind it out. I'm afraid you may only be qualified to be an academic, not a pastor. Ministry is a lot harder than scholarship."

These two anecdotes are revealing symptoms of a deeper problem, a vision problem that afflicts the twenty-first-century church, especially in North American evangelicalism. Though there are some shining exceptions, by and large there is widespread confusion about the nature, identity, and role of the pastor.

Elsewhere Kevin has said that the pastor-theologian ought to be evangelicalism's default public intellectual.[1] This claim intrigued Owen, a former doctoral student, eventually prompting him to ask Kevin to coauthor the present book. Kevin and Owen had earlier worked together in connection with the Center for Pastor Theologians (formerly known as the Society for Advanced Ecclesial Theology), a fellowship of pastors with PhDs committed to engaging in biblical and theological scholarship for the twin purpose of the theological renewal of the church and the ecclesial renewal of theology. We briefly toyed with the title *The Pastor as Public Intellectual*, only to realize that, as a stand-alone title, it would probably be misunderstood. The original idea has nevertheless sneaked its way back into these pages. Readers are therefore advised to pay special attention to what we mean by "public" and "intellectual," and why we qualify both with "theological."

So much for the origins of the book. As to the actual process of coauthoring, we quickly came up with the book's general structure after a little brainstorming. Owen wrote chapters 1 and 2 while Kevin wrote chapters 3 and 4, as well as the preface, introduction, and conclusion. Next we read and commented on each other's drafts, then revised accordingly. We are particularly grateful to "the twelve"—not our disciples but rather our partners in the ministry of the gospel—who have contributed testimonies to the importance of reclaiming the vision of the pastorate as a theological vocation. These twelve affidavits—testimonies from everyday ministerial life—provide concrete evidence that the vision we set forth, far from being an abstract ideal, is indeed being lived out on the ground. They also provide practical advice about how to make our vision more visible in the local church. These twelve minor (i.e., in terms of length) prophets give our book's argument, if not street cred, perhaps a bit more pew cred.

Speaking of credibility, what gives us, two *professor* theologians, the right to issue statements about the nature and role of the *pastor*? We are acutely conscious of our lack of qualification. To be a theologian in the academy is to risk becoming a disembodied mind. To return to the graveyard: the theologian who is not a pastor is like a soul that, after death, has been separated from its body (i.e., the church). We regret this unnatural "intermediate state," but as believers in resurrection, we look forward to the time when body and soul are reunited.

Theological minds belong in ecclesial bodies. We don't wish to exaggerate: there is a place for academic theology, but it is *second* place. First place—pride of theological place—belongs to the pastor-theologian. It is therefore only fitting that we dedicate this work to Gerald Hiestand and Todd Wilson, cofounders of the Center for Pastor Theologians, and to all the members of the Center's two Fellowships. These exemplary pastor-theologians embody the vision our book seeks to reclaim. May they be fruitful and multiply!

Owen Strachan
Kevin J. Vanhoozer

Introduction

Pastors, Theologians, and Other Public Figures

KEVIN J. VANHOOZER

"Societies become secular not when they dispense with religion altogether, but when they are no longer especially agitated by it."[1] The church, the society of Jesus, is similarly in danger of becoming secular, and in the very place where we would least expect it: its understanding of the clergy. This is not because churches are dispensing with the pastorate, but because they no longer find its theological character particularly exciting or intelligible. The idea of the pastor as a theologian—one who opens up the Scriptures to help people understand God, the world, and themselves—no longer causes the hearts of most church members to "burn within" them (Luke 24:32).

Too many pastors have exchanged their vocational birthright for a bowl of lentil stew (Gen. 25:29–34; Heb. 12:16): management skills, strategic plans, "leadership" courses, therapeutic techniques, and so forth.[2] Congregations expect their pastors to have these qualifications, and if pastors have an MBA, well then, so much the better. In these circumstances, it is hardly surprising that newly installed pastors so often complain that their seminaries failed to prepare them for the "real work" of ministry. Meanwhile, seminaries race to catch up to new expectations, reforming their curricula in ways that result in an even greater loss of theology in the church.

The story is complex and has been told elsewhere.[3] The basic gist: theology has been more or less banished from Jerusalem. Theology is in exile and, as a result, the knowledge of God is in ecclesial eclipse. The promised land, the

1

gathered people of God, has consequently come to resemble a parched land: a land of wasted opportunities that no longer cultivates disciples as it did in the past.

This book is written to hasten theology's return. It sets out to *reclaim* the land—the place where God dwells—by viewing the people of God as the principal medium with which the pastor works. The underlying conviction is that theological minds need to return to where they belong: in the body of Christ. The present book aims to reclaim the theological pedigree of the world's boldest profession and to awaken the church to the immensely challenging, exciting, and joyful vocation of being an evangelical pastor.[4] Specifically, the present book sets out to reclaim a lost vision for three sets of people.

We are writing to you, pastors (and not senior pastors only!), because you need help in recovering the theological heart of your vocation, whether it is defined narrowly in terms of "youth ministry," "Christian formation," "congregational life," "worship leader," or something else. It is no mean feat to speak of God, or to relate to people, yet pastors often (always?) have to do both things at once, regardless of their area of primary responsibility. Every pastor is responsible for communicating Christ and for ministering God's Word, at all times, to everyone, and in many ways. Ministering the Word of God to the people of God is the pastor's lifeblood.

We are writing to you, churches, because you need to be encouraged to rethink the nature, function, and qualifications of the pastors whom you appoint to serve you. In particular, you need to think hard about how to create the conditions in which the pastor is able to serve, and grow, as a public theologian (on which see below). We also think you need to reclaim your heritage as a theological community created by God's Word and sustained by God's Spirit, and to remember that you are part of God's story, not that God is part of your story (pastor-theologians ought to be able to help you with this!).

We are writing to you, seminaries, because you exist to train pastors and serve the church. You are in the broader academic world, but you must not simply be of it, for the simple reason that God's Word is "not of the world" (John 17:16). In particular, you need to do everything possible to minimize the ugly (and embarrassing) ditch between the so-called theoretical and practical theological disciplines. We also think that seminaries should do more to encourage their brightest students to consider working in the church rather than the academy, precisely because cultivating the wisdom of Jesus Christ on the ground requires more intelligence and creativity than writing scholarly articles does.

"Parched land" is a harsh but accurate term, describing a place where nothing can grow or be built. The "world"—men and women who have no personal knowledge of or relation to Jesus Christ—is indeed a land that has become barren (fruitless), overgrown with material, psychological, and ideological weeds that choke out life. This is indeed a tragic waste, a matter of deep heartache. The church, by way of contrast, should be a land flowing with milk and honey, and especially with the fruit of the Spirit. The pastor-theologian is a farmer of men and women, charged with working and keeping the promised land—the gospel of Jesus Christ—and with bringing streams of living water to urban and suburban deserts in order to cultivate the new creation in Christ. But we are getting ahead of ourselves. First, the bad news. . . .

Problem: A Lost Vision

Without theological vision, the pastors perish. Vision is what allows us to see where we are and where we are going. Sometimes what we see frightens and intimidates us: Peter walked on water with his eyes fixed on Jesus until he saw the wind (and presumably the waves), at which point he began to sink (Matt. 14:28–31). In Peter's case, physical vision overwhelmed his faith in Christ. Yet ultimately it is faith in Christ that enables us to see the world as it truly is: created, redeemed, and loved by God. This was the message of the prophets,

> *The faithful pastor will always be a countercultural figure.*

spokesmen for God who *said* what they *saw*, namely, that God is renewing all things through his covenant servant and his covenant people. If this is the vision, why are so many pastors sinking into the sea?

Sea storms are not the problem. What causes pastors to sink—or rather, to shrink from the theological task—are the waves of public sentiment and winds of public opinion that act as obstacles and temptations, hindering progress toward their vocation of bringing others to maturity in Christ (cf. Eph. 4:14). Make no mistake: it is not easy to go against the cultural grain, and in a real sense, the faithful pastor will always be a countercultural figure: what else can pastors be when they proclaim Christ crucified and then ask disciples to imitate their Lord by dying to self? The call to self-emptying will always be unpopular to those whose pockets and closets are full.

What makes the pastor's role even more challenging is the existence of three different sets of people, *three publics*, each with its own kind of opinion. By three publics, I mean three social realities, three locations into which pastors may speak of God and Jesus Christ: (1) the academy, (2) the church, and (3) the broader society.[5] Because God is the maker of everything that is, visible and invisible, and because the good news of God's self-giving love concerns the whole world, there is not a square inch in the cosmos, nor a single aspect of human existence, that does not somehow relate to God and the gospel. However, most of us live in more than one cultural world, and the way we talk about truth or the meaning of life varies considerably, depending on our social location (e.g., classroom, church, megaplex, etc.).

> *It is Scripture that illumines the life story of everyone who has come into the world.*

If there are college students and professors in a congregation, then the pastor needs to address all three publics, sometimes—in particular on Sundays—at the same time. How does one speak of God to a teenager, a graduate student, an unemployed carpenter, a working mother, a mayor, and a physics professor simultaneously?

David Tracy claims that the way a person does theology is largely a function of the particular public identified as one's primary audience. Each public has its own norms and forms of discourse and particular concerns, and these generate three types of theology: fundamental, systematic, and practical.[6]

Tracy is right to be concerned about religion dwindling into one more private option or personal choice. But his separation of theology into different modes of discourse may leave pastors either scratching their heads—or burying them in the sand. Clearly, the pastor's primary location is the church, but do pastors therefore get a free pass (no obligation) when it comes to speaking the truth in ways that address the general populace and college population? It is not easy to divide real people into three publics. The reality is that many of us indwell two or more of these social locations. Tracy is aware of this, and he argues that the task of systematic theology (the one most closely associated with the church) is to interpret Scripture in critical correlation with the contemporary situation. This comes close to the role of the pastor-theologian that we shall propose as well, though we are inclined to give pride of critical place to Scripture rather than the contemporary situation, not least because it is Scripture that illumines the life story of everyone who has come into the world.

Tracy's analysis nevertheless helps clarify the nature and scope of the challenge in reclaiming the vision of the pastor-theologian. Pastor-theologians must be trilingual, able to speak the language of all three social locations, or at least speak it well enough to ask directions (and give them). Our task in this book is to argue, first, that pastors must be theologians; second, that every theologian is in some sense a public theologian; and third, that a public theologian is a very particular kind of generalist. We begin by tracing how the vision of the pastor-theologian was lost in all three publics.

Academy: Power and Principality of Theology?

It is difficult to pinpoint the precise moment when pastors lost interest in theology, though clearly its migration to the academy was an important factor. Whereas the separation of church and state empowers the church to practice its faith and order its life as it sees fit, the separation of church and academy, combined with the migration of theology from the one to the other, has had a debilitating effect.[7] "No one can serve two masters" (Matt. 6:24). The sobering question for would-be theologians is whether one can both serve the needs of church communities and simultaneously satisfy the demands of contemporary scholarship.[8]

Theology first became a classroom endeavor in the medieval period, when cathedral schools developed into the first universities. For centuries afterward, theology nevertheless continued to thrive in the church, in large part because the most important theologians were also churchmen.[9] The more decisive break took place in the early nineteenth century, when Friedrich Schleiermacher, a pastor appointed professor at the University of Berlin (and widely considered to be the father of modern theology), restructured the theological curriculum into its now-familiar fourfold division—biblical studies, church history, systematic theology, and practical theology—and viewed their unity in terms of vocational training rather than subject matter. This "Berlin" model has proved influential in North American theological education and has led to a division between the classical or academic disciplines (the first three divisions) and the professional or practical disciplines (the fourth).

The perception that academic scholarship is abstract and "theoretical," disconnected from the issues of daily life, neither relevant nor necessary for "practical" ministry, is perhaps the single greatest prejudice against theological education (I can't say "misconception" because, alas, there is an element of truth in it as a description of many academic programs).[10] Relatedly, but from the other side as it were, the perception that the "practical" disciplines are nontheological, driven by pragmatism and influenced by secular models in the human sciences, is another prejudice that works against the notion of the pastor-theologian.

The further division in the academy between biblical studies and theology has only made matters worse. Scholars who study the Bible belong to their own professional organizations (e.g., the Society of Biblical Literature), read their own journals (e.g., *Journal of Biblical Literature*), and typically specialize not only in Old or New Testament but often in one genre or author (e.g., Pauline studies; apocalyptic). Theologians, likewise, have their own professional organizations (e.g., the American Academy of Religion), journals (e.g., *International Journal of Systematic Theology*), and areas of specialization (e.g., analytic theology; Reformed theology; Christology).

The would-be pastor-theologian wrestles not with flesh and blood, but with institutional powers and academic principalities. In particular, pastor-theologians must fight on two fronts. Pastor-theologians must contend, first, with the fact that much theology is written by academics for academics (i.e., "professor-theologians"). It is often difficult to translate or apply these technical treatments of specialized topics to the everyday needs of one's congregation. What has Thomas Aquinas's understanding of the persons of the Trinity as subsistent relations to do with visiting a deacon who has just learned he has pancreatic cancer, or the economic Trinity with church members struggling with unemployment? For that matter, what bearing does the doctrine of the Trinity have on the life of the church at all? To think that it has no bearing is as unfortunate as it is false. The doctrine of the Trinity is the lifeblood of the church and has everything to do with the identity and saving work of Jesus Christ, though it is true that professor-theologians do not always make this as clear as they should.[11]

Second, pastors also have to contend with the disciplinary Berlin Wall separating biblical studies and theology that is now a fixture in the academy.[12] Given the centrality of preaching in most pastors' lives, it stands to reason that, if forced this day to choose whom they will serve, most would opt for biblical studies. The problem, however, is that much of what pastors find in many scholarly commentaries on the Bible is hard, if not impossible, to preach. The standard biblical commentary produced in the modern academy typically treats the Bible as a historical document, often focusing more on the world *behind* the text (e.g., historical backgrounds, ancient Near Eastern parallels) than on what God is saying to the church today *in and through* the text about the subject matter *of* the text: God's plan of salvation summed up in Jesus Christ (cf. Luke 24:27; Eph. 1:9–10). Not a few biblical scholars think that the biblical commentary ought to be a theological no-fly zone.[13]

Institutional powers and academic principalities have put asunder what had originally been joined together under God: theology and church life, biblical studies and theology, pastor and theologian. While theologians shoulder the primary responsibility for demonstrating the importance of doctrine for discipleship, pastors cannot afford to neglect theology or to wait for someone to broker peace talks between biblical scholars, systematic theologians, and practical theologians. The way forward is for pastors and theologians to bear one another's burdens, responding together both to the ecclesial amnesia of the academy and to the theological anemia in the church. It is to the latter that we now turn.

Church: Pictures That Hold Pastors Captive

The past fifty years or so have seen a bewildering variety of images describing what pastors are and what they do. There continues to be widespread confusion about just what a pastor is. Indeed, the term "pastor" itself is a metaphor, taken from the Latin *pastor* for "shepherd." Metaphors are powerful imaginative instruments that can color our daily experience. George Lakoff and Mark Johnson speak about metaphors we live by, like "Time is money."[14] We can also speak about metaphors pastors minister by.

Metaphors pastors minister by often gain such a grip on the imagination that it sometimes becomes difficult to dislodge them. Such metaphors become pictures that hold us captive. These pictures often reveal more about the concerns of the age in which they were produced than they do about pastors themselves. Indeed, the prevailing picture of the pastor almost always reflects the broader intellectual and cultural influences of the day.[15] We can go even further and hazard the suggestion that pictures of the pastor are themselves tossed to and fro by waves (i.e., cultural trends) and by every wind of doctrine (i.e., academic trends).

Others have enumerated some of these leading pictures, so I can be brief. William Willimon rightly observes: "Contemporary ministry has been the victim . . . of images of leadership that are borrowed not from scripture, but from the surrounding culture—the pastor as CEO, as psychotherapeutic guru, or as political agitator."[16] There is nothing wrong with organizing programs and helping people, to be sure; the only question is whether these things *distinguish* the pastor's vocation. What, if anything, is distinct about the person and work of Christian pastors? This is the point on which there is ongoing confusion.[17]

Images of what pastors do affect what seminaries do in turn. Everything hinges on the dominant metaphors that guide pastors' ministries. Joseph Hough and John Cobb trace the rise and fall of four models that prevailed at different times in American church history: the "master" of biblical and theological knowledge (late eighteenth and early nineteenth centuries), the "revivalist" (nineteenth century), the "builder" of churches and congregations (late nineteenth and early twentieth centuries), and the "manager" of people and programs (twentieth century).[18] Willimon has helpfully updated this list of images that hold us captive, or threaten to do so, in the twenty-first century. In addition to older images (e.g., political negotiator, therapist, manager) that continue to enjoy considerable influence, he mentions the media mogul and community activist.[19] Still other images include the "living human document," the wise fool, the moral coach, the agent of hope, the diagnostician, the indigenous storyteller, and the midwife.[20]

This proliferation of images is a sign of the lack of consensus, even widespread confusion, over just what pastors are and are supposed to do. As one observer of the pastoral scene puts it: "It is hard to conceive of persons in other lines of work—construction workers, hair stylists, dentists, tennis pros, even systematic theologians or biblical scholars—bothering to concoct so steady a diet of metaphorical equivalents to their chosen fields."[21] Yes, there are more literal descriptions of the pastor's work, like "soul care" or "preacher." But these beg the question as to what kind of care is worth giving and what preachers have to say that no one else does.

What do pastors have to say and do that no one else can say and do? This question brings to a boil the issue of the pastor's distinct identity. In 1967 Karl Menninger delivered the Stone Lectures at Princeton Theological Seminary and was struck by the number of seminarians who had doubts about their profession. Menninger suggested that one reason for their doubts was the disappearance of sin. Many aberrant behaviors previously considered "sins" (e.g., gluttony) are now considered symptoms of some underlying psychological or social condition, and others (e.g., cohabitation before marriage) have largely been declassified as sins due to widespread social acceptance. Menninger rightly describes the significance of this semantic development:

"The disappearance of the word 'sin' involves a shift in the allocation of re-sponsibility for evil."[22] This shift from sin to symptom also means that people are more likely to turn for help to those who understand the problem. If the problem no longer is sin, but some underlying psychological, social, or perhaps even biological condition, one may wonder, "What distinct help can a pastor give? What distinct service can a pastor perform?

Uncertainty about what pastors are good for is not good for a minister's soul. This was undoubtedly one factor that explained a headline in the *Chicago Sun-Times*, April 9, 1971: "Young Clergymen Bewildered, Disillusioned." It is easy to see why. If the metaphor by which you minister is "helping profes-sion," then you had better be prepared to say what kind of help you have to give.[23] But this was precisely the problem. What do pastors have to say and do that other people in the helping professions—psychologists, psychiatrists, social workers, and so forth—are not already doing, and often doing bet-ter? Today there are many "experts" in a variety of helping professions who are offering solutions and strat-egies for coping with diverse personal problems. Mental and social health services offer up a smorgasbord of

Pastor-theologians must have confidence that the ministry of the gospel is more than another helping profession.

theories and therapies for what ails us. Pastor-theologians must have confi-dence that the ministry of the gospel is more than another helping profession.

John Leith makes a similar point by asking, "What do churches have to say and do that no other institution can?" His Reformed answer: minister God's Word, in preaching, teaching, and counseling. To this we shall want to add, "and shape God's people so that they reflect the new humanity that is in Christ." Leith's follow-up question to Presbyterians could easily be broadened to include evangelicals: "Can we today claim that in terms of competence our Presbyterian preaching matches the performance of the best professional people in the community in the discharge of their duties—that is, the best lawyers and doctors?"[24] One need not accept the suggestion that pastors are professionals (professional *what*?) to grant Leith's point: it is hard to apply standards of excellence to what pastors do unless we first determine what it is they are (or should be) doing.

One especially powerful metaphor for the pastor is therapist: someone who addresses personal or interpersonal problems and effects healing.[25] The temptation here is to rely overmuch on gold taken from other mines (e.g., clinical psychology) in order to appear "professional": "Seminarians would learn the rudiments of human nature from psychiatrists, psychologists, and social workers who knew those rudiments; that is, from the professionals who currently control the definitions of them."[26] The net result of this heavy conceptual borrowing, however, was that the clergy as a group "had lost any vestige of cultural jurisdiction over personal problems."[27] No longer can one apply theological categories to personal problems. This leads to the disappearance not only of "sin," but also of "grace" and even "God."[28]

Another powerful metaphor for the pastor is manager of religious people and programs. Indeed, the image of the pastor as manager resonates so well with contemporary culture that it has captured the imagination of mainline Protestant, Roman Catholic, and evangelical churches alike. According to George Weigel, for much of the twentieth century the Roman Catholic Church "came to conceive the Bishop of Rome as the chief executive of a global enterprise whose local leaders (the bishops) were, in effect, papal delegates (or branch managers) for their respective areas."[29] Individual parish priests were thought of "as men who had been licensed to conduct certain types of ecclesiastical business: baptizing infants, hearing confessions, celebrating Mass, presiding at weddings and funerals."[30]

Eugene Peterson has been especially critical of the managerial metaphor: "The vocation of pastor has been replaced by the strategies of religious entrepreneurs with business plans. . . . I love being an American, . . . [but] I don't love the rampant consumerism that treats God as a product to be marketed."[31] The most insidious image of all is that of the pastorate as professional *career*: "American pastors, without really noticing what was happening, got our vocations redefined in terms of American careerism. We quit thinking of the parish as a location for pastoral spirituality and started thinking of it as an opportunity for advancement."[32] A cultural picture holds pastors captive, even in the church. It is therefore to the loss of vision of the pastor-theologian in broader society that we now turn.

Society: The Predicament of Public Discourse

Once upon a time, as recently as the nineteenth century, pastors were revered and respected public figures with a certain degree of social status. Pastors were frequently the best-educated persons in small- and medium-sized towns, the village intellectuals. When we fast-forward one hundred years, we see how radically things have changed: the popular portrait of the pastor these days is often no more than a stereotypical caricature (e.g., the self-righteous and repressed prude, the self-inflated and well-dressed megalomaniac). Sadly, there is more than an element of truth behind these cardboard cutouts. David Rambo's 1999 play *God's Man in Texas* (based on a true story) features an eighty-one-year-old pastor of a megachurch who cannot bring himself to hand over the reins of power to his younger assistant. The pastor's arrogance, stubbornness, paranoia, and self-doubt are on conspicuous display.

David Wells worries that the average churchgoer confesses faith in Christ but ingests the same cultural fare as everybody else. Television shows and films shape our perceptions of everything from the good life to the "normal" family. Wells does not mention it, but popular culture both reflects and influences how people view pastors. Novels, television, and films exercise far more influence than live plays on the general population. What kind of public figure does the pastor cut in these media?

David Larsen, professor emeritus of preaching at Trinity Evangelical Divinity School, has undertaken a labor of love in combing Western literature and examining the various models of ministry depicted by works of fiction over the centuries. This is serious business: fiction is not simply the realm of make-believe but rather a laboratory of human possibility, where the human condition is being examined and tested. A serious work of fiction can explore the challenges and yield insights into the life and work of a pastor more effectively than textbooks because they give readers a taste of the reality, not a lesson but a vicarious experience.[33] Pastors can learn important things about the possibilities and pitfalls of their vocation by seeing how others respond and act in diverse particular situations.[34] Moreover, works of fiction both reflect and inform a society's understanding of what it is to be human—and what it is to be a pastor. Larsen observes: "More in Western literature is negative about the ministry than is positive. This is evidence which requires reflection not a knee-jerk reaction."[35]

Name a work of fiction in which the hero is a faithful pastor (extra points if you can think of a novel whose protagonist is an *evangelical* pastor). It is an interesting, though painful, thought experiment. Two come to mind: John Buchan's *Witch Wood* (published in 1927 but set in the seventeenth century) and Marilynne Robinson's *Gilead* (published in 2004 and set in the twentieth century). Larsen devotes one chapter of his book to images of the faithful pastor ("Cameos of Character and Courage") and examines "A Parson's Tale" in Chaucer's *Canterbury Tales*, Oliver Goldsmith's *The Vicar of Wakefield*, Anthony Trollope's *The Warden*, and the character of Father Tim from Jan Karon's *Mitford* series, among others. Alas, these promising pastoral profiles give way to five chapters focused on novels that cast a less flattering light on ministers, where one encounters images of inadequacy, immorality, intellectual infidelity, familial instability, and vocational obscurity respectively. Along the way readers are treated to ministers in the fiction of Jane Austen ("peerless prigs"), George Eliot ("the stately, stiff and starchy"), and Charles Dickens ("ministerial menagerie").

Earlier I mentioned my pet theory that, like biblical commentaries, our images of pastors serve as barometers for larger ideological and cultural trends. Much work needs to be done to make good on this hypothesis. Although many books have been written on the way in which God or Jesus Christ have been portrayed in film, studies that focus on church leaders are far less common.[36] Yet film and television are probably more instrumental than books in influencing public perceptions of the pastor. Richard Wolff's *The Church on TV: Portrayals of Priests, Pastors, and Nuns on American Television Series*[37] is one of only a handful of studies attempting to discern what popular culture tells us about Americans' attitudes toward the church and its leaders. His book studies television series that feature members of the clergy (e.g., *The Flying Nun*, *Father Dowling Mysteries*, *7th Heaven*). What does it say about pastors, or contemporary culture, that one is much more likely to find a television show about a pastor-detective than a pastor-theologian?

To be a pastor-theologian—to speak of God before some public—is to be squarely in the public eye. And this is the pastor-theologian's predicament: to make truth claims about God in a way that satisfies the requirements of public discourse. Karl Barth, a pastor-theologian, expressed the predicament this way: "*As minister we ought to speak of God. We are human, however, and so cannot speak of God.*"[38] Here Barth reflects not only on the limits of human language and reason but also on the difficulty of giving an account of one's *authority* to make claims about God. What creature is qualified to speak of its Creator? How dare we, or anyone, speak of God?

Who has the authority to speak of God? Whose say-so counts, and why? Coming up with a satisfactory answer—satisfactory in the sense of being acceptable in the public square—is no easy feat, in part because a hermeneutics of suspicion holds sway there. A well-known postmodern suspicion holds that all truth claims are either partial, a reflection of one's particular social situation, or oppressive, a reflex of the will to power. These suspicions increase exponentially when the subject of our public discourse is God and when the discourse appears to benefit either an individual (in terms of status, money, or power) or a special interest group.

Sinclair Lewis's novel *Elmer Gantry* encapsulates the contemporary predicament of public discourse about God. The novel follows the life and career of Elmer Gantry from the time of his conversion in college to his ascent as a pastor with national recognition. The book became the number one fiction bestseller in 1927 and in 1960 became a film, with Burt Lancaster playing the part.[39] In the story, Elmer Gantry confuses his desire for praise with a call to the ministry: he is addicted to "the drug of oratory" and finds the most receptive crowds in churches.

Elmer Gantry is exactly what postmoderns warn us about: a person who cares more about rhetoric, and the recognition that dramatic speaking brings, than about truth, and the suffering that speaking truth might entail. Lewis says, "Elmer assumed that he was the center of the universe." For Gantry, God is an ingredient in Gantry's own story, rather than Gantry being a bit player in God's story. To paraphrase Milton's Satan: better to reign in my own narrative than to be a minor character in God's.

Elmer Gantry is a cautionary tale of ministerial hypocrisy. Gantry personifies exactly what worries Eugene Peterson: that pastors will pursue successful careers rather than vocations, the magnification of their own names rather than the name of Jesus Christ. Sinclair Lewis has word-crafted a portrait of the pastor as a young professional. In some respects, the story is remarkably contemporary even though it is now almost a hundred years old. The temptation for pastors to view themselves as the heroes of their own story is even more palpable in an age of televangelists and megachurches: "If the ministry is simply a profession, then everything about the ministry is professionalized. For the minister, then, the only question becomes, how will this promote, or impede, the advancements of my ministerial career?"[40]

Here is the central paradox: the pastor is a public figure who must make himself nothing, who must speak not to attract attention to himself but rather to point away from himself—unlike most contemporary celebrities. The pastor must make truth claims to win people not to his own

> *The pastor must make truth claims to win people not to his own way of thinking but to God's way.*

way of thinking but to God's way. The pastor must succeed, not by increasing his own social status but, if need be, by decreasing it.[41] Moreover, when pastors do refer to themselves, they must follow the example of the apostle Paul, acknowledging themselves to be public sinners who have received yet continue to need God's grace and mercy (1 Tim. 1:15). Finally (again like Paul), pastors must engage in public speaking about general matters, such as the meaning of life, for which there are no publicly acknowledged credentials, unlike specialists whose expertise is publicly recognized.[42] The situation is even more difficult and paradoxical when we factor in the widespread assumption that public figures are neither trustworthy nor truthful. As recent opinion polls make clear, people are largely disenchanted with public figures, especially those connected with some institution or organization whose interests they are seen to represent.

To be sure, people tend to trust neurosurgeons when they need operations or pilots when they fly. However, neurosurgeons and pilots are specialists with demonstrable instrumental knowledge (i.e., they operate on brains, they operate jet planes). Here, then, is the pastoral predicament. To explain what contribution they make to the public good, pastors must either specify the kind of specialist knowledge they have *or* take up the mantle of the intellectual: one who claims a certain kind of intelligence and authority to speak about matters of general philosophical and social import (e.g., the meaning of life). Let us take one example: Alexander Solzhenitsyn's 1978 commencement address at Harvard University, "A World Split Apart," tackles no less a topic than the trajectory of Western civilization. Solzhenitsyn states—in public!—that the West has lost its civic courage, perhaps because it is materially well off and organizes itself in legalistic (i.e., procedural) ways that focus on rights and freedoms more than responsibilities and purpose. No doubt he raised many American eyebrows when he discussed whether he could in good conscience propose the West as a model for his country to follow (at the time, he lived in the Soviet Union): "No, I could not recommend your society as an ideal for the transformation of ours. Through deep suffering, people in our own country have now achieved a spiritual development of such intensity that the Western system in its present state of spiritual exhaustion does not look attractive."

Solzhenitsyn's address becomes more pointed, even sermonic, toward the end. The fight for our planet, he says, is "physical and spiritual, a fight of cosmic proportions." Solzhenitsyn concludes with something like an altar call: a summons to recover a spirituality beyond materiality. He mentions Evil (with a capital *E*), and locates the problem at the very foundation of modern thought: "the proclaimed and practiced autonomy of man from any higher force above him." Remember, he is speaking at Harvard, making grand claims at a secular university with hundreds of academic specializations. And then he goes and does it. He risks offending polite society by mentioning God: "The West has finally achieved the rights of man, and even to excess, but man's sense of responsibility to God and society has grown dimmer and dimmer."

Solzhenitsyn's address impresses because of the scope of its claims. There are some grand assertions: not predictions, but predications. To "predicate" is to affirm something about something. Predication is the preeminent act of the preacher (the French term for "sermon" is *prédication*). "Predication" is also linked etymologically to the term "predicament," and we need only consider Solzhenitsyn's address, or a sermon, to see why. To affirm something about something as large as Western civilization, not to mention *God*, is no easy task, particularly when one is speaking in front of an audience. If speaking in public is people's greatest fear, how much more fearful is making public predications about God and the world! It is precisely this ability—to speak meaningfully and truthfully about broad topics of ultimate social concern— that is the mark of what I shall call a public intellectual. The question before us is whether a pastor-theologian is also a public intellectual.[43]

Proposal: The Pastor-Theologian as Peculiar Public Figure

To this point we have painted a negative picture of the contemporary situation: many churches have lost the vision of what a pastor is and should be doing. As we have seen, pastors have a plethora of metaphors from which they can choose a ministering style to follow. Consequently, pastors are leading the people of God in a number of ways and different directions. Without a biblical vision of the pastor, the people of God may indeed perish; they certainly will fail to prosper. How, then, are pastors to lead? The rest of our book attempts to answer this question by setting out a positive proposal, thereby leading the church out of its wanderings in the wilderness of modernity.[44]

So we lay out our argument: First, pastors are and always have been theologians. Second, every theologian is in some sense a public theologian, a peculiar sort of intellectual, a particular type of generalist. A key underlying conviction of our argument is that one need not be an academic to be an intellectual. Pastor-theologians are not necessarily persons with high IQs, but they must have high TQ (theology quotient).[45] Third, the purpose of the pastor-theologian being a public intellectual is to serve the people of God by building them up in "the faith that was once for all delivered to the saints" (Jude 3). Let me briefly comment on these three points.

Theologian: Saying What God Is Doing in Christ

Pastors are and always have been theologians: yet this, one of those things that should not have been forgotten, was forgotten . . . and lost. As we saw in the brief narrative above, theologians and pastors have been torn asunder, relegated to separate publics (the academy and the church, respectively). "The invention of 'theologians' as the professional authorities on Christian belief may turn out to be one of the really damaging things that have occurred in the history of the church."[46] This claim may be startling, but the rationale is straightforward: the existence of "professional" theologians suggests that pastors and laypeople—those who are not paid to do theology—either cannot do theology (because they don't have the "smarts") or do not have the authority to do so (because they do not have the right academic qualifications).

> *To be a Christian theologian is to seek, speak, and show understanding of what God was doing in Christ for the sake of the world.*

Theology is too important to be left to the "professionals." Every human being is accountable before God for responding to the knowledge of God that is available in the things that have been made, including the human heart (Rom. 1:19–21). "Ordinary" Christians (if such a thing exists) are able to read the word of God with a measure of understanding and, again, are responsible for responding in love, trust, and obedience. Theology is part and parcel of faith's incessant drive for greater understanding. Theology is inevitable: William Ames says it is simply the teaching [*doctrina*] of "living to God."[47] Theology is about speaking and doing the truth divinely revealed in Jesus Christ.

Thus theology is the attempt to speak well of God, and to live to God's glory, on the basis of the story of God recounted in the written Word of God (the Old and New Testaments). The adjectival qualifier "Christian" signals the centrality of Jesus Christ to the theological project. Jesus Christ is God's final word (Heb. 1:2), God's fullest disclosure (1:3a), and the agent of God's greatest work (1:3b). Jesus Christ is the alpha and omega of both revelation and redemption. He is the sum of divine wisdom and the fulfillment of the divine plan for the world (Eph. 1:8–10). The risen Christ claimed that everything in Scripture centers on him (Luke 24:27). *To be a Christian theologian is to seek, speak, and show understanding of what God was doing in Christ for the sake of the world.* Christian theology sets forth in speech *what is in Christ*: God; true humanity; all visible and invisible created things; the reconciliation of the world to God (2 Cor. 5:19).

Public: Involved with People in and for Community

We have already provided a brief account of the three publics or social realities in which theologians speak of God. Which public—church, academy, or society—do we have in mind in speaking of the pastor as public theologian? One might think that "public" is the most obvious of our three terms, but in fact it is the most elusive, largely because there is an already-established sense of public theology in use (see below). This conventional meaning is partly, but not wholly, what we have in mind when we use the term. Our use is more radical because it reclaims the etymological root (*radix*) of the term "public" (from Latin *pubes*, "adult population," and *populus*, "people"). Pastors are public theologians because they work in and for the public/people of God, for the sake of the public/people everywhere.

Public theology: The prevailing view. The standard meaning of public theology is "theology in and for the public square." The particular public in view is society: the broader *polis*. Public theology is therefore theology that addresses common concerns in an open forum, where no particular creed or confession holds pride of place. Specifically, public theology concerns the forms and means by which individual Christians (and churches) should bear witness to their faith in the public square (i.e., society at large). A brief discussion of how this kind of public theology relates to public policy, political theology, and the social gospel will help clarify the ways in which our proposal for pastors as public theologians is distinct.

Public theology is first and foremost a reaction against the tendency to privatize the faith, restricting it to the question of an individual's salvation. As we shall see in later chapters, the church is not a collection of saved individuals but the culmination of the plan of salvation: to create a *people* of God. More-over, Christ is Lord over all areas of life, and it is important that Christians avoid dualistic ways of thinking so as not to compartmentalize discipleship (for Sundays and the privacy of one's home only) from citizenship (for the rest of the week, schools, and the workplace). As Max Stackhouse, one of the leading pioneers of public theology reminds us, the public world—schools, businesses, clinics, theaters, restaurants, factories, and so forth—is the place where disciples live out their faith: "If these public worlds are the larger con-text of our ministries, we need a public theology to deal with that reality."[48]

According to Stackhouse, there is a sharp distinction between public and political theology. Political theology is the analysis and criticism of politics (the art or science of governing) and the relationship of church and state. The focus is on the organization, distribution, and use of political power to address social issues. By way of contrast, public theology does not treat every problem as if it were a political problem, nor does it solve every public problem through reforming the state or by creating a moral majority.[49] Public theology aims to win not elections but arguments: "It intends to offer to the world not 'our confessional perspective,' but warranted claims about what is ultimately true and just that pertains to all."[50] Stackhouse would have the pastor be a public theologian in the sense of "the philosophical-theologian of universally valid truth and justice, . . . [able] to equip the people to discern how and where, *in the world*, the traces of God's truth and justice may be unveiled."[51] Hence Stackhouse worries that theology, "the only thing pastors have to offer the world not already better offered by others,"[52] is too often cut off from public discourse, as if no public warrant could be offered. Consequently, Stackhouse calls pastors to take on "the additional burdens of recovering and recasting the fundamental notions of truth and justice in the larger domain of public discourse."[53]

The editors of a volume honoring Max Stackhouse put it this way: "As Chris-tians are in the world, so must the church be, and thus the church must have a public theology."[54] Public theology involves critical reflection on how Christians should bear witness in the public square. One of the key issues is whether, and to what extent, Christians can and should make common cause with those of other faiths, or no faith at all, over social issues. The prevailing view, represented by Stackhouse, is that public theology should employ forms of discourse and arguments that are in principle intelligible and acceptable to all, regardless of their faith (or lack thereof). In short: public theology is theologically informed discourse aimed at the general public. Interestingly, Stackhouse believes that seminaries ought to be preparing pastors to be public theologians who can in turn teach their congregants to be "lay public theologians."[55]

Richard Mouw speaks of an earlier generation of North American evangelicals who believed the church's primary task was to get people ready to go to heaven: "Paying too much attention to major issues of public policy was viewed as bordering on a God-dishonoring 'worldliness.'"[56] The ethos today is quite different, especially among evangelicals in their twenties and thirties, many of whom are "public intellectuals not driven by a partisan political agenda."[57] Evangelicals are now speaking out on a variety of public policy issues, from the more familiar moral issues such as abortion and poverty to newer ones like immigration and health care.[58]

Does being a public theologian mean that pastors must be proponents of the social gospel, focusing their ministry and energies on this-worldly problems—peace and justice issues such as economic inequality, racism, and so forth?[59] The basic problem with early twentieth-century debates about the so-called social gospel was that they were too polarized: its proponents emphasized the this-worldly nature of the kingdom of God, the proclamation and practice of liberating people from oppressive institutions here on earth; its opponents stressed the otherworldly nature of the kingdom of God, a proclamation of the individual's liberation from sin and death. Pastor-theologians should not have to choose between a "social" and a "spiritual" gospel, for there is only *one* gospel (Gal. 1:6–7), "an eternal gospel" that concerns the heavens *and* the earth (Rev. 14:6).

> *Pastor-theologians should not have to choose between a "social" and a "spiritual" gospel, for there is only* one *gospel (Gal. 1:6–7).*

The good news is not merely that individual souls go to heaven but especially that God has established "a kingdom of priests and a holy nation" (1 Pet. 2:9; cf. Exod. 19:6; Rev. 1:6), that he has established social peace in reconciling Jews and Gentiles (Eph. 2:14), and that all this will come to fruition on a new earth. While the gospel has implications for public affairs—after all, the whole created order is being renewed in Christ (2 Cor. 5:17)—it must not be reduced to a series of positions on public policy issues. Rather, public theology is, or ought to be, the church's demonstration of life in Christ—to the glory of God and for the sake of the world.

Public theology: An ancient-future alternative. Conventional public theology is therefore not what we have in mind. We're reclaiming a lost vision, not jumping on a bandwagon. Miroslav Volf is closer to what we have in mind when, sailing between the Scylla of the social gospel and the Charybdis of old-time gospel, he encourages Christians to be neither a domineering presence in society nor an otherworldly absence, but rather a witnessing presence. There is no one single way that the church ought to relate to contemporary culture, though the goal in every cultural encounter is to be salt and light by bringing the Christian vision of God and the good life into the public sphere: "A vision of human flourishing and the common good is the main thing the Christian faith brings into the public debate."[60] Public theology is, for Volf, a matter of the church bearing public witness to Jesus Christ, the embodiment of the good life. Living well to God—which is to say, along the grain of the created order being renewed in Christ—cannot be anything other than public theology; Christian doctrine gives specific content to the meaning and lived shape of love, justice, and being human.

Rowan Williams provides another good example of a public theologian. The lectures that make up his *Faith in the Public Square* treat issues that are of concern for the academy, church, and broader society alike: secularism, the environment, justice, religious diversity, to name but a few. These lectures are "worked examples of trying to find connecting points between various public questions and the fundamental beliefs about creation and salvation from which (I hope) Christians begin in thinking about anything at all."[61] His aim is not to influence public policy directly, nor to proclaim the gospel directly in the public square, but rather indirectly to communicate a vision of Christian faith in corporate life oriented around God. A religious life is a material life in a particular place, a life that takes on "the task of ensuring a habitation for God, . . . [who] is visible only when a human life gives place, offers hospitality to God, so that this place, this identity, becomes a testimony."[62]

The present book shows "a still more excellent way" of conceiving and practicing public theology. It is radical in that it returns to the etymological roots of the term *public* (see above). Public theology, as we are using the term, means "theology made up of people": "God is at work to bring into being a people under his rule in his place. The idea of the people of God, therefore, stands at the heart of biblical theology."[63] The church—not a building but the people of God speaking, acting, and perhaps suffering—is that "place" where God and the kingdom of God best come into focus.

Lesslie Newbigin describes the life of the local congregation as a "hermeneutic of the gospel," the best indication of what it really means to speak of the new creation in Christ.[64] This too is public theology—and public truth. It is precisely as a hermeneutic of the gospel that the church is a hermeneutic of the Triune God, for what the church lives out, as the people of God, is the life of Jesus Christ and the fellowship with the Father in the Son through the Spirit, made possible by Christ's person and work.

> *The church is thus a public spire in the public square.*

Trinitarian faith is not a private opinion but a public truth. The doctrine of the Trinity underscores how the Father extends familial relations through the Son and Spirit to those who were formerly not his people.[65] The church is thus a *public spire* in the public square, the visible, sharp-pointed part of a structure "knit together" [*symbibazō*] in God's love made flesh in Christ (Col. 2:2, 19).[66]

The church is wherever the people of God—the public of Jesus Christ—live out their faith and fellowship in the Triune God. This is public theology: children of light being "the light of the world" (Matt. 5:14), bringing to light "the plan of the mystery hidden for ages" (Eph. 3:9), namely, "to unite all things in [Christ]" (Eph. 1:9–10). In Newbigin's words: "This *koinōnia* is indeed the very being of the Church as a sign, instrument, and foretaste of what God purposes for the whole human family."[67] The church, as public spire, is the vanguard of the realization of this plan. As such, the church is the public truth of Jesus Christ, and not only truth, but also the public goodness and public beauty of God's plan of redemption.

The church is a set-apart public whose life and witness serves the interests of the broader public (i.e., "every nation and tribe" [Rev. 14:6] as well as every social caste and class). Public theology has to do with shaping the people of God to be a hermeneutic of God's love. Eugene Peterson comments: "But our vocation is very public in what we do in relation to God and a life of love. . . . [People] see and are influenced either for good or bad by the seriousness and reverence in which we order our response to God (the showcase for this is Sunday worship); and they notice the way we live with our families and our friends."[68] In sum: the people of God are the public place where what is in Christ is remembered, celebrated, explored, and exhibited. Stated simply: the pastor's task is to help congregations "to become what they are called to be."[69] This is the ancient-future task of the pastor as public theologian.

Pastor: A Public Theologian qua Organic Intellectual Who Builds Up People in Christ

While all Christians participate in the ministry of building one another up in Christ, the pastor's distinct office is to serve others by building them up into Christ through the ministry of Word and sacrament in particular. Ordination means that a person is set apart for a special purpose, namely, for special service in the house of God. The pastor is thus the *prime* (but not the sole) minister, the first (servant) among equals. The pastor is a household manager [*oikonomos*]—a "steward of the mysteries of God" (1 Cor. 4:1 altered). Our immediate concern is to describe the pastor's work as a public theologian, a person who works with people, both in the sense of working alongside them as their colaborer but also in the sense of working with people as the very medium ("material" sounds too impersonal) of the ministerial art. The pastor's special role is to edify or build people up: in particular, to build them into the house of God, the body of Christ, and the fellowship of the Holy Spirit.

Stanley Woodworth, my high school French teacher, once described the peculiar passion for his own vocation in the following terms: "The joy of teaching lies not in one's own enthusiasm for the students, or even for the subject matter, but rather for the privilege of introducing the one to the other." If this is true of French, chemistry, or history, how much more is it true of the pastor's passion, which is not simply love of God or love of people, but rather the love of introducing the one (people) to the other (God)? The pastor's special charge is to care for the people of God by speaking and showing and by being and doing God's truth and love. Success in ministry is determined not by numbers (e.g., people, programs, dollars) but by the increase of people's knowledge and love of God. This is the only way "to present everyone mature in Christ" (Col. 1:28).

By this point, I trust that it is clear why pastors must be public theologians. But why must pastor-theologians, in order to minister truth, be "intellectuals"? Recall the example of Solzhenitsyn: an intellectual is one who speaks meaningfully and truthfully about broad topics of ultimate social concern. The truth of God's plan for the world is clearly such an issue! Indeed, even to speak of "God" is to address a topic of potentially universal concern. Surely we would not want those who speak of God's plan for the world to be *anti*-intellectual?

The way forward is to clarify further what we mean by "intellectual." There are intellectuals in the academy as well as society, but they are few and far between. Most academics are specialists: they know a lot about a little, but they are often tongue-tied when forced to address the big questions. Yet on a regular basis pastors address the big questions: issues of life and death, meaning and meaninglessness, heaven and hell, the physical and spiritual. To be sure, no church wants a pastor to be an intellectual if this means being so cerebral and preoccupied with ideas that one cannot relate to other people. This kind of intellectual is so theoretical as to be practically good for nothing. However, the kind of intellectual we have in mind is a particular kind of generalist who knows how to relate big truths to real people.

Tom Oden examines a number of titles for a minister (e.g., curate, rector, priest, reverend, etc.) and finds that each illumines an aspect of the pastor's work; he concludes by stating his preference for pastor as the central paradigm, with shepherding as the pivotal analogy.[70] Our English term "pastor" comes from the Latin *pastor* ("shepherd"). More important, Jesus designates himself the Good Shepherd (John 10:1–18) and commissions Peter to "Feed my sheep" (John 21:17). Oden thinks the shepherding analogy still works in a postindustrial society because the Bible spells out how the shepherd relates to the flock. Interestingly enough, one of the marks of a good shepherd also characterizes intellectuals: "The shepherd characteristically is 'out ahead' of them, not only guiding them, but [also] looking out, by way of anticipation, for their welfare."[71]

> *The kind of intellectual we have in mind is a particular kind of generalist who knows how to relate big truths to real people.*

The flock of Jesus Christ is threatened not by lions, bears, or wolves (1 Sam. 17:34–35) but by false religion, incorrect doctrine, and ungodly practices—not to mention "principalities and powers" (Eph. 6:12 KJV). Consequently, pastors who want to be out ahead of the congregations must be grounded in the gospel and culturally competent. Public theologians help people understand the world in which they live and, what is more important, how to follow Christ in everyday as well as extraordinary situations. "Ministerial leadership is, first and finally, discipleship,"[72] though to follow Jesus one has to know where one is, what is happening, and which way is the way of truth and life. *The pastor-theologian is the organic intellectual of the body of Christ, a person with evangelical intelligence who is "wise unto salvation"* (2 Tim. 3:15 KJV).[73]

An organic intellectual is neither a genius—an individual thinker alone with their own brilliant thoughts, detached from everyone else—or a member of an elite intelligentsia. Rather, the organic intellectual articulates the needs, convictions, and aspirations of the social group to which they belong. The organic intellectual brings to the level of speech the doctrines and desires of the community.[74] The organic intellectual is not a product of the Ivy League but homegrown, as it were, on the farm. Most important, the organic intellectual does not speak down to people: "The mode of being of the new intellectual can no longer consist in eloquence, which is an exterior and momentary mover of feelings and passions, but in active participation in practical life, as constructor, organizer, 'permanent persuader,' and not just a simple orator."[75]

> *The pastor-theologian is the organic intellectual of the body of Christ, a person with evangelical intelligence who is "wise unto salvation."*

In chapter 4 we shall return to the role of the organic intellectuals in exposing and combating cultural hegemony—the pervasive worldview that circulates in so many ways and places that we are often not even aware of it.[76] The immediate focus is on the organic intellectual as one who serves the interest of a minority or oppressed social group by giving it prophetic and poetic voice—speech designed to clarify the situation, express the aims and objectives of the community, and rouse it to act in ways consistent with its vision.[77] The organic intellectual knows that ideas matter, that they have the power to give shape to certain forms of life. The organic intellectual is therefore no abstract theorist but rather a social activist and political organizer.

The term "organic intellectual," we submit, gives concrete content to the analogy of the pastor as shepherd. The pastor-theologian is an advocate for the community of God's people. The pastor-theologian takes every false thought captive to sound doctrine (2 Cor. 10:5)—christological "ideas" (i.e., truths) that are both indicative of life and life-giving. David Wells points out that historically church leaders were scholar saints, pastors who were "as comfortable with books and learning as with the aches of the soul."[78] Reading books—not only of theology but also of fiction (see chap. 3 below)—ought to be part of every pastor's plan of action for staying out ahead of the flock.

It bears repeating: pastor-theologians ought to be not academics but intellectuals, and organic intellectuals at that. Pastor-theologians do not need to be the smartest people in the room—but then again, neither did the apostles. When Peter and John were arrested for preaching the gospel and dragged before the Sanhedrin, they had to do some impromptu—or rather inspired—public speaking: "This Jesus is the stone that was rejected by you, the build-ers, which has become the cornerstone. And there is salvation in no one else" (Acts 4:11–12). When the high priests, elders, and scribes—all highly trained in rabbinic schools—saw the "boldness" of Peter and John, they were aston-ished, for "they perceived that they were uneducated, common men" (4:13). Peter and John were not geniuses but apostles: they knew something that the Sanhedrin did not know ("He is risen!"), and they knew it not because they were clever but because they were told. They *had* learned something, something that astonished the Jewish leaders, but they had not learned it at school. Luke tells us that the Jewish leaders recognized that Peter and John "had been with Jesus" (Acts 4:13)—an understated way of acknowledging their educational qualifications.

Pastor-theologians know something that others do not know, and they know it because the Bible tells them so. To be instructed by the Spirit in the school of the Scriptures is to be, as Peter and John had been, "with Jesus." What pastor-theologians know is something quite particular (what God was doing in Christ) but has enormous, even universal, implications. The organic intel-lectual resembles not the fox, who knows many things, but rather the proverbial hedgehog, who knows one big thing: in this case, what God is doing to create a people for his treasured possession (Exod. 19:5; Deut. 7:6; 14:2; 26:8; Mal. 3:17; Titus 2:14; 1 Pet. 2:9).[79] Pastor-theologians, like Sol-zhenitsyn, are generalists, yet with a differ-ence: pastor-theologians give voice to the church's understanding of the meaning of life—or rather, the meaning of the life hid-den in Christ (Col. 3:3). Pastor-theologians know something particular and definite,

> *The pastor-theologian is an organic intellectual who is present as the mind of Christ, which animates the body of Christ.*

but strictly speaking, it is not specialized knowledge. The pastor-theologian is rather a special kind of generalist: *a generalist who specializes in viewing all of life as relating to God and the gospel of Jesus Christ.* Better: the pastor-theologian is an organic intellectual who is present as the *mind of Christ,* which animates the *body of Christ.*

Prospect: The Ministry of What Is "in Christ"

> For I decided to know nothing among you except Jesus Christ and him cruci-
> fied. (1 Cor. 2:2)

> I count everything as loss because of the surpassing worth of knowing Christ
> Jesus my Lord. (Phil. 3:8)

This book sets forth a vision for reclaiming the vocation of the pastor-
theologian, but that does not mean that it is for clergy only. On the contrary,
we have written this book for congregations as well; they too need to reclaim
a lost vision. Every Christian is a living exposition of the Bible, charged with
responding to God's Word for using the Spirit's gifting to build up the church:
"Let the word of Christ dwell in you richly, teaching and admonishing one
another in all wisdom, singing psalms and hymns and spiritual songs" (Col.
3:16). Still, our primary focus is on the work of the pastor-theologian. What
should organic intellectuals—minds activating the body of Christ—actually do?

We have introduced the pastor as a public theologian, a participant in the
divine economy of "public works." The pastor is one who works with people,
ministering the reality of Jesus Christ in order to build people up into the
house of God. To minister the reality of Christ is to do more (but not less)
than inform others about him. The apostle Paul speaks of the "surpassing
worth" of knowing Christ. Paul wants to know the Christ, the whole Christ,
and nothing but the Christ. The pastor-theologian communicates this knowledge not to swell people's heads but to transform their hearts. Ultimately
what pastor-theologians want their people to know is "the love of Christ that
surpasses knowledge" (Eph. 3:19).

A brief outline of what follows may prove helpful. Our four chapters treat
the biblical, historical, systematic, and practical theology of the pastorate
respectively. Chapter 1 examines the way in which Scripture, both Old and
New Testaments, describes those who lead the people of God. God has never
left his treasured possession without some kind of shepherd leaders to guide
them. Special attention is given to the distinct theological nature of the pastoral
office. Chapter 2 surveys the rich tradition of the pastor-theologian in church
history. Special attention is given to certain figures that either exemplify or
wrote on the theological nature of the pastoral office. Together, these two
chapters make the case that we are indeed reclaiming a lost vision rather than
creating a novel version.

Chapters 3 and 4—the systematic and practical theology of the ministry of the word of God—were conceived of and are best read together, two edges of the same sword (Heb. 4:12). Chapter 3 focuses on systematic theology, the attempt to say in a coherent and culturally intelligible way *what is* "in Christ" (and then conform to it). We present a threefold ministry of theology: a ministry of reality, understanding, and edification of the people of God. Chapter 4 likens the pastor-theologian to a master craftsman whose work is to build God's house. Special attention is given to the pastor-theologian's practical work of preaching, catechesis, celebrating the Lord's Supper, and organizing the people to do works of love that are simultaneously demonstrations of the gospel's truth.

The book concludes with fifty-five summary theses on the pastor as public theologian. These theses bring the pastor's theological work with God's people into sharp focus. Some readers may object that our vision is too idealistic: pastors are too busy or too finite to do everything we say they should be doing. We understand the concern, but we believe that the problem has less to do with time, energy, or native intelligence than it does vision and priority. Theology is not a luxury, an optional extra (like leather trim), but a standard operating feature (like a steering wheel) of the pastorate. The briefer essays interspersed throughout the book from twelve pastors attest in various ways to the possibility and practicality of our vision. These contributions provide evidence that theology is part and parcel of ministry on the ground, not least because the pastor's task is to conform disciples, here on earth, to Christ as he is in heaven.[80]

Six Practical Steps toward Being
a Pastor-Theologian

GERALD HIESTAND

If there's one thing I've learned as a pastor, it's this: being a pastor-theologian requires swimming against the current of the atheological swamp that is contemporary evangelicalism. I don't claim to have it all figured out, but over the years I've developed an increasing sense about some of the moves a pastor can make to help facilitate the pastor-theologian vision. Here are six steps I've found helpful, in a roughly descending order of importance.

1. *Hire staff with the vision.* Building a staff that values theology will go a long way toward creating a robust theological culture at your church. I don't recommend making staffing changes solely with a view to the vision for pastor-theologian. But if you oversee hiring at your church and are in need of new ministry staff, let me strongly encourage you to look for ministry partners who share your sense of calling to theological leadership. If you can find a like-minded ministry partner who is serious about theological leadership, you will have overcome perhaps the most significant hurdle of the pastor-theologian: isolation. This is a significant disability to the pastor-theologian. In previous church contexts, I didn't have a working environment where I could pop my head into the room next door and talk about how Aquinas's prioritization of the intellect in

conversion causes him to arrive at a different *ordo salutis* than Calvin, and the implications this has for the doctrine of total depravity (for example). Now I do, and the difference it has made is significant.

2. *Get networked.* Not all of us are in a position to hire a fellow pastor-theologian. Perhaps your church is too small. Regardless, the next most important thing you can do is to become involved in a network of like-minded pastors. Whether a denominational gathering, or an informal meeting of outside colleagues, having a network of pastoral peers who desire to engage theologically is crucial to sustaining your theological calling. Use Skype, connect at ETS, or start a blog. I meet monthly with two other pastors via Skype to discuss what we've been reading and writing. The regular exchanges help to provide a sense of camaraderie and motivate me to keep sharp theologically. However you do it, find a group of pastors who are committed to engaging theologically.

3. *Make your study time a priority in your weekly schedule.* The expectations and demands of your congregation will almost certainly push you away from theological study and writing. If you're going to do it, you need to make it a priority in your schedule. I've found that setting aside my mornings works best. I spend the first hour or more in prayer and Scripture reading. The next hour is given to my Latin primer (I'm working on a PhD in classics), and the next three hours or so are spent engaging with theology. This year I'm reading Augustine on Mondays, Barth on Wednesdays, and contemporary theology/scholarship on Thursdays. Tuesday mornings I spend on church-vision matters. Staff meetings, counseling appointments, and administrative duties are reserved for the afternoon. Of course, sometimes I have to pull up from studying: funerals, emergencies, and so forth press in occasionally. Don't just study for your next sermon or teaching assignment. Too many pastors are merely one step ahead of the theological train. The lifeblood of the pastor—whether your congregation realizes it or not—is a steady intake of rich theology, prayer, and Bible reading. Stop feeling guilty about prayerfully reading Calvin's *Institutes*, or Athanasius's *On the Incarnation,* or Augustine's *The Trinity*. Theological study isn't something a pastor fits into his schedule after fulfilling other pastoral duties; rather, theological study *is* the pastor's duty. For the good of your congregation—for the good of your preaching, teaching, counseling, and capacity to offer pastoral care—it is vital that you not neglect to feed yourself.

4. *Get buy-in from the leadership of your church.* If you're doing your job right, the leadership of your church should eventually come to value the time you spend in your study. After all, they should reap the benefits of your theological labor more than anyone else. But depending on the history of your church, robust theological study might be seen as a distraction from your pastoral duties. Go slow here. Since theology has been separated from the church for so long, it is no longer self-evident to many congregations that sustained theological engagement by their pastors is a good thing. This will need to be demonstrated, not simply argued. In any case, it's important that you help your church leadership see that your pursuit of theological scholarship is not ancillary to your calling as a pastor but rather a vital part of it. And this leads to my next point.

5. *Don't forget that theology exists for the church—your own church first and foremost!* If the people in your congregation don't feel valued as your first priority, then you are being a poor pastor-theologian, regardless of how smart you become. Your congregants should feel like your study time is about them, not simply your next writing project or sermon. If they start to begrudge you your study time (e.g., "He spends all his time holed up in his office"), you will need to take a hard look at yourself and your priorities. It is very likely that your study time isn't really as much about God and his kingdom as you think it is. Theology serves the church, not the other way around. Love for God and his people should drive us to our books. If love for God and our congregations isn't the fuel that powers our study, then what are we really studying for?

6. *Stop calling the place where you work an "office" and start calling it your "study."* Never, under pain of excommunication from the pastor-theologian club, refer to your study as an "office." If this is the first time you've heard this rule, you get three free passes to break the habit. After that, your pastor-theologian license will be suspended. Semantics matter. If you call your study an office, the people in your church will have a certain set of expectations regarding what you do during the day. If you refer to it as your *study*, they will come to have a different set of expectations. The room with all your books, where you read the Scriptures and pray—that room is your study. Start referring to it as such, and your people will come to expect that studying is part of your calling.

Seven Ways to Theologize as a Pastor

JOSH MOODY

I am grateful for the opportunity to share some thoughts on the theme of this volume, and I view its task as one of utmost importance. I also, strangely, view the subject itself to be of almost intensely ironic proportions! Perhaps some of that will come across as I briefly remark the following.

1. It seems to me principally *impossible* to be a pastor at all without doing some sort of theology (good, bad, or indifferent)! The role of the pastor, however understood in whatever tradition we are from, is in some shape or form about bringing people face-to-face with the reality of God, responding to his call upon their lives, and shaping their existence by the truth of eternity. If that is not *theological*, I do not know what it is. This seems to be a statement of such sheer obviousness—it probably appears so to you—that I feel somewhat embarrassed to begin by mentioning it. Perhaps we can rapidly move on to the next remark. But before we do, I make an observation: a pastor is inevitably doing theology in some shape or form; that this is not obvious to all is surely at least in part because of the intimidating nature of the word "theology," which appears to mean "academic," when it should mean something more like "with relation to God, or the study of God, or the word of God," or something along those lines (which is not my purpose to define here).

2. In my view our *core* task as pastors is to "preach the word" (2 Tim. 4:1–2), whether via the pulpit, hospital bedside, small groups, personal conversations, or however. If that is the case, then we *are* engaged in theology. The way to do that is to give ourselves to that core task of proclamation and to do it as well as we can.

3. Pastoral (practical) questions/issues have *theological* roots. For instance, suppose you are meeting with a leader who seems perpetually involved in various hidden machinations and manipulations to get his own way, even at the cost of relationships with other people; and you discover that he cannot accept that if he is uninvolved with something personally, he can leave it to God to bring good into the situation. You are (again, at least

if not more) *at root* dealing with a theological issue related to God's sovereignty. Tracing these connections from the practical, to the theological, and back again is frequently the key to making pastoral progress; did not Jesus say "out of the heart the mouth speaks" (cf. Luke 6:45)?

4. Practicing as a theologian pastor means devoting *time* to word ministry. That means such deceptively simple matters as . . . carving out time in the calendar to study the Bible, avoiding interruptions, prioritizing preparing to preach, and so forth. Lest anyone feel that it is only possible for someone like me to say this, who has a large supportive staff team, I briefly mention that in my first senior pastor role at a church revitalization, my desk was an upturned box in our rented living room. My laptop had a screen saver that said, "Preach the word," and I prioritized that. (It didn't mean I avoided visitation, counseling, administration; I just did that after I had done the study time in the morning each day.)

5. Practicing as a theologian pastor means becoming expert in *translation*. That is, we need to translate the big words of our systematic theologies, textbooks, and fancy academic hoopla into the vernacular of everydayness. And we need to do it without being patronizing, remembering that technical words usually function as a shorthand. Avoiding technical terminology does not mean you have to say less; it merely means you have to take more time to say it.

6. Practicing as a theologian pastor means continuing to develop *confidence* in the Word itself (not just books about the Bible); thus from the Scriptures you can find new light to address the particular situations you are facing. Elite professors at elite universities who produce lengthy volumes can end up intimidating some into thinking they need to sound like them, or copy them; far from it. By all means read their stuff, but then be inspired to get your own stuff from the Bible itself (*sola Scriptura*).

7. Practicing as a theologian pastor means doing the task of *evangelism*. If anyone feels that to be a theologian, they need to give up personal evangelism, or proclamation evangelism, or evangelistic events, then I would rather see them give up theology and keep on doing evangelism. That said, evangelists need to be careful; most heresy in the Christian church historically has come from well-meaning evangelistic efforts to reach people by shifting important theological concepts to make them more acceptable in ways that have unforeseen effects. As a rule of thumb,

if you are primarily an evangelist, my strong counsel to you is this: read theology, but don't try to write it. More bunk has been written by brilliant evangelists who should have just stayed with doing evangelism than I have time to mention. Evangelists are frequently the most gifted among us, be it noted, but their overwhelming God-given desires to reach the lost have a strong tendency to lead them up the garden path, theologically. Pastors should do evangelism too, of course, and as they do it, they will be faced with theological challenges, apologetic challenges, to which they need to formulate theological responses, to guard and guide the evangelism of the churches.

Foundationally, because of the biblical description of pastor as "pastor-teacher" (cf. Eph. 4:11), those who are earning their living from the church as pastors must teach. Yet those who are earning their living from the academy as teachers, though they must be committed to the church and its flourishing, need not necessarily pastor.

PART 1

Biblical Theology and Historical Theology

1

Of Prophets, Priests, and Kings

A Brief Biblical Theology of the Pastorate

OWEN STRACHAN

In the middle of the world's greatest city, he prayed.

It was 11:20 a.m. in London on June 18, 1944, the era of Churchill, Hitler, Roosevelt—larger-than-life figures. It was a period of terrible, totalizing war, when all the world seemed a mix of fire and smoke. The British Empire had effectively ended. In recent decades, it had controlled nearly a quarter of the globe's land area, making it the largest superpower in human history. Now the city at the center of it all was under siege. In the midst of the aerial invasion, with sirens blaring and chaos reigning, D. Martyn Lloyd-Jones stood before his people. He was a few hundred feet from Buckingham Palace, but he sought the ministrations of a higher kingdom.

It was a frightening time in London. The Germans' remote-controlled bombing of the city had begun only days before and had already caused tremendous casualties—over ten thousand in a week, according to historian Iain Murray.[1] It was the stuff of madness, catastrophic for the city. "The Doctor," however, was not deterred. The whole church could hear the plane closing in, but Lloyd-Jones had begun his "long prayer," his pastoral prayer, and did not stop. The whine overhead grew too loud, though, for him to continue, and so he paused. All the congregation held their breath.

Then the bomb fell. There was a massive explosion, debris fell from the ceiling, and the structure of the chapel cracked. One woman had closed her eyes moments before; she opened them, saw fine white dust covering her fellow parishioners, and thought she was in heaven. The congregation rose to their feet; panic was in the air. The church members waited to see how their pastor would react. Would he weep, or run, or·panic?

He would not. With sirens screaming, the doctor resumed his pastoral prayer. At its close, he told the people that any who wished to do so could move under the gallery for safety. A deacon then went to the podium, dusted it off, and returned to his seat. Lloyd-Jones resumed his place at the chapel's front and opened his Bible. Without missing a beat, he began to preach God's Word to the people.

The text was Jude 20, which reads in context with verse 21: *But you, beloved, building yourselves up in your most holy faith and praying in the Holy Spirit, keep yourselves in the love of God, waiting for the mercy of our Lord Jesus Christ that leads to eternal life.*[2]

The Ministry of the Old Covenant in the Old Testament

In this remarkable scene, we witness a stunning portrait of public courage. We also find a memorable portrait of the nature of Christian ministry in a fallen world. Even as the world burns, the pastor leads the church to continually build itself up in the Spirit's power.

We may not all minister in such a visceral setting, but there is indeed a battle in which every pastor fights. Pastoral ministry is a local campaign in the broader war between the living God and the principalities and powers of the air (Eph. 6:12). We see the effects of this conflict: Dispirited people. Fighting. Constant criticism of the staff. Adultery. Susceptibility to false teaching. Families riven by poor leadership. Once-vibrant disciples walking away from the faith. Despair at finances. Depression. Many modern battles are fought block by block; the spiritual conflict is fought person by person. The site of this conflict is the human heart, the inner core encompassing all the hopes, thoughts, dreams, schemes, and conflict of a God-imaging person.

If the site of this conflict is the human heart, standing at the center of the congregational battlefield is the pastor. In the momentous conflict between

God and the devil, the pastor goes ahead of the people, representing them to God, protecting them from Satan. Yet despite the central role of the pastor in the church's work to advance the kingdom of Christ in the great war of the ages, there has been relatively little biblical-theological reflection. Accordingly, there has been minimal effort on the part of exegetes and theologians to connect what one could call the "covenant officers" of the Old Testament to the pastor-theologian of the New Testament. This is not to say that priests, prophets,

Pastoral ministry is a local campaign in the broader war between the living God and the principalities and powers of the air (Eph. 6:12).

and kings have been left outside the doctrinal camp. Calvin and many others have used the term *munus triplex* (trifold office) to great profit, for example, in piecing together how Christ fulfilled these offices. We are all the richer for these cross-covenantal connections—conditioned, as they must be, by both Israelite expectation and realization in Christ.

With respect to Calvin and those who have followed in his wake, however, we must also ponder how the offices of priest, prophet, and king are connected to the pastor. In what follows, we invite the ancients back into the conference room. We make the crucial and rather commonsense point that the work of priests, prophets, and kings informs our understanding of the work of the pastor. It is true, of course, that the pastor of the new covenant does not directly fulfill these roles. The priestly line, for example, is both ended and fulfilled in the person and work of Jesus Christ. However, essential elements of the work of the old-covenant priest, prophet, and king have transferred to the pastorate of the new covenant. To put this more plainly, the threefold Old Testament offices show us the rough outlines of who, by virtue of biblical-theological inheritance, the pastor is and is to be: one who holds, before God and the people, the office of covenant minister.

In our reconstruction, then, the pastor is no recent innovation, but the occupant of the office that is the realization of the ministry of past figures. The pastor is the inheritor of the privilege and responsibility of leading the people of God, specifically, via the new-covenant ministry of reconciliation. As we shall see, this divine appointment too requires pastors—like prophets, priests, and kings before them—to speak God's Word to God's people, intercede to God on behalf of the people, and model the wisdom of salvation life.

The Priest: Set Apart for a Set-Apart People

As the Old Testament progresses, we meet three classes of covenant officers. Individuals filling this role might be a priest, prophet, or king;[3] the common denominator was that each played some crucial role in leading the people of God to live according to the gracious covenant made by God with Abraham in Genesis 12 and affirmed by God with Isaac, Jacob, Moses, and David.[4] "I will be your God, and you will be my people" is the capstone promise of the Old Testament, with Yahweh's direction to Abraham to look at the stars and see the number of his descendants as the spectacular representation of the fulfillment of this promise. Grace is what Yahweh promised his descendants, and grace is what he provided.

Yahweh mediated his grace through a number of set-apart individuals. He did not have to act in this way, but he chose to use human mediators to bless and guide his people. The Lord has always desired a kind of holy kinship and partnership with humankind, the pinnacle of his creation, and he has always appointed stewards to serve his people and draw them deeper into the experience of his mercy and favor. Nowhere is this seen more prominently than in the three covenant offices. The priest was at the center of the divine-human relationship. The priest was a man set apart by the Lord to be an on-the-ground mediator of holiness between God and the people. The Levitical priests were charged with the performance, oversight, and even enforcement of numerous rituals, prescriptions, and ceremonies. When the people strayed from God's law and failed to keep it, the priest called them back and made sacrificial provision to cure their unholiness. The driving concern of the priest's ministry was the cleanness of the people. In all their duties, whether conciliatory or didactic, the priests sought the actualization, even the enfleshment, of God's holiness, his set-apart nature, in the life of Israel. Yahweh was holy, and his people were to be holy.[5]

Holiness was no abstraction in ancient Israel.

The priest was appointed to seize on this reality and make it practical. He was called to provide means by which an unclean people could share a vital bond with a holy God. In his teaching and ceremonial work, the priest brought the greater claims of the law to life in the everyday experience of the people. Holiness was no abstraction in ancient Israel. To be sure, it had been declared in summary form on Mount Sinai. The source of this declaration signaled its inherent character. What God had said was far above the earth, originating in the counsel of heaven. But the law itself was rigorously relevant to the life of God's people. "You shall have no other Gods before me" was not only a directive, but also a statement about the way things are: there *is* no God other than Yahweh.

When Moses came down from the mountain, he brought the law with him. His descent symbolized the fate of God's code: it was to travel into the bloodstream of Israel. It was to be enculturated in the life of the nation. Holiness was not only becoming to the people of God; they were also to become holy. They were to take on the character of God himself by setting themselves apart from the nations, by living the law, inviting it to shape every part of their lives. When they failed to do so, as they inevitably did, they needed the priest to atone for their sin. The law was designed to influence their lives by setting them apart for a holy way of life; when they failed to own this high calling by obeying the law, they depended (as we elaborate below) on the sacrificial min-

> *Holiness was not only becoming to the people of God; they were also to become holy.*

istrations of the priest. The law was thus an all-encompassing reality for the people of God; it was their standard and their steadfast guide. If we borrow from the book of Revelation at this point, we could say that the people were to eat the law, ingest it, and be made healthy and holy by it (Rev. 10:10). The priests were those, then, who came to the people and said "Eat this law."[6]

The priest of the old covenant filled a high and holy office. No priestly servants more exemplified the set-apart nature of this work than the Levites. In Numbers 18:3–7, Yahweh's words to Aaron, head of the Levitical order, demonstrated that the Levites directly served the Lord and stewarded the holy directives of God, under penalty of death if they failed to do so:

> They shall keep guard over you and over the whole tent, but shall not come near to the vessels of the sanctuary or to the altar lest they, and you, die. They shall join you and keep guard over the tent of meeting for all the service of the tent, and no outsider shall come near you. And you shall keep guard over the sanctuary and over the altar, that there may never again be wrath on the people of Israel. And behold, I have taken your brothers the Levites from among the people of Israel. They are a gift to you, given to the LORD, to do the service of the tent of meeting. And you and your sons with you shall guard your priesthood for all that concerns the altar and that is within the veil; and you shall serve. I give your priesthood as a gift, and any outsider who comes near shall be put to death.[7]

Fulfillment of this momentous call meant that the nation would follow the Levites in worshiping the Lord in a holistic sense, on pain of death if they stray. All of life was to be normed by the law of God, and the priests were to ensure that the people embraced the gracious and beneficial rule of God's law. The daily prohibitions and commands—what fabrics to wear, what foods to eat, how to handle cases of adultery, and much more—were not, contrary to the suggestion of some popular books, arbitrary.[8] The law initiated the people of God into a way of life distinctly different from all others around them. The focus of the law, then, was not the performance of certain bizarre rituals. All the people's obedience to the law created a community that not only worshiped the Lord, but also was transformed by their worship into a righteous nation, a holy people who would do right as God does right. The set-apart God instituted a set-apart class, the priests, in order to administer a set-apart nation.

The instrument of this sanctifying process was the law. It was good, and good for the people (see Ps. 119). But though pure and righteous, the law could not save the people, and it never did (see Gen. 3:21; 15:6). As steward of the law, the priest was charged with overseeing the sacrificial system of the Old Testament, which provided symbolic cleansing of the sinfulness of the people. In this role, the priest "exercised a mediatorial function, standing between God and human beings."[9] The priest, then, was no mere code enforcer of ancient Israel, no divinely instituted regulator buried in scrolls and stipulations. The Levites were heralds of divine grace.

This is clear in Leviticus 16. On the Day of Atonement, the Levites performed the central sacrificial rites of the believing community, stewarding annual ceremonies that in graphic detail pictured the evil nature of sin and the bloody nature of divinely provided atonement for sin. The Day of Atonement was a visceral affair, filled with blood and fire and death and, at the pulsing core of it all, the realized hope of forgiveness through repentance. The people could be pure. The priest symbolized all this as he made atonement for the pervasive uncleanness of himself, his surroundings, and his nation:

> Then he shall kill the goat of the sin offering that is for the people and bring its blood inside the veil and do with its blood as he did with the blood of the bull, sprinkling it over the mercy seat and in front of the mercy seat. Thus he shall make atonement for the Holy Place, because of the uncleannesses of the people of Israel and because of their transgressions, all their sins. And so he shall do for the tent of meeting, which dwells with them in the midst of their uncleannesses. (Lev. 16:15–16)

We should read all of Leviticus 16, and beyond this the ministry of the law, as an early—though not ultimate—fulfillment of the Lord's promise to make for himself a covenant people. Because of sin, this people needed cleansing. The priests provided ritual cleansing. As James M. Hamilton Jr. has said, "The transfer of guilt from the worshiper to the sacrificial beast, and then the death of the beast, cleanses the worshiper of sin." Accordingly, "The worshipers are saved by faith through the judgment that falls on the sacrifice."[10] It was not the ceremony that saved the worshipers in the old covenant, but faith in the one who staged the dramatic ceremony, trust in God's gracious provision for sin. Following the symbolic enactment of atonement, the priest worked on a daily basis to ensure that this cleansed identity passed over into the daily life of the nation.

The ministry of the priests was thus a performance of hope. It was grace that the priests offered the nation, not in a physically deliverable way, but in the promise of cleansing offered all the penitent of the community. We must not miss, then, that this was directly *theological* work. So far from the mere observance of arcane rituals, the Levites acted out the very story of redemption before the people of God. They showed the people who they were, drawing their attention to their uncleanness and to the bloody solution to this problem. They showed the people, most importantly, who Yahweh was. He had not left his people in their impurity. Instead, Yahweh stipulated sacrifices so that they could stand in his presence and represent him to the nations.

Through a human mediator, Yahweh communicated his gracious action to his people. He did this not so that they would content themselves with their innate superiority, but that they might reach out in hope to others and "mediate his presence to the world."[11] To be set apart in biblical terms is not an escape in any sense: it is actually a call to be plunged into the work of saving others. Israel was not created and chosen by God simply for their own edification. Even when the nation was just a glimmer in Abraham's eye, the reflection of the unnumbered stars on the nighttime sand, Yahweh intended it to be a blessing to the world beyond (Gen. 12:2; cf. 22:18).

> *To be set apart in biblical terms is not an escape in any sense: it is actually a call to be plunged into the work of saving others.*

The Prophet: Proclaimer of Objective Revelation

What the priests offered the people in tangible form, the prophets rendered in speech. The prophet was set aside by the Lord to speak the will and announce the mind of God. Through declaration, exhortation, scorching rebuke, and entreaties to taste God's lavish mercy, the prophets interpreted the times through an unflinchingly theocentric perspective. Fools for God, they were seized by Yahweh, and they spoke for him. As Walter Brueggemann has said, "In their appearance, Yahweh is taken to be directly and palpably present in Israel."[12] The prophets manifested not only the mind of God but also his very presence. He was with his people. He had not left them. When they wandered, as they frequently did, he wanted them back.

As the ruler of all things, Yahweh appoints his prophets to speak with no less than divine authority. The call of Jeremiah to the prophetic office shows that he was given just this role.

Then the LORD put out his hand and touched my mouth. And the LORD said to me,

"Behold, I have put my words in your mouth.
See, I have set you this day over nations and over kingdoms,
to pluck up and to break down,
to destroy and to overthrow,
to build and to plant." (Jer. 1:9–10)

Many years before Jesus interpreted these words as a statement of his own kingship, Jeremiah spoke them as an act of transcendent proclamation. Jeremiah's words, we could say, ruled. Hearers might reject his declarations and teachings from God, but that would not mean they could choose a different path from that promised them by the Lord.

The prophets exercised the ministry of truth-telling. Truth is not something outside of or beyond God. Truth is rather a matter of the reliability of God's Word, of God's covenant faithfulness. He *is* truth, according to the prophets (see Isa. 25:1; 65:16), for there is nothing more reliable than the promises of Yahweh. His character never wavers; his word never fails (Isa. 55:11). The prophets served the people of Israel by continually reminding them of this fact. God's promises would not fail. Even when it seemed otherwise, when his faithful remnant felt Assyrian boots and Persian spurs on their neck, Yahweh had not forgotten his covenant people. Even in the worst of times for God's chosen, grace was at hand, even as judgment would eventually come for sin.

God was not shouting across no-man's-land. There were no empty threats. God's warnings too were truths stated to a wayward people, a people who continually strayed from the covenant of grace that called them to faithful trust and holy living. The prophets reminded the people of their identity even as they took on the role of prosecutors on behalf of God's broken covenant. Even in times of captivity, the people had a divine commission. The prophets shouted themselves hoarse in exhorting Yahweh's people to keep the covenant and not forget it.

If God's people would listen, they would find another way that did not lead to destruction. This was the way of preservation and salvation. Despite the terrors of Yahweh's justice, the people of Jacob—the wrestler—were not to cower before their Lord.

> But fear not, O Jacob my servant,
>   nor be dismayed, O Israel,
> for behold, I will save you from far away,
>   and your offspring from the land of their captivity.
> Jacob shall return and have quiet and ease,
>   and none shall make him afraid. (Jer. 46:27)

We learn much about what prophets did from such texts. Jeremiah warned of judgment and assured the people that they could not outpace the Lord. He called them to account for their sins and urged them to repent, promising them the grace of God if they follow the Lord—and even, because of Yahweh's regular forbearance, if they did not. Walter Kaiser has observed that Jeremiah, with fellow prophets, offered "objective revelation" that was true—and not only true, but also "food for the prophet's own soul," a summation that captures the living nature of prophetic witness.[13] The prophets were the media for communicating the word of God, a word that was divine, steadfast, and true. What God said came to pass. When the people doubted this, or denied the truthfulness of God's ways and the certain outcomes of his plans, the prophet stood up in their midst and refuted their wisdom, which was no wisdom at all.

To be a prophet was not only to declare what was unchangingly true but also to address the changing times of the people of God from a God-centered perspective.

To be a prophet was not only to declare what was unchangingly true but also to address the changing times of the people of God from a God-centered perspective. Egypt might seem promising; Babylon might seem indestructible; but the prophet existed to handle these contextual challenges, to remind the followers of Yahweh that a greater sovereign reigned in the world of men. In this way the office of prophet was an office unlike any other. "Accurate mediator of God's will," as Paul House has said, "interpreter of the world, and herald of lavish, even shocking, grace"—this was the prophet.[14]

In sum, the prophet spoke for Yahweh. Such a claim sounds audacious in the present day, when one scarcely dares to speak even for one's own mind, unsettled as it may be. The prophets did not have the luxury of citing cognitive dissonance for their inability to speak up. They were charged by Almighty God to voice his mind, and they were given the very words of this divine figure to say. This was a powerful commission. As Wayne Grudem has explained, "The prophets' words are words of God; therefore the people have an obligation to believe and obey them. To believe God is to believe his prophets (2 Chron. 20:20; 29:25; Hag. 1:12), for the words of the prophets are the very words of God (2 Chron. 36:15–16)."[15]

The prophet trembled at this responsibility. When called to his office by Yahweh, the prophet did not customarily beat his chest and roar. One thinks, for example, of Ezekiel. Confronted by a vision of the likeness of God's appearing, he did not instinctively bask in the light of the holy. He fell to the ground, eyes nearly bleeding from the sight of the holiness of the divine presence, straining to crawl into the ground for shelter from the luminous, air-compressing weight of the Lord (Ezek. 1). Yet then Ezekiel rose, empowered by the Holy Spirit to speak the words of the Lord to a people who, shockingly, did not often want them. So it was for Isaiah, and Jeremiah, and many others.

The prophet did not generally minister from a position of earthly power but rather by entering into the people's suffering. Abraham Heschel describes Hosea's ministry as one of "suffering together."[16] Suffering visited many of the prophets, not in spite of God's word, but because of it. In a world corrupted by a lie—the devil speaks just three false sentences in Genesis 3—truth-telling is neither easy nor easily accepted. In situations laden with temptations to worship false gods—and when does idolatry not abound?—the prophet dares to speak the truth, taking captive every convenient illusion.

The King: Personification of Divine Wisdom

There is no Old Testament office more tied to the nation of Israel than that of its king. Ancient Israel was a theocracy, a nation with an expressly religious cast, ruled by Yahweh himself. Yahweh, in fact, seemed to prefer that he rule his followers without a human intermediary. So goes the narrative in 1 Samuel 8, when the Lord speaks through Samuel to his people in answer to their clamoring for a king "like all the nations":

> So Samuel told all the words of the LORD to the people who were asking for a king from him. He said, "These will be the ways of the king who will reign over you: he will take your sons and appoint them to his chariots and to be his horsemen and to run before his chariots. And he will appoint for himself commanders of thousands and commanders of fifties, and some to plow his ground and to reap his harvest, and to make his implements of war and the equipment of his chariots. He will take your daughters to be perfumers and cooks and bakers. He will take the best of your fields and vineyards and olive orchards and give them to his servants. He will take the tenth of your grain and of your vineyards and give it to his officers and to his servants. He will take your male servants and female servants and the best of your young men and your donkeys, and put them to his work. He will take the tenth of your flocks, and you shall be his slaves. And in that day you will cry out because of your king, whom you have chosen for yourselves, but the LORD will not answer you in that day." (1 Sam. 8:10–18)

This message is clearly to be taken as a warning to those who wanted an earthly king (and to pastors today who lead the people of God). The repetition of "taking" language indicates that this monarch will fundamentally serve and enrich his own interests, putting them ahead of the prosperity of his subjects. The Lord blesses his people and wrenches nothing from them; the king promised by Samuel will possess no such character and enact no such ministry. His will be a hard kingship, hard to the extent that the people will become his "slaves" and "cry out" because of him. These may be allusions to the past experience of the people of God in Egypt; if so, not only did the nation grumble against the Lord following the exodus; they also have effectively resubmitted themselves to an Egypt-like ruler.

The people persisted in their desire despite this dire warning. So it was that the office of the king was inaugurated, with the decidedly up-and-down Saul as its first holder. Following Saul, David ascended to the throne. Here the office of the king received an important reconfiguring: the king was now to be not an alternative to God's rule but its earthly representative. David ruled wisely and well, keeping close to the Lord despite his sin. The Lord gave him a title far beyond "king," namely, "a man after [God's] own heart" (1 Sam. 13:13–14;

Acts 13:22). A good king rules righteously: "The rule of the Davidic kings is representative of the rule of God over his kingdom."[17]

Kings too served as covenant officers, alongside priests and prophets. In particular, the king led the people of God with humility and sagacity, listening to the divinely appointed ministers who serve the spiritual life of the nation. But the king was nonetheless a servant leader of the covenant of grace, and his role has direct value for our discussion. The king was "instructed directly by God" and "gifted by God with wisdom by which to rule."[18] In the reign of Solomon, for example, the note of greatest triumph was found not in one of his many military conquests, great and worthy as they were, but in the moment when his abilities of discernment unmasked a false mother and revealed the true one, an act that saved the life of an infant, an innocent unable to protect itself (1 Kings 3).

The Scripture makes clear that this otherworldly wisdom came not from Solomon himself, but from God, from whom he had requested it. In petitioning God for the wisdom, strength, and grace to lead the people well, Solomon prefigured the greater king to come.[19] The wise king heeds the word of God. Other monarchs were judged by their military prowess, their fearlessness, and their displays of strength that allowed them to defeat and even shame the weak. In contrast, the king who led Yahweh's people was judged by whether he did what was right in the eyes of the Lord, whether he obeyed the word of God. The king was not above the law; he was rather "prime minister," first worshiper of the nation, called to exercise and exhibit true humility and covenant obedience before God and his people.

God took greatest note not of bravado, but of prayer. Long before the greatest king came to earth, the righteous kings of the old covenant modeled, however imperfectly, the nature of Christ's kingship. Blessed with tremendous power and vast resources, the Israelite king ruled in holiness, led with wisdom, and personified righteousness: "And he did right in the eyes of the Lord" (1 Kings 15:5; cf. 15:11; 2 Kings 10:30; 12:2; 14:3; 15:3; etc.).

Participating in Jesus's Ministry of the New Covenant: The New Testament

The Pastor as Priest: Ministering Grace

The foregoing has revolved around two key ideas. First, we have observed how the covenant officers of the Old Testament period—the priest, the king, and the prophet—foreshadowed and in some way presently inform the work of the pastor, and in particular, the inescapably *theological* work of the pastor. The focus of the previous section was on the covenantal precedents of the pastor in Israel's history. The focus of the present section is on the work of the pastor in the new covenant era. In this section we seek to complete our "biblical theology" of the pastor by examining how the New Testament builds upon and fills out the preceding material.

> *Priestly ministry was centered around the teaching and performance of the law. Pastoral ministry is centered around the person and work of Christ.*

Priestly ministry was centered around the teaching and performance of the law. Pastoral ministry is centered around the person and work of Christ. In speaking of his love for his church, Jesus used numerous metaphors and images to indicate his sacrificial centrality. In John's Gospel, we learn that he is the good shepherd:

> I am the door. If anyone enters by me, he will be saved and will go in and out and find pasture. The thief comes only to steal and kill and destroy. I came that they may have life and have it abundantly. I am the good shepherd. The good shepherd lays down his life for the sheep. He who is a hired hand and not a shepherd, who does not own the sheep, sees the wolf coming and leaves the sheep and flees, and the wolf snatches them and scatters them. He flees because he is a hired hand and cares nothing for the sheep. I am the good shepherd. I know my own and my own know me, just as the Father knows me and I know the Father; and I lay down my life for the sheep. (John 10:9–15)

Jesus did not intend his ministry as "good shepherd" to involve merely generic protection. On the contrary, ministry is pictured here in terms of bloody conflict with a foe—"the thief"—that would savage the sheep, the people of God. Jesus, however, will not let this happen. The good shepherd protects not by defensive maneuvers but by laying his life down for his flock (John 10:11, 15). Here Jesus expands on the psalmist's conception of Yahweh's shepherding ministry in Psalm 23. Not only will Christ lead his people to true and lasting peace, but he will do so by a vicarious and effectual death. Without this wretched self-sacrifice, there can be no lasting peace beside still waters, no restful sleep in green pastures.

The institution of the Lord's Supper, the cross-centered fulfillment of the Passover meal, further clarified Jesus's high-priestly work. When Jesus directs his band of disciples to feed on him in the upper room, he teaches them that his blood will be the provision for their sins. The old covenant has passed away. In Christ the new has come:

> Now as they were eating, Jesus took bread, and after blessing it broke it and gave it to the disciples, and said, "Take, eat; this is my body." And he took a cup, and when he had given thanks he gave it to them, saying, "Drink of it, all of you, for this is my blood of the covenant, which is poured out for many for the forgiveness of sins. I tell you I will not drink again of this fruit of the vine until that day when I drink it new with you in my Father's kingdom." (Matt. 26:26–29)

Just hours after this meal, Jesus did indeed go to the cross, gave his body, and poured out his blood. The new covenant had dawned, and at the apex of its inauguration is Jesus, the center of all things, hanging on cursed wood for the "forgiveness of sins." The great high priest, long anticipated and long desired, served, as his predecessors had, by making sacrifice for the people of God. But Jesus did not offer the blood of bulls and goats (Heb. 9:13; 10:4). He offered himself, and he invited all who called upon his name, and who ate his holy meal, to be washed, once and for all time.

The priest, as we have seen, had the responsibility of teaching the law to the people of God and, still more directly, of bringing the law to life by "sanctifying" the people through instruction, training in righteousness, and bloody provision for their ongoing sins. The set-apart covenant officer trained the set-apart people in living a set-apart life to glorify the set-apart God. The pastor's role is to minister the new covenant in Jesus's blood (Luke 22:20; 1 Cor. 11:25). Pastors are called, like priests, to shape the lives of the people through the instantiation of holiness in the church such that all the people of God, constituted a "royal priesthood" in Christ (1 Pet. 2:9), offer sacrifices of praise and prayers of intercession. Pastors lead the holy nation stretching across every tribe and tongue to worship the Lord in the name of Jesus, the great high priest (Heb. 4; 10). Pastoral ministry is nothing other than the ministry of the good news of God's grace made available in Jesus Christ through his Spirit. To minister grace is to communicate Christ's own mediation of God's covenant forgiveness and love through the work of reconciliation accomplished on the cross. The pastor does not "dispense" grace in physical acts or spiritual formulations; rather, the pastor proclaims the gospel of grace in Christ to a people who desperately need it.

For the apostles and the early church pastors they trained, the gospel was not merely one resource among several. It was rather the very core of their work:

> The fundamental element of Paul's ministry was the preaching of the gospel (1 Cor. 1:17). This, he recognized, was the means by which God had chosen to make himself known to people (1 Cor. 1:21); this was the power of God for salvation (Rom. 1:16; 1 Cor. 1:18). He was under obligation to preach this gospel, and faced dire consequences if he did not (1 Cor. 9:16–17).[20]

The pastor's work centers in and derives from the gospel message, the good news of reconciliation in Christ, and hence life with God. As the priest led the old covenant people to draw near to God through the law and its conciliatory sacrifices, the pastor now leads the people to draw near to God through the preaching of the Word and the gospel of Christ crucified. Like the priest, the pastor draws the people into what Eugene Peterson has called "salvation life," the unique existence chartered by the holiness of God, empowered by union with God in Christ, and shaped by the word of God.[21]

The pastor images the old-covenant priest by modeling for the church a set-apart life. This righteous model is designed to inspire, edify, and if necessary critique the people—all for the sake of encouraging them to pursue the Lord with zeal so that they too may be transformed. The pastor is no more (or less) righteous than the people. Ministry does not scrub away personal imperfections and weaknesses, but rather magnifies them, drawing pastors to first lay claim to divine grace before ministering it to their people. The pastor is not separate from the people, but lives and moves in the midst of them, counseling, visiting, and training them to live not a fleshly life, but salvation life. The ministry of grace does not remove the pastor from the people. Like the great high priest whose life and work animate the pastor, the minister goes and seeks out the flock, drawing near to them in order that they might draw near to God.[22]

In sum, the pastor emulates the priest through self-sacrificial ministry of the gospel, participating in Christ's own high-priestly ministry as his earthly delegates. The church, then, is not the pastor's own possession. It is Christ's. Ministry to the church, accordingly, owes not to the pastor's ingenuity or multitasking facility. It owes only to the gospel of grace, only to the work of Christ. This is ultimately what pastors have to offer people: God's forgiveness and steadfast love in Christ.

When pastors consider how they may minister grace to their people in all their pastoral duties, we may simply answer "Christ!"

Here we may recall Karl Barth's famous response when asked what pastors should preach. Instead of indulging his expectant listeners with tricks of the homiletic trade, Barth simply responded "Christ!" Similarly, when pastors consider how they may minister grace to their people in all their pastoral duties, we may simply answer "Christ!"[23] The law is fulfilled. The rituals are retired. The bloody sacrifices have ended. But in all the preaching, teaching, counseling, training, visitation, and so forth, the pastor, like the priest ministering grace before him, offers gracious provision on behalf of the people: all of Christ for all of life.

The Pastor as King: Ministering Wisdom

The kings of ancient Israel were to rule not with an iron fist, or by way of overbearing authority, or by consulting only the oracles of their own mind. They were to be kings of a different kind. They would become great by embracing humility, discernment, and wisdom. The Israelite king was in reality an "under-king," one who ruled only by the gracious calling and provision of Yahweh. The monarchical leader of God's people was not high and mighty, but lowly and meek, charged with modeling these attributes to the people.

How does the office of king relate to our conception of the pastor? On the one hand, pastors herald the universal claims of Christ's kingship ("the earth is his footstool"). They speak a powers-and-principalities-defeating, life-remaking, cosmos-reorienting message. However, because the world has fallen under the spell of Satan, the glory of the pastoral office and the truth about the kingdom of God are veiled. In a darkened world, the gospel seems foolishness. The message of Christ, the wisdom of God, appears in this upside-down world as something silly, irrelevant, or too good to be true. The new covenant pastor who takes up the ministry of Christ must mediate the wisdom of a message about a crucified king—and thus be willing to sound like a fool.

Paul discusses this problematic in 1 Corinthians 1–2:

> For the word of the cross is folly to those who are perishing, but to us who are being saved it is the power of God. For it is written,

> "I will destroy the wisdom of the wise,
> and the discernment of the discerning I will thwart."

Where is the one who is wise? Where is the scribe? Where is the debater of this age? Has not God made foolish the wisdom of the world? For since, in the wisdom of God, the world did not know God through wisdom, it pleased God through the folly of what we preach to save those who believe. For Jews demand signs and Greeks seek wisdom, but we preach Christ crucified, a stumbling block to Jews and folly to Gentiles, but to those who are called, both Jews and Greeks, Christ the power of God and the wisdom of God. For the foolishness of God is wiser than men, and the weakness of God is stronger than men. (1 Cor. 1:18–25)

Nowhere is the paradox of the gospel of Christ clearer than in these words. The truth about Jesus slain and raised is the event on which history turns and the chief need of the human heart. But because of the power of sin, it is seen as "foolishness" to Gentiles and albeit a "stumbling block" to Jews. Humankind wants a gospel that does not require the weakness of suffering and death. We inherently thirst for what Martin Luther called *theologia gloriae*, a theology of glory that celebrates a God created in our own best image.[24]

Paul did not oblige the Corinthian lust for worldly glory. On the contrary, he preached "Christ crucified," and he explicitly rejected the possibility that we could secure salvation through our own moral efforts, as moral logic dictated. Paul refused to play to his cosmopolitan Greco-Roman audience, hungering as it did after credentials, sophistication, and worldly standing. Instead, he offered his hearers the wisdom of God, the divine word that judged all human words, rendering ineffective their worldly stratagems for making a name for themselves. To listeners who wanted to become great, Paul testified of the need to be struck down and made nothing. Paul simply taught what Jesus taught, modeled, and personally suffered.

Jesus was and is a king, but not a king like the world still yearns to follow. Jesus's kingship was not of this world. He reigned by serving and suffering, and never was Jesus more powerful than in his moment of death. All this was wisdom, truth, and power—but of an upside-down kind. So it is with the pastor, who serves like the old covenant king as a minister of wisdom. The pastor's participation in Jesus's kingly office is not grounded in grandeur, in striking fear into the hearts of the church staff, or in conducting meetings in a lordly manner. On the contrary: the pastor is most like King Jesus when serving the church in wisdom and weakness, leading the congregation with humility and bearing its burdens in prayer.

The wisdom of God, like the kingdom of Christ, turns the world on its head. Pastors do not shy away from making decisions and leading with conviction, of course; they must put things into order, as Paul instructed Timothy to do (1 Tim. 1). This speaks to the necessity of courage and vision and insight for faithful pastoral ministry. Recognizing the cruciform nature of kingly pastoral work does not mean that a shepherd never reaches a conclusion, steps out in faith, or champions an initiative. The Old and New Testaments are full of kings and apostles and other leaders who acted boldly, yet humbly, in the name of God, and who were commended for doing so.

The core of pastoral leadership is the reality that Jesus has, by his personal holocaust, inaugurated the kingdom of God on earth.

But the pastor who leads well owes less to "best practices" or strategic vision and more to biblical theology and the way of the cross. The core of pastoral leadership is the reality that Jesus has, by his personal holocaust, inaugurated the kingdom of God on earth. To belong to the church is to have been "transferred" into "the kingdom of [God's] beloved Son" (Col. 1:13). Pastors are not kings. They do, however, participate in Jesus's kingly office; but as we have seen, Jesus's kingdom does not come in Caesarean power but in cruciform weakness. He who reigns is he who was crucified, a paradox that must be believed in order to be understood.[25] Pastors can learn from the biblical model of the crucified king who leads not only by serving but also by humbling himself to the point of death. If the pastor does not live by this paradoxical calculus, the church will not understand the nature of the cross, and the world will not comprehend the glory and beauty of the gospel.

Too often, pastors are lured away from their kingly work by counterfeit versions: CEOs who never take counsel, politicians who master the art of persuasion. Pastoral leadership ought to march to the beat of a different, world-defying drummer, participating in Christ's kingship by personifying the cruciform wisdom of God.

We find resonance with this view of the pastorate in a very different context: the logic of "fairy stories" in the work of C. S. Lewis and J. R. R. Tolkien. These men drew considerable critique in the 1930s and beyond for their interest in what we would call today "fantasy literature." Such writing was not appropriate—not academically respectable enough!—for Oxford dons. Lewis and Tolkien nevertheless persisted in their shared conviction that *faerie* could illuminate truths about our world that no "science" could:

> In its fairy-tale—or otherworld—setting, it is a sudden and miraculous grace: never to be counted on to recur. It does not deny the existence of dyscatastrophe, of sorrow and failure: the possibility of these is necessary to the joy of deliverance; it denies (in the face of much evidence, if you will) universal final defeat and in so far is *evangelium*, giving a fleeting glimpse of Joy.[26]

So it is with pastoral ministry, which is a kind of *faerie* inasmuch as it discloses the deep truth about the real world that other stories miss. No other vocation offers such a sustained "glimpse of Joy" to be found "beyond the walls of the world." When pastor-theologians proclaim the gospel, they allow us to see, hear, and even taste the wisdom of God that entered into history yet lies beyond the world of sense experience that is the object of science.[27]

The Pastor as Prophet: Ministering Truth

Sometimes we are told that preaching is outmoded. Once, in an age of grandiloquent speechmakers, it made sense to ascend an aged pulpit and preach a lengthy sermon. Yet today we treat the homily with reverence, like an aged family member whose glory days are long behind him, but no longer see it as the centerpiece of our worship. We're in a posthomiletical age, which communicates in tweets and emoticons, not declamations and discourses.

The era of the spoken word is, in point of fact, not over. Media personalities continue to fill the air with political analysis, dissection of sporting events, and the personal confessions of the podcast. In such a time as this, pastors do well to reclaim their prophetic mantle. It is not the psychologists, advertising executives, or life-coach gurus that should train the pastor. It is not the latest sociological trend but the prophet, charged with the often-unpopular task of speaking forth God's word, who should inspire pastors to preach with fresh power and zeal today. The pastor, like the apostles, stands firmly in the oratorical tradition of the prophets, who heard the word of God and explained it, applied it, and commended it to the people. The prophet's ministry was a ministry of God's word and hence a ministry of truth.

To understand the prophetic aspect of ministry in the New Testament, consider the sermons in the book of Acts. Peter preaches the first recorded apostolic sermon in Acts 2. He quotes Joel 2 to inform his Jerusalem audience that the day of Pentecost, marked by the outpouring of the Spirit on all hearers, has now come. This event has signaled that the day of salvation has dawned: It has "come to pass that everyone who calls upon the name of the Lord shall be saved" (Acts 2:21). Peter grounds this call of salvation in the person and work of Jesus Christ:

> Men of Israel, hear these words: Jesus of Nazareth, a man attested to you by God with mighty works and wonders and signs that God did through him in your midst, as you yourselves know—this Jesus, delivered up according to the definite plan and foreknowledge of God, you crucified and killed by the hands of lawless men. God raised him up, loosing the pangs of death, because it was not possible for him to be held by it. (Acts 2:22–24)

Peter's sermon was not delivered in a formal ecclesial setting. He was outside, preaching in Jerusalem, just after flaming tongues of fire had descended from heaven. If the setting was slightly atypical, the content of Peter's message was not.

The apostolic preaching of the gospel of Christ flowed from the conviction that Christ has fulfilled the Old Testament, that he is the exclusive Savior and pathway to God, and that everyone who hears the message is summoned to respond in faith. Like the prophets, the apostles offered their hearers truth, not in the abstract, but truth that impinged on every aspect of each person's life. All have fallen short of the glory of God, all have been judged by the kerygma, yet all have also been offered eternal life in Christ.

The apostles preached Jesus, and they preached him fearlessly, even in the midst of tremendous hostility and opposition to their message (as did the prophets before them). The world was their parish, and they were soon dispatched to the Gentiles. When Paul came to Mars Hill, he delivered a remarkable sermon in the Areopagus. After mentioning the religious instincts of his audience, Paul revealed the identity of the unknown God:

> And he made from one man every nation of mankind to live on all the face of the earth, having determined allotted periods and the boundaries of their dwelling place, that they should seek God, and perhaps feel their way toward him and find him. Yet he is actually not far from each one of us, for

"In him we live and move and have our being";

as even some of your own poets have said,

"For we are indeed his offspring."

Being then God's offspring, we ought not to think that the divine being is like gold or silver or stone, an image formed by the art and imagination of man. The times of ignorance God overlooked, but now he commands all people every-where to repent, because he has fixed a day on which he will judge the world in righteousness by a man whom he has appointed; and of this he has given assurance to all by raising him from the dead. (Acts 17:26–31)

Paul's message might initially seem rather different from those of Peter, but in reality, it is similar. Both apostles reference the canonical authorities of the culture in which they speak. Both built upon the Old Testament. Paul cited not only the teaching of Genesis but also the great poets and philosophers of the Greek world, including Epimenides and Aratus. Especially noteworthy, however, is Paul's explanation of the purpose of the resurrection, which is not simply the vindication of the church but also the "assurance" of future judg-ment of the world, including those who live in "ignorance" of the living God. Once again, the kerygma leaves an audience without excuse. The resurrection entails the truth of Christ's lordship, and the apostles were at pains to make it subjectively relevant, whether in Jerusalem, the religious center of the ancient kingdom, or in Athens, the philosophical center of the pagan superpower.

The apostles did not perform rhetorical flights of fancy or participate in the Greco-Roman codes of public discourse but kept their discourse prophetically simple. As Paul said to the church at Corinth: "My speech and my message were not in plausible words of wisdom, but in demonstration of the Spirit and of power, so that your faith might not rest in the wisdom of men but in the power of God" (1 Cor. 2:3–5).[28] As an apostle and pastor to many churches, Paul's was largely a verbal ministry, a ministry exercised through words.[29] He spoke not his own words, but God's, and thus offered his listeners the mind of Christ.[30] Paul trained the next generation of pastors to do the same, and to guard the gospel, the "good deposit": "By the Holy Spirit who dwells within us, guard the good deposit entrusted to you" (2 Tim. 1:14). If this deposit, the gospel, was lost, then all was lost.

Pastors must not only guard this message but also feed their people a steady diet of it. According to Hebrews 5:11–6:3, preachers have the divine charge of

giving their people "meat" and not "milk." There is no clearer call in Scripture
for pastors to embrace a theological pastorate and an expository preaching
ministry than this. The people will not grow and flourish and find full health
through a diet of milk alone. They need to grow up, to eat more complex food,
to be richly sustained for a life of spiritual exertion. This means knowing the
Scripture better, acquiring a knowledge that flows out of hard pastoral work
and careful study of biblical and systematic theology. To offer this, however,
the pastor must first have embraced the very nature of pastoral work, which is
to say, its theological identity: helping the
word of God to dwell richly in the people of
God (and vice versa). The pastorate is a position that would not exist without a body
of God-fired revelation. It exists to offer
people a nourishing meal of the same.[31]

> *The pastorate is a position that would not exist without a body of God-fired revelation. It exists to offer people a nourishing meal of the same.*

Every pastor, then, stands with Peter as
Jesus tells him three times, "Feed my sheep"
(John 21). This is a remarkable charge. Jesus
does not say "Teach my sheep," as he con-
ceivably could have. The metaphor he uses
is much more evocative and informative. It tells us what the core of gospel ministry is: feeding the people of God the Word of God. The church is not submitting
itself to an odd but historically prominent practice by sitting underneath the
preaching ministry of the pastor each week. The church is eating together. In
restoring his benighted disciple, Jesus summons Peter to a feeding ministry that
is in truth a preaching and teaching ministry. The takeaway is clear: if Christians today are hungry, if they wonder why they wrestle with a certain malaise
and a less-than-vital spiritual walk, perhaps it is because they are not being fed.

The foregoing leads to a simple but deeply meaningful conclusion: pastoral ministry, like prophetic ministry of ancient times, is largely a ministry of
words. The pastor, like Peter, is a shepherd, but this shepherding work is not
physical, with rod and staff, but spiritual, with verbs and nouns. The burden
of the pastor's work is the declaration of the mind and will of God, as Carl
Trueman has pointed out:

> It is hard to see how the identity of God and his action in Christ and in the
> church could be more adequately expressed than by the use of words. In fact, the
> sermons in Acts and in the epistles indicate that the prophetic model of Moses

(exposition, application, exhortation rooted in God's revelation) is the standard; and as this action is clearly connected to a theology of God as a speaking God, the preacher simply cannot see his task as mere communication of information.[32]

God is not a pantomiming or playacting God. His fundamental product is a body of verbal revelation and the human body of Jesus Christ, the word made flesh. The work of the preacher is found not in walking through the Bible as in a how-to seminar, but in expositing the biblical text, applying it, and exhorting the people to live according to it, in union with Christ and by the power of the Spirit.[33]

The pastor, seeing in full what his predecessors knew only in type and shadow, speaks not his own mind, but the mind of God. Like the prophets of old, the pastor calls the people not to misery and anxiety, but to the world-righting, soul-renewing station of repentance. Babylon has faded and Persia is no more, but the world is still ruled by forces of darkness that would enslave the people of God. The pastor, as one captured and enraptured by biblical doctrine and theological truth, takes up the prophet's mantle, calling the church to remember the covenant and to be transformed

The pastor's preaching ministry is the ministry of God's truth: the way and life of Jesus Christ.

by the grace that pours from it. All this is a ministry of words—not words for their own sake, but words invested with the authority of the divine. The pastor's preaching ministry is the ministry of God's truth: the way and life of Jesus Christ.

Conclusion: The Pastorate as Theological Office

When D. Martyn Lloyd-Jones stood up in Westminster Chapel to pray and to preach in the midst of a wartime attack, he offered powerful testimony to the work of the minister in a fallen world. To a people besieged by Satan and pulled away from God by sinful temptation, the pastor acts as priest, calling them to freshly partake of God's grace, which overcomes sin and creates a new way of life, salvation life. To a people who desperately need wisdom in a world order built on powerful lies, the pastor acts as king, training the people's eyes on the humility and meekness of Jesus Christ, who by his death overcame the enemy and destroyed the forces of darkness, a victory veiled from the natural man but gloriously visible to the eyes of faith. To a people who crave reliable words in a culture of unstable images, the pastor acts as prophet, delving into all the Scripture to exposit Christ and call the people to fresh repentance and reinvigorated faith.

In all these roles, in this collective work, pastors serve the covenant of grace as priests, prophets, and kings did long ago. Today, as in ancient times, pastors act as theologians of the church, shining into yearning hearts "the light of the knowledge of the glory of God in the face of Jesus Christ" (2 Cor. 4:6). This is not to lay upon ministers the mantle, much less the yoke, of academic theology. It is to say that the pastorate is, like covenant officers of old, an office grounded in theological realities: salvation, wisdom, and truth—in a word, Christ. If we take away God and the gospel of Jesus Christ, then the pastorate ceases to exist. From this christological foundation, the pastor preaches, counsels, disciples, leads, acts, stewards, manages, administers, puts chaos into order, evangelizes, rebukes, and teaches. In all this work, the set-apart pastor serves the set-apart God by feeding his set-apart people. This is inherently theological work: hence every pastor works as a theologian.[34]

The set-apart pastor serves the set-apart God by feeding his set-apart people.

The pastor does so whether stones rain down in the encroachment of death, as in the martyrdom of Stephen, or rockets splinter the surrounding city, as in the ministry of Lloyd-Jones. All pastors minister amid sin and a satanic foe that would undo them. Bombs may fall or they may not. Whatever the case, every pastor has the privilege of ministering in the power of Christ and taking great hope from this truth. The buildings may crash, the sirens may wail, the culture may implode, but the pastor, and the kingdom he serves, will never be shaken.

Pastoral Perspectives

The Pastor as Public Theologian

MELVIN TINKER

Missiologist David Bosch writes: "The New Testament writers were not schol-ars who had the leisure to research the evidence before they put pen to paper. Rather, they wrote in the context of an 'emergency situation,' of a church which, because of its missionary encounter with the world, was *forced* to the-ologize."[1] As a pastor-teacher I am therefore "forced" (willingly!) to theologize every time God's people meet.

What is more, if theology is a conversation between God's Word and God's world, then I have a duty to exegete both Scripture and the world so that the hearer of God's Word (Christian or not) is enabled to enter the world of the Bible, and the world of the Bible is allowed to critically impact upon the world of the hearer, under the illuminating work of the Spirit. The result is "engage-ment" with God through his Word. I do this by recognizing three coordinating twin points in the pastoral teaching ministry.

1. *Public theology is contextual and expositional.* I minister in the context of the most unchurched city in the United Kingdom, with less than 1 percent church attendance. The congregation is mixed; made up of blue-collar and white-collar workers, young and old, white Anglo-Saxon, black, Chinese, and increasingly Polish (a total congregation of 300–400 on a Sunday). I need to be aware of the worlds they inhabit and ensure that a connection is made

between what is taught and how it is applied. This involves "walking the factory floor" by meeting people and talking with them; the regular reading of secular books, papers, and magazines (as well as watching movies, a favorite pastime!) and reflecting on these biblically.

The primary means of public teaching is regular expository preaching. Whether it is working through a book like Colossians or a series of topics, the method is to unpack the meaning of Scripture in terms of its various contexts (literary, historical, canonical), and then *throughout* the sermon to draw out its significance. As the world of the Scripture is opened, then the world of the hearer is opened too; whatever cultural differences there may be, it is the same fallen world with glimpses of "Godlight" by common grace—and the life-changing power of the gospel is brought to bear.

I'll give one example. Several years ago I was coming across a number of pastoral problems among the church members, issues that, on the face of it, seemed unrelated (troubling children, issues of sexuality, stress at work) until I realized that there was a common thread connecting them all. The Christians were simply not aware of the changing nature of society in which they found themselves; hence they were experiencing a kind of "cognitive dissonance" and couldn't understand what was happening. To attempt to remedy this, I devised a sermon series titled "By the Rivers of Babylon—Living Christianly in Today's World." I presented the idea that the church was in captivity in "Babylon," and Christians were "strangers and pilgrims" (1 Pet. 1:1; 2:11 KJV; 5:13). The nature of the "captivity" shows itself in the United Kingdom by relativism in public and private ethics, valuing people by their looks and work, secularization with the marginalization of religion in public life ("privatization"). Taken together, the Christian certainly *feels* like an alien and is alienated. The gap between what is believed and how it can be practiced (without guidance) can reach cavernous proportions in people's minds, and so the temptation to capitulate to the world by privatizing religion is strong. By deliberately drawing on a variety of different genres (psalms, prophecy, law, wisdom, gospels, epistles, apocalyptic), a wide variety of issues were addressed: idolatry, sexuality, marriage, work, raising children, the future hope, and so on. This not only helped the congregation see that the whole Word of God in its splendid variety touched upon the whole of life, but also gave them confidence to work at relating Scripture to their day-to-day existence. Small Bible-study groups and special events in which we tackle issues such as consumerism, superstition, and "Dawkins and the New Atheism" reinforce this approach.

2. *Public theology is christological and doxological.* Taking Luke 24:27 seriously, that the whole of the Scriptures relate to Christ (although not all in the same way), biblical theology shapes the teaching that is public. The aim in every sermon is to exalt Christ. This is achieved not by tacking on Jesus as a tagline at the end but by displaying Christ through whatever Scripture is being handled. Christ is the hermeneutical key, and folks are excited to see this. The threefold role of Christ as prophet, priest, and king clearly relates to the way we view the world as we see his relationship to the world in these roles. And so as pastor-teacher, my aim is also to present theology as doxological. The temptation to be "with it" and practical is to end each sermon with a list of to-dos. But by allowing the genre as well as the content of the text to be determinative in preaching, seeing God's Word as "doing" (performative) and not simply "instructing" (informative), means that more often than not there is a "wow!" element (the "heat" as well as the "light" spoken of by Jonathan Edwards), leading to sheer adoration of the Triune God. The "light" element is afforded by dealing with any major doctrine that is allowed by the text. The value of systematic expository preaching ensures that over time all the major biblical doctrines (i.e., systematic theology) are covered. At the very least, this will affect the stance that the believer will take in relation to the world on a Monday morning, shaping their affections as well as informing their decisions and sharpening their perceptions.

3. *Public theology is missional and pastoral.* If the programmatic unfolding of the gospel of righteousness by faith in Romans leads to a "renewal of [the] mind" (12:1–2), it is not surprising that Paul construes Christian living in terms taken from Old Testament worship, which is then worked out in Christians' relationships with one another (12:5–13) and with a hostile world (12:14–21). The climax of the letter is Paul's concern to proclaim the gospel in unchartered territory and for the Christians in Rome to support him in his "priestly service" (15:14–16:27). Thus in my Bible teaching there are always elements of relating to the world in terms of service and evangelism, and relating to each other in love and good works. This involves working with the people to understand their world from a biblical viewpoint in order to adopt a Christlike stance toward it.

Given that the church is the great goal of God's saving purposes (Eph. 1:22), I want the local congregation to get ready for the coming bridegroom by being more bride-like. So the teaching cannot be divorced from other aspects of public worship. This means that at the beginning of our time together, there is a clear reminder of what we are: the expression of the heavenly church on earth; what we are doing: meeting in the presence of the Most High, with Christ in our midst by his Spirit, and responding to his Word in faith, repentance, and praise. Engaging with God is uppermost in our minds rather than entertaining ourselves before God. We believe God engages with us through Word and sacrament (audible and visible Word). Space is made for relating to each other too, especially after the main act of worship. Church is family, and it is hoped that when outsiders come in, they will not only see the relevance of the Christian faith but also *feel* it.

Human Origins:
A Test Case for Pastor-Theologians

TODD WILSON

Recently I received a phone call from a fellow pastor asking for help. "I'm preaching through Genesis 1–11," he told me, "and I need some advice on the whole creation and evolution thing." The anxious sound of his voice let me know he was worried about how this might go down in his congregation. Understandably so, since there is hardly a more controversial subject these days than human origins.

Pastor-theologians, however, shouldn't shy away from engaging with controversial issues. Indeed, those responsible to bring God's Word to bear on the world need to take every thought captive to Christ, and the more controversial an issue, the more important it is for pastor-theologians to deal with it.

The church's best public theologians, its pastors, are uniquely gifted to grapple with the myriad issues involved in the question of origins, yet without losing sight of the forest because of the trees. But they're also well equipped to model for their congregations the intellectual virtues of humility and hospitality, so that this issue doesn't generate more heat than light within the body. In short, pastor-theologians are well suited to navigate the Scylla of blissful ignorance and the Charybdis of hotheaded contention, so their congregations don't crash on the shoals of a divisive issue to the detriment of their own growth and witness.

Several years ago, rumor began circulating within my congregation that the senior pastor was of the opinion that "we came from apes." This alarmed some who held a different view on these matters, and thus I, together with the leadership, needed to wrestle with the question—in light of our church's ecclesial tradition and articles of faith, as well as the Word of God itself.

While we might have been tempted to view this as a distraction from the business of ministry, we agreed that it was a good investment of our time and energy, and for several reasons.

First, the question of human origins is a major cultural and apologetic issue for the church. If you get *National Geographic*, you'll find in almost every issue something related to origins and evolution. Or if you follow the news closely, you'll regularly read about new archaeological discoveries that have made headlines and that present a fresh challenge to a traditional Christian understanding of origins.

Second, human origins is a major discipleship issue, especially for our young people. It's not at all uncommon to hear of students from the church's youth group losing their faith in college as a result of gaining exposure to evolutionary biology and its attendant worldview.

Third, human origins is a fascinating issue in its own right, requiring that one develop some facility across a range of different disciplines, from the life sciences and history to theology and exegesis. It's a challenging and invigorating intellectual workout!

Within our church, I held a view not shared by everyone. Thus I needed to articulate and, yes, argue for my own position. As part of this process, I read dozens of books and journal articles to get up to speed on the issues. This took me the better part of three months, at the end of which I produced a fifteen-page white paper for our church leadership. This was an invaluable exercise because it not only gave me an opportunity to express my views in writing, but it also provided an occasion for our leadership team to grapple with the biblical, theological, hermeneutical, historical, cultural, scientific, and philosophical issues surrounding the question of origins. In the end, regardless of where we came down on the issue, every one of us came away sharper because of the process.

Preparing and discussing a white paper, however, wasn't the only or even the most important task. I also needed to provide guidance on how to think about this issue in light of Scripture and our tradition, as well as in view of the diversity of views within our church. I therefore prepared what we called our "Elder Affirmations on Creation & Evolution." This was an effort to articulate, in a series of short and succinct statements, how to live together as Bible-affirming believers who hold different views on this issue yet stand together within a particular stream of evangelical Christianity. This was, of course, no easy task, but it was profitable.

Pastor-theologians, as ministers of God's Word in this world, are on the frontlines of theological engagement, for the good of the church. They're also ideally positioned and uniquely equipped to help congregations deal with the major intellectual issues of the day in a way that not only sharpens thinking but also shepherds souls. For this is the ultimate goal of the pastor-theologian.

A Practical Theology of Technology

JIM SAMRA

"My twelve-year-old claims that he is the only child in his class without a smartphone, and he desperately wants one. What should I do?"

"My mother has recently joined Facebook and is constantly worried about how many people 'liked' her status update. This doesn't seem healthy to me—is it?"

"All the other big churches I know have off-site video venues to reach more people; shouldn't we?"

"If a pastor is right now not on Facebook and Twitter, he should repent and start using them immediately."[2]

These questions and comments have in common a focus on the role that technology should play in the life of the church and in the lives of faithful Christians. As a former engineer, I was enamored with technology. As a pastor, I am now leery of what it is doing to the people that God has entrusted to me to shepherd. We all know that technology can be used for either good or evil and that Christians should use it for good and not for evil. Is technology neutral? Or is it possible that even when we are using it for good, there still may be negative consequences? Can it tempt us to put our faith in it even as we are using it to accomplish great good?

How is one to go about answering these questions? One approach is to let what "works" dictate what we do. If Twitter makes people feel more connected to the pastor, then I should use it. But doesn't God have anything to say about technology? As a pastor, I am not simply an adviser encouraging people to adopt the latest trends in technology, but a prophet speaking on God's behalf to his people. What does God have to say about technology and how to use it responsibly?

We need a theology of technology in order to answer this question. But I did not receive a theology of technology in any of my seminary classes, nor did I come across a theology of technology in my PhD work. I do not usually find sections about technology in standard systematic theologies or biblical theologies. When I read commentaries on what I now realize are biblical passages relevant to technology, most commentators do not mention anything about it.[3]

A theology of technology is an especially practical theology. People need help translating theological principles and ideas about technology into daily decisions unique to each person and family. New technologies are arising every day, and people need personal guidance in navigating the ever-changing technological world with sound biblical and theological principles. This too is the job of a pastor.

Over the past few years, I have been trying to formulate a theology of technology. This has involved spending time praying through this issue, studying the Bible, reading what others have written, combing the media for studies about technology's effects on people, observing people's use of technology, listening to questions, and working through the material with our pastoral staff and congregation.

God has led me to realize that the Bible has much to say about technology—as long as we are willing to use a sufficiently broad definition: "Technology includes all tools, machines, utensils, weapons, instruments, housing, clothing, communicating and transporting devices and the skills by which we produce and use them."[4] Stories from the first eleven chapters of Genesis give foundational principles relevant to the use of technology: (1) Technology is possible because man is created in the image of God (Adam and Eve). (2) Technology often hinders our ability to recognize our need for God and can be used to attempt to render God unnecessary (Cain). (3) Technology can free us to sin by attempting to shield us from some of the consequences of sin (Lamech and Tubal-Cain). (4) Technology is used by God to rescue us, to help alleviate some of the consequences of the fall, and to help us worship God (Noah). (5) Technology is inherently dangerous because it is the product of purposive human activity, and we need help from God in limiting its use (Tower of Babel). Of these five, I have found the last one to be the most difficult for people to grasp.

Studying the cross as a form of technology led to my recognizing that technology is dangerous inasmuch as it is constantly tempting us to imagine a better life available to us through technology: to covet and to put our faith in technology rather than God. The cross is associated with the Jewish leaders coveting a world without Jesus (Luke 20:9–19) and their idolatry in embracing Caesar rather than God (John 19:13–16).[5]

Because technology is a means by which the world tries to influence our lives toward coveting and idolatry, the symptoms of being infected by technology are the same as those of being infected with worldliness. These include speaking evil of others (James 4:11–12), making plans without God (4:12–17), being financially selfish (5:1–6), being impatient with God (5:7–12), and being individualistic rather than community oriented (5:13–20). By providing these practical symptoms for which they can look in their own life and in the lives of others, James helps us recognize the often-concealed effects that technology is having on us.

The solution is not to abstain from technology. This is not only impractical but also wrong. God used the technology of the cross to accomplish the greatest possible good, and he continues to use human technology to alleviate some of the consequences of the fall and to advance his kingdom. Technology can be a blessing from God and an integral aspect of serving him. Yet the dangers inherent in technology require the same solutions that James gives us regarding the things of this world in general: humility, submitting to God's law (the second and the fourth commandments are especially relevant to technology), and drawing near to God in prayer, because prayer is in many ways the opposite of technology.

Watching Christians trying to navigate this technological world is like watching sheep without a shepherd. It is my job as a pastor to help my people think biblically and theologically about technology so that they can live faithfully in this technological world.

2

Of Scholars and Saints

A Brief History of the Pastorate

OWEN STRACHAN

Few films have more chillingly depicted the uncontainable nature of original sin than *No Country for Old Men*, based on the lyrical story by Cormac McCarthy. Near the film's conclusion, Sheriff Ed Tom Bell sits with his wife, drinking coffee. He reflects on a dream he had the night before, in which he saw his father, a lawman, ride past him:

> It was like we was both back in older times. And I was a-horseback, going through the mountains of a night. Going through this pass in the mountains. It was cold, and there was snow on the ground. And he rode past me and kept on going . . . never said nothing going by, just rode on past. He had his blanket wrapped around him and his head down.
>
> When he rode past, I seen he was carrying fire in a horn . . . the way people used to do, and I . . . I could see the horn from the light inside of it . . . 'bout the color of the moon. And, in the dream, I knew that he was . . . going on ahead.
>
> He was fixin' to make a fire somewhere out there in all that dark and cold.

The setting of *No Country for Old Men* is bleak. As an apocalypticist, McCarthy will hardly be accused of gross optimism about the future. This passage, however, introduces a discordant note in the funereal symphony of evil that precedes it. In this strange dream, we hear a chord of hope. The darkness, it seems, had not overcome the world.

This vision of hope resonates with the purposes of this book. For those who view the pastorate as a theological office, encouragement in light of broader evangelical trends is sometimes hard to come by. Pastors today are asked to be so many things, and it is quite possible for these many duties to submerge the essentially theological work of the ministry. As noted in the introduction (above), perhaps no job in the world has taken on so many facets: leader, organization builder, administrator, coach, inspirer, endless problem solver, spiritual pragmatist, and so much more. There is major pressure, in addition, for today's pastors to be relentless inventors and creative visionaries. The culture is influencing the church in this regard; the "creative," not the stoic business executive, is the coveted career today, as the covers of *Fortune* and *Inc.* show.

> *Pastors have a tremendous spiritual heritage, though one wouldn't necessarily know it from today's evangelical media.*

How invigorating, then, to realize that pastors need not endlessly invent. The shepherd is not alone. Many have gone before. Pastors have a tremendous spiritual heritage, though one wouldn't necessarily know it from today's evangelical media. Many of those who preceded us resisted the harmful pressures surrounding them, both cultural and theological, and have unapologetically taken up theological pastoral work. In other words, they have seen the pastorate as a theological office, a vocation to communicate—in word, deed, and body—the new life available in Christ: fellowship with God the Father in God the Son through God the Holy Spirit.

This is our fundamental claim: in numerous eras of church history, the pastor was a theologian. Indeed, we can go further, with Douglas Sweeney, who says, "*Most* of the *best* theologians in the history of the church were parish pastors."[1] Though this sounds counterintuitive to a modern, academy-enthralled office, the pastor, as David Wells has recognized, was historically "the scholar-saint, one who was as comfortable with books and learning as with the aches of the soul."[2] This is no mere attempt to gild the pastoral lily.

Such a judgment is a point of historical fact, as the following material makes clear. For the dispirited and confused, there is great hope to be harvested from the church's faithful pastoral heritage.

The Early Church

Irenaeus and the Rule of Faith

The bishops of the early church drank in the Scripture like water in the desert. They meditated solemnly on the truths they learned. Of course, they had no formal seminaries. They did not accrue degrees. But pastors, frequently called "priests" by the end of the second century, clearly understood themselves as teachers of the people of God, and thus as thereby responsible for knowing biblical doctrine. They did not separate from the people and the ministry to learn theology but instead tilled the rich soil of Scripture in the context of pastoral work. We can put it more sharply: it would have been unthinkable for these early pastors to give up the grind of weekly Bible exposition in order to sequester themselves in theological meditation to mine more deeply into the Bible's doctrine. On the contrary, reading the Bible for sermon preparation was itself an opportunity for real theological work, a glorious exegetical grind.

One of the earliest of the pastor-theologians was Irenaeus, bishop of Lyons. We possess little extant material from Irenaeus (130–200) but do have access to two of his major works: *Against Heresies* and *Proof of the Apostolic Preaching*. With Tertullian (160–225), an early Christian author and theologian, Irenaeus promoted the *regula fidei*, or "rule of faith," which was a summary of the core message of the Bible and its gospel. The following is an approximation of the fuller creed:

> The Church, though dispersed throughout the whole world, even to the ends of the earth, has received from the apostles and their disciples this faith: in one God, the Father Almighty, Maker of heaven, and earth, and the sea, and all things that are in them;
>> and in one Christ Jesus, the Son of God, who became incarnate for our salvation;
>> and in the Holy Spirit, who proclaimed through the prophets the dispensations of God, and the advents, and the birth from a virgin, and the passion, and the resurrection from the dead, and the ascension into heaven in the flesh of the beloved Christ Jesus, our Lord.[3]

This rule is a summary of the whole sweep of the history of salvation, a history that required the professing believer to view the work of Father, Son, and Spirit as equally important and equally divine, contra the false teaching that demoted the Son or Spirit from this standing. The Rule of Faith could be seen in minimalist terms—in other words, here is the minimum one needs to believe to know the truth. The opposite, however, is true. This rule outlined the superstructure of all Christian theology, providing the church with biblically drawn parameters. For Irenaeus and his peers, then, theology was not an exercise in intellectual speculation. It was a matter requiring the highest precision. Life and death, even eternal life and eternal death, depended upon this work.

In handling intricacies of trinitarian theology, the early church's theologians were not doing "pre-gospel" work; they were calibrating the categories through which gospel truths flowed. We can paraphrase theologian Fred Sanders on this point: the doctrine of the Trinity is the most evangelical of all Christian doctrines.[4]

The Development of Early Church Polity

At this point we should briefly detour our investigation of the pastor's theological work for a broader consideration of the duties of the pastorate in the early church. How, precisely, did Irenaeus and others come to hold the office of bishop as suitable for a pastor presiding over a defined geographic area and thus leading multiple churches?

The development of what is called the "monarchical episcopate," the ecclesial oversight of a region by a bishop, is shrouded in some mystery, we must admit. It is not immediately clear how this system of polity came to be adopted by the early church; there was no once-and-for-all decree handed down to the early church that led to the formation of this ecclesial system. In the *Shepherd of Hermas*, we find an expanded set of offices laid out for the government of the church. The document mentions "apostles and bishops and teachers and deacons."[5] By this point the office of bishop was separated from that of teacher.

The church's adoption of the monarchical episcopate spread widely in the early part of the second century. By this point, the monarchical episcopacy had achieved widespread adoption. At the Council of Nicaea in 325, the church formalized elements of these developments.[6] Bishops were instructed to appoint other bishops, with confirmation by the metropolitan.[7]

Chrysostom, Augustine, and the Pastor as Teacher

Irenaeus, our first subject, was not alone in viewing the pastor as the church's teacher, its theologian. John Chrysostom (347–407), the greatest preacher of his era and author of *On the Priesthood*, invested great significance in the spiritual life of the "priest," or pastor, as we would identify the role today. While this was the treatise's focus, though, Chrysostom at length expressed the need for the overseer of God's people to preach true doctrine and refute false teaching:

> But when a dispute arises concerning matters of doctrine, and all take their weapons from the same Scriptures, of what weight will any one's life be able to prove? . . . None; no more than there will be in a sound faith if the life is corrupt. Wherefore, for this reason more than for all others, it concerns him whose office it is to teach others, to be experienced in disputations of this kind. For though he himself stands safely, and is unhurt by the gainsayers, yet the simple multitude under his direction, when they see their leader defeated, and without any answer for the gainsayers, will be apt to lay the blame of his discomfiture not on his own weakness, but on the doctrines themselves, as though they were faulty; and so by reason of the inexperience of one, great numbers are brought to extreme ruin; for though they do not entirely go over to the adversary, yet they are forced to doubt about matters in which formerly they firmly believed, and those whom they used to approach with unswerving confidence, they are unable to hold to any longer steadfastly, but in consequence of their leader's defeat, so great a storm settles down upon their souls, that the mischief ends in their shipwreck altogether.[8]

Chrysostom's focus here is largely negative. That is, he argues the importance of doctrine from the standpoint that getting it wrong will lead "great numbers" of congregants "to extreme ruin." For reasons mentioned above, this was a common perspective in the early period. Biblical doctrine was not, in Chrysostom's eyes, "faulty." To give such an impression would make "shipwreck" of the faith. It fell to the pastor, the leader of the people, to teach the people sound words about God and his Word, a message that could only bring health to the church.

For Chrysostom, the pastor was a teacher: the pastorate was a theological office that steered the people safely to God.

We carefully notice Chrysostom's conviction that ultimately the pastor must teach and must answer "gainsayers" who would train the people to doubt biblical teaching. In his view, the pastor had no choice but to equip himself in the Scriptures so as to triumph over unbelief and to present those in his care safe before God's dread seat of judgment. For Chrysostom, the pastor was a teacher: the pastorate was a theological office that steered the people safely to God.[9]

One of the leading bishops of the first five hundred years of church history was the North African pastor Augustine of Hippo (354–430). His was a theological ministry, to be sure, but it was aimed first not at his philosophically minded friends but at the ordinary men and women who crowded his pews and needed his gospel. Writing to his gifted peer Jerome, the bishop of Hippo indicated that he had no time for flights of theological fancy. He had to study to minister, and to minister in his view was to *instruct*:

> Whatever abilities I may have for such study, I devote entirely to the instruction of the people whom God has entrusted to me; and I am wholly precluded by my ecclesiastical occupations from having leisure for any further prosecution of my studies than is necessary for my duty in public teaching.[10]

We must listen closely to Augustine's self-conception. Even this sharply defined understanding of his work speaks volumes about the nature of his chosen ministry. God had granted him a people. "Instruction" was his obsession. He saw his capital work as "public teaching." As Michael Pasquarello III has said, for Augustine "pastoral formation occurs by means of contemplation or reverent attention, loving God with the intellect and the will, a way of knowing acquired by constant immersion in Scripture to become participants in its 'storied' way of life."[11] Theology for the bishop of Hippo creates habits of thought and action that in turn produce a life of godly wisdom.[12] There is no wisdom, then, without theology.

Augustine believed that the ministry of the truth would lead, by divine grace, to the miracle of transformation.

Augustine believed that the ministry of the truth would lead, by divine grace, to the miracle of transformation. In his classic work *On Christian Doctrine*, he straightforwardly expressed the need for Christian teachers to teach the right and correct the wrong:

> It is the duty, then, of the interpreter and teacher of Holy Scripture, the defender of the true faith and the opponent of error, both to teach what is right and

to refute what is wrong, and in the performance of this task to conciliate the hostile, to rouse the careless, and to tell the ignorant both what is occurring at present and what is probable in the future.[13]

Augustine viewed the ministry of truth in both positive and defensive terms. The right must be promoted while the false must be corrected. To be sure, Augustine devoted much attention to commending what was true to his people and to the audience of his writings. But he was no less an "opponent of error," using Scripture to correct heresies. In both roles, often filled at one and the same time, Augustine served the church as a theologian. This ministry meant not a leaving of the people, but a binding of himself to them. If he did not teach them well in a full-orbed way, encompassing both promotion and defense, they would remain "hostile" to God, "careless" before God, and "ignorant" of the very nature of their lives.

This last comment is instructive: unlike some pastor-teachers, Augustine could not content himself with only declaring the verities of days past. The pastor was called, even required, to wake the people to see what was "occurring at present," to make sense of their existence in their own particular context. For this reason, Augustine wrote *The City of God*, a text that seeks to make sense of why Rome fell after it became formally Christian while providing, more broadly, a Christian theology of history. The ministry is anchored in the proclamation of what is timeless, but as practiced by Augustine and many others, the ministry is to bring the timeless to bear on the present.

The Pastorate as an Office

Those who steward the mysteries of God's grace in Christ (cf. 1 Cor. 4:1) enter not a trade but an "office." In a letter to Bishop Valerius in 391, Augustine opined that there was "nothing in this life, and especially at this time, easier or more agreeable or more acceptable to men than the office of bishop or priest or deacon."[14] This scathing critique is noteworthy not only for the changed prospects of the post-Constantinian minister, but also for the use of "office" to describe the pastoral vocation.

Augustine's usage of "office" to describe the pastorate followed the earliest theologians of the church. Tertullian used the term in the early third century to speak against female pastors.[15] Hippolytus used it in 215 to speak of the rite of pastoral initiation: "If a confessor has been placed in chains for the

Name of the Lord, hands are not laid upon him," for such a figure "has the honor of the office" through his suffering.[16] By Augustine's day, it seems, it was common to speak of the pastorate as an office. This usage continued throughout the medieval period. Gregory I decries those who seek "the office of pastoral care" without humility, for example, in his *Pastoral Rule*.[17] Centuries later, Thomas Aquinas used the term, speaking in one instance in his *Summa theologica* of the need for only priests, "whose office it is to baptize solemnly," to carry out the initiatory rite.[18]

To jump ahead in our chronological survey for a moment, the Reformers used the title as well, though they rejected a division between "spiritual" or churchly offices and lay callings. Calvin, for example, spoke of "four offices" of the church, including the pastor or doctor.[19] From the Reformation onward, the pastorate as "office" became nearly ubiquitous in Protestant conceptions of the pastor, though it becomes less prominent in the twentieth century. In its historic deployment, in the early, medieval, and Protestant church, the term is often deployed to signal either the set-apart nature of the pastor or the unfitness of a person for such a role.

"Office," whether preceded by "pastoral" or "theological" (the terms seem to be relatively interchangeable in ancient usage), is linked in diverse eras to a high view of the pastorate and the holy seriousness of its work, which might begin to explain why this term sounds vaguely outmoded to modern ears. These terms indicate the solemnity and significance of the pastorate. One does not choose this office: one is called to it by the Lord and appointed to it by the church. A theological office is a role set apart for God's service, and accountability for its holy duties is not simply to an entire congregation but also ultimately to the God who rules heaven and earth.

The Medieval Period: Scholasticism and Monasticism

The conception of the pastor's work shifted during the medieval period. We are at pains to summarize such a sprawling pastoral and priestly movement stretching over a millennium, roughly 500–1500. Nevertheless, we can identify at least two major trends in the development of pastoral practice and understanding in the Catholic Church in the medieval era.

First, theology became more the province of what we could call "academic theologians." The scholastics, of course, made many important contributions to Christian doctrine, with Anselm and Aquinas among the most noteworthy thinkers of the period. Anselm's "satisfaction theory" of the atonement faithfully captured a key thread of biblical teaching on the crucifixion that the Reformers would develop in their project to recover "penal substitution" from Scripture. Anselm's *Cur Deus Homo* (*Why God Became Man*) argued for the necessity of the incarnation and connected it to the atonement, a vital theological link. Aquinas made many and varied contributions to Christian theology, not least of them his doctrine of just-war theory, his "five arguments" that ground a belief in the existence of God, and his development of Augustinian predestination.

These figures and others—Abelard, Ockham, and Scotus prominent among them—made deeply meaningful contributions to the theological guild. But this was part of a growing problem: as the Catholic Church grew and expanded, the teaching of theology became more the province of academic teachers and less the responsibility of learned pastors. Here we see the second major trend of the medieval pastorate: it became the province of practical ministry, deeds-driven service, rather than the central location of the theological task. Leaders like Gregory I, Bernard of Clairvaux, and Francis of Assisi trained many followers to take up mendicant ministry and to perform holy works. To be sure, such duties overlap with the biblical portrait of the pastor. For our purposes, however, this shift toward "practical ministry," as we could call it, meant that many local church leaders saw themselves less as theologians, as in past days, and more as spiritual aid workers.

The Reformational Awakening: Protestant Pastors

By the early sixteenth century, the established European church had moved away from the early church's teaching and model of the pastorate. The Reformation represents both a reclamation of biblical doctrine and a restoration of the pastoral model of the early church. From his post in muddy Wittenberg, Martin Luther taught that the pastor existed for no greater purpose than to make clear the gospel and to present Christ to the people. There is considerable continuity between Augustine's vision of the pastor and Luther's, as we see in Luther's lectures on Galatians:

> Therefore we always repeat, urge, and inculcate this doctrine of faith or Christian righteousness, so that it may be observed by continuous use and may be precisely

distinguished from the active righteousness of the law. (For by this doctrine alone and through it alone is the church built, and in this it consists.) Otherwise we shall not be able to observe true theology but shall immediately become lawyers, ceremonialists, legalists, and papists. Christ will be so darkened that no one in the church will be correctly taught or comforted. Therefore if we want to be preachers and teachers of others, we must take great care in these issues and hold to this distinction between the righteousness of the Law and the righteousness of Christ.[20]

The work of the pastor is at once a deadly serious business and a life-giving appointment in Luther's mind. If we get the law and gospel wrong, we fall away from "true theology" and obscure Christ himself, for one cannot know and understand Christ apart from a correct understanding of his righteous work. Preaching the righteousness that is by faith is, in Luther's view, fulfilling the fundamental mission of "preachers and teachers of others." The pastor is thus commissioned by God to "inculcate this doctrine of faith." The work of proclaiming "true theology," that which literally saves and transforms the people, requires "great care" and unusual theological discernment. Thus Luther held a high view of the pastoral office.

This conception of the pastorate was supported and even enhanced by Luther's brother in spiritual arms, John Calvin. Appointed in human terms to the Genevan pastorate by the fiery persuasion of Guillaume Farel, Calvin witnessed the profound blessing of the Lord on his doctrinally charged ministry. More than Luther, and more than any other pastor in his day, Calvin fashioned a self-consciously theological pastorate in Geneva. In his *Institutes of the Christian Religion*, Calvin defined the office of pastor as indissolubly connected to the Scripture:

Here, then, is the sovereign power with which the pastors of the church, by whatever name they be called, ought to be endowed. That is that they may dare boldly to do all things by God's Word; may compel all worldly power, glory, wisdom, and exaltation to yield to and obey his majesty; supported by his power, may command all from the highest even to the last; may build up Christ's household and cast down Satan's; may feed the sheep and drive away the wolves; may instruct and exhort the teachable; may accuse, rebuke, and subdue the rebellious and stubborn; may bind and loose; finally, if need be, may launch thunderbolts and lightnings; but do all things in God's Word.[21]

The ministry owes its power, all of it, to the Word of God. Calvin's definition ties all agency and power in ecclesial service to Scripture. His full confidence as a minister was in the Bible, which he clearly believed called all to account, including those possessing "worldly power." As the pastor-ruler of Geneva, it is not surprising that Calvin had such a perspective; he was not a magistrate of the city, but he exercised profound moral influence in it.

Calvin's primary act of influence was the sermon, and the model of his preaching was expository. Calvin, like so many other Reformers (including a great many whom he trained), preached continually through books of the Bible, interpreting the text in a simple yet learned style. At the end of his life, in his will, he summarized the aim of his preaching: "I have endeavored, both in my sermons and also in my writings and commentaries, to preach the word purely and chastely, and faithfully to interpret His sacred Scriptures."[22] To do so, Calvin studied ferociously during the week, straining the limits of his body in order to know the passage in question and give the right sense of it, a sense always conditioned by the grace of God in Christ. Then, his preparation concluded, he ascended to the high pulpit, opened his Bible, and preached without notes. This was a grand ministry, but it

Calvin's primary act of influence was the sermon, and the model of his preaching was expository.

was grand not because of ornamentation or affectation, but because Calvin's preaching lifted up a great and gracious God, who built his kingdom through the humble yet powerful work of regular, focused, weekly exposition, one Sunday after another, one sermon after another.

In his preaching and his broader program, Calvin sought to provide not only exegetical instruction but also "moral oversight."[23] Calvin knew he could not make people Christian, despite what some contemporary scholars would argue. But he did see to it that the pastors under his watch shepherded the city's moral life. As Scott Manetsch has observed, "Geneva's unique brand of church-sponsored discipline emerged from biblical and theological reflection, as well as everyday practice."[24] Calvin, Beza, and the band of ministers they trained put great stock in the biblical fact that Jesus entrusted the "keys" of his kingdom to his disciples (see Matt. 16:19; 18:18–19). The Genevan pastor-theologians took the "power of the keys," as the Reformers called it, to mean that they were responsible to exercise ecclesiastical discipline. In the city, this led to the formation of "an elaborate system of surveillance and pastoral supervision within the city and countryside parishes."[25] This system represented the realization, however imperfectly, of a theological vision for the Genevan church, one driven by the preeminent pastor-theologian of the era. To be sure, the Genevans did not always live up to their own high standards. It was their goal, however, to instantiate the holiness of God in the life of the people.

Calvin was not alone in seeking the transformation of his surroundings through a revitalized pastorate. Other Reformers invested considerable authority in their pastoral corps. In their ministries Ulrich Zwingli in Zurich and John Knox in Scotland, to name just two other leading Reformers, acted on the conviction that the Scripture, to a degree that many modern pastors might shy away from, was for all of life, including one's society. It was confidence in the Word of God that led the Reformers to this conviction and that transformed sixteenth-century Europe. Knox's peer, Thomas Randolph, famously summed up the effect of the preacher: "I assure you the voice of one man is hable in one hower to put more lyf in us than 500 trumpettes continually blustering our eares."[26] These are strong words in any era, but in the age of the Reformation, there was abundant evidence to their truthfulness.

Theological Shepherds: The Puritans and the Practicality of Truth

The Puritans, heirs of the on-again, off-again English Reformation, viewed the office of pastor in similar terms. The pastor was a physician of souls, a theologian who brought all the force of biblical doctrine to bear on the lives of his needy people.

This was true to the core of their ministry. The Puritans defined theology in churchly terms. William Ames, author of the classic Puritan theology manual *Medulla ss. theologiae* (*The Marrow of Sacred Theology*), defined theology itself as "the doctrine of living [un]to God." In his book Ames argued that "since the highest kind of life for a human being is that which approaches most closely the living and life-giving God, the nature of theological life is living to God."[27] In Ames's construal, theology is for living. It is for the people of God and designed so that they might flourish before God. It belongs to those who would live for God, know his will, and treasure his goodness. This is a premodern, precritical definition of theology that has much to commend it, as successive chapters will make clear.

The Puritans loved theology, but they loved it in large part because it was fitted for life. Few of their ilk advocated for the practicality of biblical truth more than Richard Sibbes, the "Sweet Dropper" of Cambridge. Sibbes famously pictured the Christian as a "bruised reed" in fundamental need of Christ and his comfort:

> The bruised reed is a man that for the most part is in some misery, as those were that came to Christ for help, and by misery he is brought to see sin as the cause of it, for, whatever pretences sin makes, they come to an end when we are bruised and broken. He is sensible of sin and misery, even unto bruising; and, seeing no help in himself, is carried with restless desire to have supply from another, with some hope, which a little raises him out of himself to Christ, though he dare not claim any present interest of mercy. This spark of hope being opposed by doubtings and fears rising from corruption makes him as smoking flax; so that both these together a *bruised* reed and *smoking* flax, make up the state of a poor distressed man. This is such an one as our Saviour Christ terms "poor in spirit," who sees his wants, and also sees himself indebted to divine justice.[28]

Because of this weakened condition, the believer needed the church, which Sibbes depicted as "*a common hospital*, wherein all are in some measure sick of some spiritual disease or other, so all have occasion to exercise the spirit of wisdom and meekness."[29] In Sibbes's hands, theology is essentially Christ-shaped comfort for a weary, needy, broken people.

We gain further appreciation for the rich connections made by the Puritans between theology and life in the ministry of Richard Baxter, the seventeenth-century catechist of Kidderminster. Baxter has passed into pastoral immortality for his unflagging efforts to train the eight hundred families in his congregation in the rudiments of biblical faith. For this reason, Baxter is often grouped as a "practical theologian." But here again we glimpse the difficulty of this descriptor. Behind the Puritan's prodigious program, after all, lay the settled conviction that the chief need of the church was theological instruction of such a kind that it produced a transformed heart.

In his classic work *The Reformed Pastor*, Baxter suggested that the members of the church needed to have things of eternal weight pressed into their souls by their pastors:

> It is these fundamentals that must lead men to further truths; it is these they must build all upon; it is these that must actuate all their graces, and build all upon; it is these that must fortify them against temptations. He that knows not these, knows nothing; he that knows them well, doth know so much as will make him happy; and he that knows them best, is the best and most understanding Christian.[30]

Without biblical truth, Christians had nothing to "build all upon," nothing to "fortify them against temptations." Baxter believed there was a one-to-one relationship between knowledge and maturity. Purves notes that Baxter operated "on the view that grace enters into lives by growth in understanding."[31]

The Puritans were not spotless shepherds; they had their foibles. Yet all their ministry was grounded in Scripture and the need, quite simply, to teach it. In this respect, they represent a faithful model for modern pastor-theologians to follow. J. I. Packer, dean of Puritan scholars, has said that their scriptural interpretation shows that they believed that "Scripture is a doctrinal book; it teaches us about God and created things in their relation to him."[32] All the Bible was "theocentric," meaning that Puritan pastors taught their people the "God-centred standpoint of Scripture." This meant that "whereas fallen man sees himself as the centre of the universe, the Bible shows us God as central, and depicts all creatures, man included, in their proper perspective—as existing through God, and for God."[33]

For the Puritans, pastoral work was not an escape from theological work but the call to instantiate truth in the life of the church.

The Puritans, we see, took theological and intellectual dominion of the created order, setting themselves up as the chief interpreters of life and thought in this world. With the Lutheran and Reformed pastors of the Reformation period, they would have boggled at the suggestion that they, as pastors, were inadequate to act as theologians for their people. They might have asked, "Who else but the pastor is capable for these things?" For the Puritans, and for many thousands upon thousands of ministers in the church's history, pastoral work was not an escape from theological work but the call to instantiate truth in the life of the church. For the Puritans, theology cannot be anything but public: the people of God living to God by living out God's truth.

Agents of "Divine Business": The Edwardseans and Pastoral Dominion

America's greatest pastor was a son of the Puritans. Because of this storied legacy, it is easy to forget that Jonathan Edwards spent little time in the ivory tower. He was never a professor in the modern sense. Edwards composed many of his treatises in the middle of a demanding pastorate, at the largest church in New England, outside of Boston. Later he wrote soaring theological works on the Massachusetts frontier while serving as a missionary.

Few pastors will match the output of Edwards as an author and theologian. That stated, his conception of ministry and his personal model offer generous encouragement for theological ministry conducted on behalf of the church. His ordination sermons, delivered in many cases in far-flung locales, made plain that the ministry the ordinand was entering was a doctrinal calling. In one such sermon preached on the nature of the bond between pastor and people, Edwards argued that the pastorate was nothing other than a gospel ministry:

> The business of the Gospel is properly a divine business. They that are called to this work are called to a work that may properly be called Christ's work. It is a business wherein a person has, in all parts of it, to do with God. It is either to act in the name of God's people towards God, or in the name of God towards the people. It all consists in acting either to God or from God. And it is to act for God. God is more immediately the end of the work of the ministry than of any other work or employment that men are called to in this world.

Edwards concluded the point by connecting the pastor to Christ:

> When a people call a minister, it is that he may be a person by whom they may carry on their affairs to Godward—a person to act for them before God, and by whom they may worship him. The office of the ministry is an office not of any human or earthly kingdom, but it is an office of Christ's kingdom. A gospel minister is Christ's officer, and his business is to be an instrument to carry on Christ's work, the work of redemption.[34]

There are many Edwardsean passages on pastoral identity worth citing, but these capture Edwards's unshakable conviction that pastors carry out "divine business," a marvelous phrase. In its totality, "in all parts of it," the pastorate deals with God, and the pastor is thus primarily a theological leader. There is little finesse in this conception of the ministry but much glory. The pastor is, one might say, set apart, a figure whose orientation is relentlessly "Godward." Acting either toward God from the people, or toward the people from God, the minister in every case has God as "the end of the work." This is a role unlike any other.

The pastor in the Edwardsean model was not to waste time looking longingly at more urbane and profitable careers. Leaders of the church were officers of Christ, instruments in "the work of redemption," the greatest work the world would ever see. So it was that Edwards focused so much of his own attention on "revival," the saving of souls through the preaching of the gospel. Edwards preached Christ to both the professing Christian and the wandering soul. His theological ministry fueled and propelled his preaching for conversions and did not squelch it. Study and deep thought produced in him an even greater desire for souls. There was no tension in Edwards between intellectual brilliance and evangelistic passion. Instead, each stoked the other, as his fervency for the Great Awakenings of the 1730s and 1740s shows in spades.

To read Edwards's sermons is to hear him roar. His was no tame pastorate. His ministry involved high-powered theological work in the sense that Freud's counseling involved psychology, Einstein's academic work involved science, and Churchill's work involved politics. Robert Caldwell has well said, "Edwards was convinced that the primary pathway to Christian transformation was through teaching the great truths of Christianity. Only when the mind is sufficiently informed with biblical theology can heart and life be transformed by the gospel." To this end, Edwards "devoted long hours to studying the Scriptures so that his congregation could benefit from his rich meditations on biblical doctrine." Beyond this, "He wrote sermons and treatises on the will, moral virtue, the mind, and much more."[35]

Week after week, Edwards preached the biblical text. He was not an expositor in the verse-by-verse sense now common among homileticians; instead, Edwards often focused his attention on a single phrase or sentence of the Bible. After explanatory remarks on the context of the passage, Edwards then delved into the textual "doctrine," typically taking one of several homiletical paths: he might ground the idea by using biblical theology, making canonical connections with his text; he might expound on the theology or philosophy that the verse substantiated; he might offer extended commentary on the plight of his people and their great need for repentance and faith. All this work built to the application, which was often just as theological as the preceding section. Consider the following from *The Excellency of Christ*:

> Let what has been said, be improved to induce you to love the Lord Jesus Christ, and choose him for your friend and portion. As there is such an admirable meeting of diverse excellencies in Christ, so there is everything in him to render him worthy of your love and choice, and to win and engage it. Whatsoever there is, or can be, that is desirable to be in a friend, is in Christ, and that to the highest degree that can be desired.[36]

For Edwards, it is not first Christ's love that induces humanity to follow and worship him, but the "admirable meeting of diverse excellencies" one finds in him, and only in him. So it was that Edwards called his hearers to become friends with Christ, to experience affection and happiness of "the highest degree."

Edwards was not departing from his tradition in ranging over whole vistas of theological, philosophical, and spiritual life. He was reared in a grand expository tradition, one that called preachers not to a lowest common communicative denominator but to the practice of a multifaceted ministry, with the stimulation of the intellect and the affections at the core. Richard Bailey has observed, "Edwards modeled his preaching after several contemporary preaching manuals, particularly Cotton Mather's *Manductio ad ministerium* and John Edwards' *The Preacher*. Both of these books appear early in Edwards' 'Catalogue,' a list of books documenting his reading interests." According to John Edwards, the preacher "must be a Linguist, a Grammarian, a Critick, an Orator, a Philosopher, an Historian, a Casuist, a Disputant, and whatever speaks Skill and Knowledge in any Learned Science," while he seeks to construct sermons "like diamonds, Clear as well as Solid."[37]

Two centuries before Kuyper would picture Christ calling "Mine!" over all his creation, Edwards was already calling "His!"

In his own preaching, Edwards felt no shame in relating all areas of life to God. If an area of God's created order seized his attention, he felt glorious freedom to situate it within his God-centered worldview and to preach it to his people. This was the outworking of being a gospel minister, the figure who served the kingdom of Christ, which stood over the world, ruling it. Two centuries before Dutch theologian Abraham Kuyper would picture Christ calling "Mine!" over all his creation, Edwards was already calling "His!" in his preaching and writing.

The followers of Edwards, creators of an indigenous theological school called the New Divinity, similarly served as pastor-theologians. Like Edwards, they sought revival wherever they went, even as they continued to ask the great questions of the Scripture and the faith. They were intellectually curious, poring over different disciplines to mine them for wisdom and insight, writing with abandon. As E. Brooks Holifield has shown, they and their contemporaries racked up an impressive publishing record in the eighteenth and nineteenth centuries:

> The Presbyterian Jonathan Dickinson attained an international reputation for blending Calvinism and revivalist piety. Samuel Johnson in Connecticut was equally at home with Anglican sacramental theology, British moral thought, and philosophy. Cotton Mather wrote the history of New England, James Blair and William Stith the history of Virginia, and Jeremy Belknap the history of New Hampshire. Jedidiah Morse was America's leading geographer. Francis Allison and John Witherspoon popularized Scottish philosophy. John Clayton and John Bannister in Virginia prepared botanical reports, while Jared Eliot wrote on iron and field husbandry in New England. Edward Taylor, Timothy Dwight, and Conowry Owen stand out as colonial poets. Toward the end of the century, lawyers and political theorists took the lead, but for most of the period the clergy were America's intellectuals.[38]

This last sentence may startle the modern reader. "America's intellectuals" would not necessarily stick to the preaching class today. Yet this summation deserves reflection. There is something vibrant, something alive, in Holifield's reconstruction. Something moves and breathes in this summary that sleeps in the present day. Pastors were once theologians, and theologians of intellectual confidence, not merely spiritual confidence. They were often their community's best-educated citizen: learned generalists. They spoke authoritatively on a wide range of matters. They believed that they were in the *best* position for this kind of work, because God's Word interpreted the world authoritatively.

The Modern Turn: Populism, Professionalism, and the Taming of the Pastorate

If pastoral ministry is divine business, then we might describe its modern crisis as a theological recession. To make sense of this claim, we must first understand the effects of the post-Edwards era, the late eighteenth and early nineteenth centuries, which upset the established order so carefully tended by the Puritans and their heirs.

The Great Awakening driven by the preaching of Edwards, George White-field, John Wesley, and a host of others shook up the colonies and, as it extended throughout the eighteenth century, the young republic. In this era, one need not be a member of the formal clergy to preach; one could emulate Whitefield, the tireless outdoor celebrity evangelist, and with Wesley claim the world as one's parish. As the First Great Awakening gave way to the Second, it produced new movements and powered upstart denominations. In the early nineteenth century, the Baptists and Methodists exploded in numbers as a generation of circuit riders and evangelists roamed the country.

The effect of these awakenings upon America was revolutionary. According to Nathan Hatch, a leading historian of the nineteenth century, it was this period and its "wave of popular religious movements" that "did more to Christianize American society than anything before or since."[39] No preacher more exemplified the spirit of the rambunctious Second Great Awakening than Charles Finney. After entering the ministry with little formal training, he promptly sought to modify the theology of the Edwardsean revivalists, whom he believed hindered sinners from coming to Christ due to their belief in the necessity of sovereign grace. Finney seized on Edwards's idea of "natural inability" but converted it to "natural ability" in terms akin to Pelagian theology. According to Finney, in their "inward being" sinners are "conscious of ability to will and of power to control their outward life directly, and the states of their intellect and of their sensibility, either directly or indirectly, by willing."[40] In Finney's scheme, conversion therefore became a matter of discovering the right agitator of the will. Turning to Christ was, in a watershed statement, "a purely philosophical result of the right use of the constituted means."[41] Because of this, Finney instituted the "anxious bench" and other methods that placed tremendous psychological and emotional pressure on the sinner. Unlike past revivalists, conversion for Finney did not require a miracle; it was, with the proper techniques, a sure thing. Finney exerted a significant influence on fellow Christian preachers. According to Randall Balmer and Lauren Winner, scores of other Protestants "began to adopt his practices when they saw just how many converts Finney could win in a single night of preaching."[42] This can-do spirit went hand in glove with a changing America. The so-called Dedham Decision of 1820 proved to be a tipping point for what had been developing for decades, even centuries: the final disestablishment of the Christian church. After the implications of this decision unfolded, local assemblies no longer enjoyed the tax support of every landowning citizen.

This brought a truly stunning change in American life that fit the political mood of the country perfectly. Innovation and no-holds-barred gospel proclamation became the means by which one won a hearing. In many places, formal training was seen as a deadening agent on a young preacher and on the church who endured his stilted preaching. The Puritan sermons with fifty subheadings were out; the freewheeling pulpiteer, master of the homespun story, was in. As Hatch has said, religious upstarts eagerly tackled the challenges of this new age, changing the nature of American ministry and preaching in the process:

> Passionate about ferreting out converts in every hamlet and crossroads, they sought to bind them together in local and regional communities. They continued to refashion the sermon as a popular medium, inviting even the most unlearned and inexperienced to respond to a call to preach. These initiates were charged to proclaim the gospel anywhere and every day of the week—even to the limit of their physical endurance. The resulting creation, the colloquial sermon, employed daring pulpit storytelling, no-holds-barred appeals, overt humor, strident attack, graphic application, and intimate personal experience.[43]

In one generation, America went from a nation featuring a carefully guarded pastoral office—marked by learning, communal stability, and staunch theological preaching—to one in which disestablishment reigned and highly gifted populist communicators like Finney dominated. At the same time, the increasingly secularized American academy, like its European forebears, expanded and made territorial claims over the intellectual life of the country.

As the nineteenth century wore on and the twentieth began, pastors yielded to academics as thought leaders, giving up much of the disciplinary ground over which Kuyper's (and Edwards's) Christ shouted "Mine!" According to George Marsden, this transition centered in a few major moves that together helped to transform the American academy, and with it, the American church. First, scholarship was "seen as a profession in its own right."[44] Second, in this framework, philosophy, philology, and later the hard sciences displaced theology as the queen of the disciplines. Third, theology itself was separated from the life of the church, in large part due to the Kantian division between "noumenal" (spiritual) and "phenomenal" (verifiable) truth.

In this context, theologians scrambled to justify their discipline as academically respectable even as their fellow intellectuals increasingly viewed them as trafficking in the reconstruction of fairy tales. In the eighteenth century, Enlightenment thinkers had declared miracles out-of-bounds, but it was not until the institutionalization of the modern research university in the midnineteenth century that the miraculous, and beyond this the supernatural, was effectively ruled out-of-bounds in academic discourse. Some respect for eminent theologians, most of whom treated the Bible as a thoroughly human historical product, lingered in Europe and America. This persisted even into the mid-twentieth century; it took some time for the Enlightenment to triumph over the Great Awakening, to use a bit of historical shorthand, and the victory was not truly recognized until the late twentieth century. But the theological guild, particularly its evangelical members, would never be the same. The queen of the sciences, the discipline that for centuries had God for its object, had dwindled into religious studies, a region of merely human (all too human!) behavior. If society were one grand dinner party, the theologians were increasingly to be found in the corner, left alone to their fantastic thoughts and their pious imprecations.

The theologians suffered from this momentous cultural shift, yet the pastors took it still harder. Theology had become a specialist's discipline, not a generalist's, as was formerly the case. As noted, theologians scrambled to justify their professions. Many pastors either ignored these developments, focusing instead on their local church work, or waved a white flag. By the early twentieth century in urban areas, with some notable exceptions, pastoring was now a practical profession, more concerned with meeting immediate personal needs than with formulating timeless truths. This was communicated not only by a growing secularist media culture but also by the very seminaries in which pastors trained. E. Brooks Holifield has observed that William Rainey Harper, intellectual architect of the University of Chicago,

Theology had become a specialist's discipline, not a generalist's.

"wanted future ministers to learn not primarily by mastering a theological system but by developing special skills in preaching, teaching, pastoral duties, music, and church administration." This meant substantial fieldwork, for the "professional minister would have specialized knowledge linked to practical skills, not necessarily theological learning in the older manner but a theologically informed capacity to carry out the functions associated with ministry to a congregation."[45]

In Harper's epoch-changing theories, we witness a sea change in the ministry. Alongside the other trends thus far mentioned, we behold the taming of the pastorate. Pastors by and large embraced this new identity, domesticated, bridled, and even secularized as it was. Theirs was a "practical" field, though many ministers sought to cling to some of their former glory by grounding their work as a "profession."[46]

With the increasing dominance of the American business climate in cultural life, churches began to seek to grow just like the mass-market enterprises rocketing into profitability all around them. "Efficiency" propelled the "church growth" model, and "administration" ascended to primacy of place in the panoply of pastoral duties. In such a climate, as H. Richard Niebuhr of Yale Divinity School wrote,

> The pastoral director becomes the "big operator." When ministers comment on the kinds of men who are failures in the ministry they frequently describe among these types the person who operates a religious club or a neighborhood society with much efficiency and pomp and circumstance. He is active in many affairs, organizes many societies, advertises the increases in membership and budget achieved under his administration and, in general, manages church business as if it were akin to the activities of a chamber of commerce. In their reaction to such secularization of the office some men try to return to the idea of the preacher or of the priest. But the needs of men and the responsibilities of office prevent them from doing so. Then they realize that the "big operator" represents a perversion of the minister's office not because he is an executive but because he does not administer the *church's* work.[47]

Niebuhr put his finger on a massive problem confronting the church. Outside of the confessional traditions, the pastorate had largely lost its character as a theological office in midcentury America; in many pulpits this conception was lost and has not returned.

None of the foregoing means that theologically minded pastors like C. H. Spurgeon failed to find an audience in the late nineteenth century. They most certainly did not fail, and Spurgeon's sermons still speak. Yet alongside the trends just covered, revivalism blazed on, as evangelists like Billy Sunday carried its torch into the twentieth century. Sunday famously—and proudly—said that he knew as much about theology as a jackrabbit knows about Ping-Pong, a quip that historian George Marsden affirmed as stated "with some accuracy."[48]

Billy Sunday's exploits were unparalleled in evangelistic history; by many estimations, he preached to more people than had any other revivalist in history—until, that is, Billy Graham exploded on the scene. Graham's rise as a world-famous revivalist helped cement the already-established trends thus far documented. Graham became a global celebrity in 1949 after newspaper magnate William Randolph Hearst (the inspiration for no less a cinematic character than Citizen Kane) told his staff to "puff Graham" after a number of celebrities publicly converted to Christ at the evangelist's Los Angeles rally. Graham and his team had learned from forebears like Whitefield, Finney, and Sunday and had publicized these conversions.

Graham's use of the market did not signal that his was a compromised ministry; it did show, though, that ministry in America had changed dramatically in two hundred years. Though there is no real contradiction between theology and evangelism, many pastors eschewed the former in favor of the latter, finding their model in the mega-evangelists. These tended to see their chief duty to be not biblical-theological instruction but rather the oversight of ongoing revival (and meeting felt needs). In this climate, influenced by the other factors mentioned above, theology seemed separate from evangelism and from the local church's everyday ministry. The church's evangelistic apparatus was strong, but its theological muscles had atrophied due to disuse.

> *The church's evangelistic apparatus was strong, but its theological muscles had atrophied due to disuse.*

Glimmers of Hope: Harold Ockenga and Neoevangelical Boldness

In the face of these developments, some pastors pursued the recovery of the historic model of the pastor—the pastor-theologian—thus seeking to repair what modern man had put asunder.

In 1937 a gifted young pastor with the unforgettable Dutch name of Ockenga had assumed the helm of Boston's historic Park Street Church. Harold John Ockenga was from Chicago, had gone to revivalist Taylor University, trained at austere and modernizing Princeton Theological Seminary, and graduated from Westminster Theological Seminary as the protégé of confessional theologian J. Gresham Machen. Ockenga took the then-unusual step of earning a doctorate from the University of Pittsburgh, showing a strong desire to equip himself for a theological pastorate. But Ockenga did not seek a scholarly ministry at the expense of evangelism. Under his leadership, Park Street personally funded dozens of cross-cultural missionaries, held annual events to prioritize global gospel ministry, and held citywide preaching events aimed at those outside the church.

Ockenga's ministry on the edge of Boston Common flourished from the start, with his preaching drawing congregants from Harvard, MIT, and the professional class, many driving in from all corners of the surrounding area. Ockenga made no apology for preaching lengthy intellectually ambitious sermons grounded in "logical doctrine." The ambitious young pastor was not content to feed only his tony Boston crowd, though. He wanted to inspire a generation of staunch young ministers. When called to the first presidency of Fuller Theological Seminary in 1947, he posited the need for a rigorously intellectual program for young Christian students:

> We do not intend to allow our Christian heritage to go because of default. A revival of Christian thought and life cannot occur in a vacuum. Our minds must first be convinced before we commit our lives, our fortunes, and our sacred honor to any cause. Since in the minds of many people the ground work for the Christian view of God, the world, man and the kingdom has been destroyed by naturalism and liberalism, it will be the solemn and sacred duty of this faculty to attempt the reconstruction of this with scholarly pursuit.[49]

Ockenga wanted to recover the historic model of the pastorate, which centered in staunchly theological ministry that took dominion of all life and thought in the name of Jesus Christ. Here we witness the confident spirit of the past raising its head once more. Christianity stood in a position to judge the world, not vice versa; pastors training under the scholarly Fuller faculty, led by its first academic dean, Carl F. H. Henry, would be equipped to interpret their world and proclaim God's truth.[50]

Several future leaders for God entered the ministry after sitting under Ockenga's own preaching. Ockenga's influence did not overturn the aforementioned trends, to say the least. Alongside contemporaries and successors like W. A. Criswell, James Boice, D. Martyn Lloyd-Jones, Sinclair Ferguson, John Stott, Mark Dever, John Piper, John MacArthur, and J. Ligon Duncan, however, Ockenga reclaimed the model of the pastor-theologian in his ministry, grounding his work in unabashedly theological preaching, teaching, and leadership. The message of the gospel informed all aspects of his ministry: he did not shrink back from instructing his people in the whole counsel of God, a charge that meant learned exegesis of the Scripture rather than entertaining homiletics. Ockenga believed that the Word fed the people, and so he devoted himself to a theological pastorate. His influence endures in the present day, as a generation of would-be pastor-theologians seek, like him, to reclaim the ministry as—in the words of Jonathan Edwards, Ockenga's New England forebear—a "gospel office."

Conclusion: Toward What Pastorate?

Christian pastors have historically figured among the brightest minds of the Christian church. The pastorate has not historically squeezed church leaders into a tiny box, shutting out the possibility of thinking—not until recently. On the contrary: for much of church history, the pastorate has unleashed godly and gifted leaders to declare and demonstrate the riches of God's Word to people. This is the activity that renders them pastor-theologians who, for the good of people and the glory of God, bring all of life and thought under the dominion of Christ Jesus.

Hope is real. Even in the grim world of Cormac McCarthy's apocalyptic fiction, after all, the fire still burns. One McCarthy story, the poleaxing novel *The Road*, features a conversation between an unnamed father and son who are alone and must surmount many and terrible obstacles to survive. The narrative is fierce, but in one piercing conversation, hope peeks through.

> SON: We're going to be okay, aren't we Papa?
> FATHER: Yes. We are.
> SON: And nothing bad is going to happen to us.
> FATHER: That's right.
> SON: Because we're carrying the fire.
> FATHER: Yes. Because we're carrying the fire.[51]

If we may transpose these words to the church, we can observe that evangelical churches do face the threat of decline. Yet in the midst of a secularizing society and a church that sometimes seems bent on exchanging its pastoral birthright for a morsel of meat, great hope is at hand. A generation of pastors has carried the fire, wedding theology to practical ministry. May God raise up others, in the present generation, who are likewise willing to carry the fire.

How the Theology of Saving Faith
Has Affected My Congregation

WESLEY G. PASTOR

In 1746, Jonathan Edwards prefaced his great work *Religious Affections* with a question that has rocked my church for the past fourteen years: "What is the nature of true religion?"[1]

Edwards asserted that there was "no question of greater importance to mankind."[2] There has certainly been no question with greater impact on Christ Memorial Church, planted in 1992. Christ Memorial saw sixteen conversions in its first seven years. But since 1999, we've averaged approximately sixteen conversions *per year,* including a number of professing believers. What follows is my own "faithful narrative" of and commentary on these surprising conversions.[3]

This journey started for me as a student at Dallas Theological Seminary under the tutelage of Dr. John Hannah, professor of historical theology. Dr. Hannah was significant in steering me into church planting in New England, mentoring me in the glorious Awakenings, and exposing me to Jonathan Edwards, the great theologian of revival. Sue and I moved to Vermont in 1991, and Christ Memorial was launched the next year.

For the first seven years, our church saw steady growth but relatively few conversions. Then, in February 1999, an active member who had professed faith as a teen was suddenly converted. Our congregation witnessed the radical transformation of this "Christian" who got saved. Responses were mixed. Some embraced this new category quickly. Others were cautious, perhaps a bit confused. Some were just angry.

Sandy was indignant.[4] A mother of four and committed to Christian homeschooling, Sandy reasoned that, if one professing Christian could be deceived, she also might be. As she wrestled through her response, God revealed that her persistent guilt came not from failing to understand grace, but from failing to have it applied to her heart. She was penitent but not repentant. Yet that summer, God moved in Sandy's heart, drawing her to true faith in Christ. With her burden now lifted, she rejoiced in her conversion and rejoices in the conversions of all those formerly deceived.

That fall we launched a series on the book of Hebrews, a letter written to people who had professed faith and even suffered for Christ's sake, but were in danger of falling away (Heb. 3:12–4:13). I was preaching regularly, therefore, on the persevering nature of true faith, which longs for the heavenly city, is obedient even amid persecution, and loves the fellowship of the brethren (Heb. 10:24–25, 35–39; 11:8–10; 13:1–3).

Chet, the son of a Methodist minister and active in his church for nearly two decades, came to Christ later that year. He and his wife were pursuing membership, so I asked them to prepare their testimonies. That night, they realized they had no testimonies. Nothing in their lives resembled true faith. They stayed awake, confessing, repenting, and finally coming to a saving knowledge of Christ. Since then they've served his church joyfully.

The conversions continued, with adults and teens both affected. And Marie was watching. As an elder's wife, Marie had struggled with a judgmental and unloving spirit for years. In my New Year's sermon in 2002, I challenged our congregation to love each other the way we love ourselves, which is the distinguishing mark of saving faith (Luke 10:25–28; 1 John 3:11–24). God opened Marie's eyes to the stranglehold of her sin, and she was dramatically converted. The following year, as I preached through Romans, God saved Claire, a staff member who was raised a Jew but had professed faith nearly two decades earlier. God showed her that her intellectual assent to the gospel had merely heightened her awareness of the law, not given her the power to obey it (Rom. 6–8; James 2:19). Both Marie and Claire continue to walk as new creations to this day.

God has been on the move. He's saved adulterers, assistant pastors' wives—even an assistant pastor who, working through *Religious Affections*, gradually realized that his own affections were unholy. Yes, God has moved through a better grasp of the theology of saving faith. But this theology is nothing new. At one level, it's the theology of the Puritans, expressed so well by Jonathan Edwards. But really, it's the theology of Scripture: of the four Gospels, of Genesis and Romans, of Exodus and Hebrews, of Deuteronomy and James, of the Pastoral Epistles, of John's Epistles and John's Revelation. It's the doctrine of salvation, focusing on the nature of true faith that (1) proceeds from the eternal election of God the Father; (2) is grounded in the death, burial, and resurrection of Christ; (3) is activated by the miraculous touch of God's Spirit; (4) delivers from sin's penalty, power, and (ultimately) presence; (5) works itself out in love for the brethren; and (6) always perseveres.

Our folk have come to understand that true faith is life-changing faith. They have embraced the understanding that not everyone who says, "Lord, Lord," will enter the kingdom of heaven (Matt. 7:21–23). They've grasped that saved soil bears lasting fruit (Mark 4:1–20). True faith, unlike that of Judas and the Jews, abides and perseveres even amid persecution (John 15:1–6; Rev. 2–3). They know it's possible to have spurious faith, vain faith, devilish faith, none of which will save (John 8:30–59; 1 Cor. 15:1–2; James 2:14–26). They're clear that real faith no longer practices sin but performs righteousness and, particularly, demonstrates love for the brethren (1 Cor. 6:9–10; Gal. 5:19–21; 1 John 3:1–10). Our church knows that there's no higher life, deeper life, second work, or gospel wakefulness, but only a faith that miraculously flows from God's quickening ray, producing new creations that "rise, go forth, and follow Christ."[5]

God has been gracious to Christ Memorial Church, awakening some two hundred souls these last fourteen years, and credibly so. And it continues. This past summer as we baptized seven teens, we heard testimony after testimony reflecting clarity on their sin, their Savior, and the signs of true life they'd already experienced. The theology of saving faith has helped our people to answer life's most important question and to experience the freedom of true faith: increasingly dying to sin and living unto righteousness (1 Pet. 2:24). As Jesus said, "If you continue in my word"—if you have saving faith—"you are truly my disciples; and you will know the truth, and the truth will make you free" (John 8:31–32 RSV).

A Place for Truth

KEVIN DEYOUNG

If I'm not mistaken, our church is known around town as the "theology church." I don't say that to pat my own back. After all, taking theology seriously is no guarantee of spiritual fruitfulness and Christlike maturity. Being known for faith, hope, or love might be safer than a reputation for theological erudition. Still, all things considered, I'll take "theology church" over the "church that recycles batteries," the "church with the Xboxes in the youth wing," or the "church with the gnarly fog machine."

Developing a church grounded in good theology, and one that is hungry for more of it, starts with the pulpit. When I arrived at University Reformed Church in 2004, I inherited a strong legacy of robust, expositional preaching. I've tried to continue this tradition with lengthy series to date through Genesis, Leviticus, 2 Chronicles, Ezra, Ecclesiastes, the Minor Prophets, Mark, Acts, 2 Corinthians, Ephesians, 2 Timothy, 2 Peter, and Revelation (just to name the major endeavors). Few churches will grow deep in the Word if they only swim in the shallow end on Sunday morning. This doesn't mean I aim for the professors and doctors in my congregation. My target audience is the college freshman—someone who is (hopefully!) in the habit of thinking and open to careful teaching, but who may need help with new terms, new names, and new concepts. In other words, I assume people can learn, but I don't assume they know what I'm talking about.

I'm sure people in my congregation would say my preaching is very theological. I think by this they would mean that they can tell I've worked hard on the text during the week, that I try to be a careful thinker, and that I'm not afraid to weave in church history, systematic theology, and even a few ten-dollar words now and then. But good theological preaching should not be confused with smarty-pants preaching. It's entirely possible for a world-class intellect preaching world-class theology to instill in his people nothing but a world-class boredom for theological reflection. Good content is not enough. There are at least two other things that must accompany theological preaching if it is to produce a theologically minded people.

First, there must be passion. People don't hear everything we say. They hear what we are excited about. There is a way to talk about the Chalcedon

Definition that communicates, "This is important for smart people who like to know more than less intelligent people." And then there's the way that says, "I can't believe we get to look at this! We are in for a real treat this morning!" It's like that story about Ben Franklin and George Whitefield. When someone asked the decidedly unevangelical Franklin why he kept going to hear Whitefield when he didn't believe a word Whitefield was saying, Franklin replied, "I know, but *he* does." Theological reflection will never matter to God's people if they know it doesn't matter to God's preachers.

Second, we must bring the best theology down to the heart and up to the glory of God. If I give a learned sermon from John 10 on the ins and outs of definite atonement, the committed Calvinists will cheer and the rest will squirm. But if I can show how Christ's dying uniquely for the elect is an expression of his particular love for the sheep and his unconquerable love for his bride, and if I can show that God is glorified by not just making us saveable on the cross but by saving us to the uttermost, and if I can make the sermon sing with the wonder of the death of death in the death of Christ—if I can connect this difficult doctrine to our hearts and to God's glory, then I'm helping people care about theological precision and care enough to get all the marrow they can from their meaty Bibles.

Of course, there is more to think through in the life of a church than just preaching. We work hard to weave theological instruction and reflection into every aspect of our church. We want to think theologically about all of life, especially our ecclesiastical life together. We try to think theologically about the songs we sing, the prayers we pray, the order of the service, and even the placement of the announcements. How can we expect people to think theologically about their vocations if we as ministers don't think theologically about ours?

And how will God's people grow in theological discernment and literacy, how will they be affected in their affections with the riches of God's Word, how will they learn to think God's thoughts after him, how will they form a theological people—unless we have a theological church? For us in our confessional Reformed context, this means we structure our new members' class around the Belgic Confession, the Heidelberg Catechism, and the Canons of Dort. Most of our new members are strangers to the Three Forms of Unity, but invariably they consider it a highlight of the class to read for themselves these theological formulations that have nurtured the faith of God's people around the globe for centuries. Recently we devoted an entire year to preaching through the Heidelberg Catechism for fifty-two Sunday evenings.

There's more I could say about our leadership training course, our vetting process for elders and deacons, our college ministry, our small groups, our children's program, and all the rest. We don't do anything out of the ordinary, unless focusing on the Word, being rooted in a confessional tradition, catechizing our people, and being unapologetically theological are unusual. Our superficial world needs substantive churches. Our shallow culture needs depth in worship. Our secular society needs a whole lot of good, holy thinking. My ministry as a pastor and our ministry as a church is based on the *assumption* that we are all theologians and the *conviction* that if this is the case we might as well try to be good ones.

PART 2

Systematic Theology and Practical Theology

3

In the Evangelical Mood

The Purpose of the Pastor-Theologian

KEVIN J. VANHOOZER

What are theologians for? What exactly is the real work of theology? We can say how theology serves the church only when we answer these twin questions. We begin by focusing on the work of theology. Then, after determining the purpose of theological work in general, the next chapter examines how pastors in particular engage it.

I've labored in the field of theology for years, but my uncle still wants to know when I'm going to get a real job. So does the handyman I sometimes hire. I get it. Those who can, do; those who can't, teach. No doubt many Christians would be happy to add: and those who *really* can't, teach theology. Jane Austen's comic creation of the Reverend William Collins in *Pride and Prejudice* puts fictional flesh and blood on the stereotype of the pastor as a relationally inept buffoon, more concerned with the pageantry and status of his office than with ministering to real people. The Reverend Collins never rises above being a clerical error. Such caricatures of pastor-theologians as practical good-for-nothings, unable to do much more than change a lightbulb, could not be further from the truth. The real work of real pastors is both brave and bracing.

Pastor-theologians are indeed handy to have around, both at special times—a child's birth, a marriage, a parent's death—and on a daily basis. They may not be able to repair the furnace or rewire a house for electricity, but their presence and activity is particularly welcome when one is struggling with issues and challenges for which there is no technology: losing one's job, struggling with marriage, coping with grief, raising difficult children, tending the dying. Pastor-theologians are helpful to have around because they know what to say and do (or not to say and do) to communicate Jesus Christ—to represent Christ in particular situations by providing consolation, advice, truth, or simply tears. Pastor-theologians are handy to have around because they know how to look at things from the perspective of the drama of redemption and to incorporate people, and moments, into Christ and his story.[1] To paraphrase our Lord: the real work of pastor-theologians is to be farmers of men and women (cf. Matt. 4:19), cultivating the image of God in each and every person, to build persons up into mature adulthood (Eph. 4:13).

The real work of pastor-theologians is to be farmers of men and women.

Christian theology is the attempt to know God in order to give God his due (love, obedience, glory). Jesus Christ is in the thick of it: he is both the ultimate revelation of the knowledge of God and the model of how rightly to respond to this knowledge. Pastor-theologians, too, are in the thick of it: they represent God to the people (e.g., through teaching by word and example) and the people to God (e.g., through intercessory prayer). Changing a lightbulb is child's play compared to teaching people to walk as children of light (Eph. 5:8). Far from being impractical, the pastor-theologian is (or ought to be) a holy jack-of-all-existential-trades.[2]

Changing a lightbulb is child's play compared to teaching people to walk as children of light.

The Many Moods of Theology: Between Death and Resurrection

What are pastor-theologians for? The short answer: for cultivating life and for coping with death. "Death" is more than the moment of dying. It is rather the sense of an ending that casts its dark shadow over everything else in our stories. Death is shorthand for the problem of the human condition: mortality, what the Roman philosopher Seneca called "the shortness of time."[3] No one yet has devised any kind of technology that can cope with the inevitability of one's own death, or that of one's parents, friends, or children. Death casts a shadow over everything else—meaning, goodness, and beauty; though we try not to think about it, death will not be denied, at least not forever. The existentialist philosopher Martin Heidegger argued that awareness of one's own death is what makes human beings different from all other life-forms. Men and women know—if they are being honest—that their time is limited, and this knowledge creates no little anxiety.

How then shall we spend the comparatively little time that we have? Will we have enough time to fulfill our destiny, to accomplish our life purpose? Will we even have time simply to discover our life purpose? It is possible to avoid such questions for only so long. Sooner or later, a debilitating illness, the loss of loved ones, or some other catastrophic event reminds us of the fragility of life. Heidegger believed that anyone who is honest about the human condition cannot help but suffer from a constitutional anxiety. To be human is to be a "being-toward-death," to use Heidegger's haunting phrase. It was largely in light of Heidegger's work that Paul Tillich described modernity as "the age of anxiety of meaninglessness."[4] We might similarly call postmodernity "the age of anxiety of truthfulness" (i.e., an anxiety over how to live in an age in which belief in truth has become difficult, if not impossible).

We are all suffering from a bad case of the twentieth and twenty-first centuries. Anxiety medications abound, as do types of anxiety: social anxiety, posttraumatic stress, phobias, depression, and panic attacks. An estimated 40 percent of Americans suffer from some kind of anxiety disorder, and antidepressant or antianxiety medications (e.g., Prozac, Paxil, Zoloft) are frequently prescribed.[5] Yet one wonders whether certain drug-induced tranquility might not count as "saying 'Peace' when there is no peace" (Ezek. 13:10 altered). The closest medical equivalent to what Heidegger meant by anxiety is probably "generalized anxiety disorder." According to Heidegger, there is no particular trigger to anxiety (in contrast to phobias, which have specific objects, like spiders or public speaking): it is rather a spiritual condition on the borderlands of despair, less a specific feeling than a mood.

"Mood" is Heidegger's term for the way in which humans experience being-in-the-world. Moods are deeper than ideas or even feelings. A mood is a mode of being, an awareness of ourselves in a given situation, a way of being at-tuned to the world. The way in which we're tuned in to the world depends on the kind of music in which we find ourselves caught up: are we in the world during a famine, a war, an economic boom, or a bust? Heidegger considered anxiety to be the default human mood because it reflects the true perception of the human condition: we are finite beings with only limited time and energy, yet we can imagine limitless possibilities and harbor infinite hopes. Anxiety inevitably results from an honest appraisal of the human condition: we *care* about existence; our existence will soon *cease*. For Heidegger, authentic human being means being-toward-death.[6]

Heidegger intended his analysis of human existence to be universal. How-ever, an analysis of the twenty-first-century human condition might depart from Heidegger in one significant respect. Not care but carelessness or even carefreeness mark some who have made the radical postmodern turn. Instead of anxiety, the prevailing mood among many millennials appears to be acedia: a kind of existential listlessness, torpor, or stupor. Like anxiety, it is a sick-ness not primarily of the body but of the soul (though often it has somatic symptoms). The Christian tradition knows it by another name: sloth. At the limit, acedia does not even care about not caring. Is there a cure for souls that inhabit this inner darkness 24/7?

Pastor-theologians deal with the despair that accompanies anxiety and acedia alike. As Søren Kierkegaard says in the opening pages of *The Sickness unto Death* (the sickness in question is despair): "Everything essentially Chris-tian must have in its presentation a resemblance to the way a physician speaks at the sickbed."[7] Pastor-theologians do not merely alleviate the symptoms; they also address the disease itself. Despair is truth-indicative inasmuch as it correctly perceives being-in-the-world apart from being-in-Christ. In contrast, faith is truth-indicative inasmuch as it perceives the believer's true condition as united with Christ. Jesus Christ is the way, truth, and life that sets finite creatures free from the anxiety of being-toward-death: "The resurrection of Jesus transformed the first disciples' picture of the world, not in an abstract or theoretical way but through their transformed *experience* of being alive."[8] Pastor-theologians treat the human condition itself, by introducing people to Jesus Christ and helping them to grow into Christ. Pastor-theologians cure souls by administering, not mood-altering drugs, but rather a mood-altering dose of reality: the good news that God raised Jesus from the dead, and that we too can be raised in Christ. Pastors minister the Word by using biblical and theological language to indicate what God has done in Christ and to shape their congregant's sense of identity as people who have died and risen with Christ.

Pastor-theologians exist to embody the evangelical mood, an indicative declaration ("He is risen! He is Lord!") and a concomitant way of being that is attuned to the world as already-not-yet made new in Jesus Christ. The pastor-theologian is part of an embassy on the part of the risen Christ and, as such, is an ambassador of the new created order that has already begun to exist amid the old disorder. The pastor-theologian communicates, in word and deed, in person and work, the reality of the new resurrection order: the renewal of human being. The pastor-theologian both proclaims and practices resurrection. N. T. Wright comments that the early Christians "behaved as if they were in some important senses already living in God's new creation."[9] Indeed, the local church is an earthly embassy of Christ's heavenly rule.

Pastor-theologians exist to communicate and disseminate this new evangelical mood: being-in-Christ. Whereas being-in-the-world in Heidegger's view gives rise to a mood of anxiety, *joy* is the mood that best accords with being-in-Christ. Joy is not a feeling, like happiness. Pastor-theologians are not here to produce happy Christians, saints with smiley faces. Happiness is too shallow a term and fickle an emotion. Happiness is dependent on circumstances, and circumstances change. Often happiness is either inappropriate or inauthentic in our in-between times, marked by finitude and suffering. By way of contrast, resurrection joy is a *mood*, a way of being attuned to the world—when one knows that the world includes an empty tomb.[10] Happiness is a surface phenomenon, but for those who through faith enjoy being-in-Christ, joy resides in the depths of their being. Joy is never inappropriate, even in the depths of suffering (e.g., funerals), because the resurrection reminds us that death, foe though it be, has been defeated, along with its cohorts, meaninglessness and hopelessness. The psalmist declares: "I will sing praises to my God while I have being" (Ps. 146:2 RSV). The Great Reversal has taken place.

The New Testament writers identify Christ as the joyful fulfillment of Israel's hope for the messianic reign of God. Thanks to Jesus's resurrection

Pastor-theologians cure souls by administering, not mood-altering drugs, but rather a mood-altering dose of reality: the good news that God raised Jesus from the dead.

from the dead, the groaning of creation is being replaced with highland singing and arboreal clapping (Isa. 55:12). The pastor-theologian communicates the joy of resurrection, not least in leading worship. Like joy, worship is not simply a particular activity but a general mood, a gratitude expressed not for a few minutes on special days only but throughout each and every day: "And whatever you do, in word and deed, do everything in the name of the Lord Jesus, giving thanks to God the Father through him" (Col. 3:17). The pastor-theologian communicates and embodies this evangelical mood—and one does not need a PhD to do so. In sum, the pastor-theologian cures despairing souls by sharing the joy of the risen Christ. This is the pastor-theologian's particular-general contribution to the human condition: to help men, women, and children learn how to deal with the shortness of time by *redeeming* it (KJV: Eph. 5:16; Col. 4:5), living each moment in an evangelical mood (i.e., being-toward-resurrection).

How do pastor-theologians communicate the joy of being-toward-resurrection? "Mood" is a remarkably supple term, with related grammatical and ontological meanings. As we have seen, in ontology (the study of being) "mood" pertains to our fundamental orientation to the world: our mind-set and heart-set. Paul says, "If then you have been raised with Christ, . . . set your mind on things that are above" (Col. 3:1–2). In grammar, "mood" indicates a speaker's attitude to what is said (i.e., whether it is a fact, command, desire, question, etc.). Given the eschatological nature of the resurrection, the pastor-theologian must communicate evangelical joy in *many* moods.[11]

A Ministry of Reality: Theology in the Indicative Mood

Whereas verb tense speaks to the *time* of an action (e.g., past, present, future), verb moods speak to the language-world relation. Interrogatives express a lack of certainty about a state of affairs ("Is the window open?"). Imperatives express a desire to have the world conform to one's language ("Shut the window!"). Indicatives express one's belief that the world is a certain way ("The window is open."). Simply put, indicatives are used to state facts. Theology requires many moods, but the gospel is in the indicative: "He is risen!" "Jesus is Lord." "Jesus now reigns." The Fourth Gospel is largely indicative testimony to what Jesus said and did: "These [things] are written so that you may believe that Jesus is the Christ" (John 20:31).

Christian theology is largely indicative. As we said in the introduction, theology is the attempt to set forth in speech *what is in Christ*. This is another way of "indicating" the truth of the gospel: what God has done, is doing, and will do *in Christ*. There are many true stories about what is going on in the world (and even more false stories), but the focus of the biblical story is on what God is doing in the world to renew the created order: "The Lord has risen indeed" (Luke 24:34). Nothing looks quite the same in the afterglow of resurrection: God, human being, the plan of salvation, the cosmos itself—all need to be rethought.

> *Public theology is the setting forth in propositions and, more importantly, in* persons *the reality of new life in Christ.*

The theologian's task is to set forth in speech and act "sound doctrine": the truth about the strange new world of the gospel. The theologian is a representative of this strange new postresurrection world, an emissary of the kingdom of God that is even now impinging on the old world in which many think they are still living. In clarifying what God has done in Christ, the theologian provides something helpful—performs a service. Stated differently: the theologian is a *minister of reality*. A minister (from Latin *minus* = "less") makes oneself less than the thing or person being served. Pastors are public theologians because they bear witness to *what is in Christ*, and there is no more basic reality than that. If the word of God endures longer than the heavens and the earth, how much more the living Word through which the heavens and the earth were made. Insofar as the theologian helps God's people to live into the reality of the resurrection, the new creation in Christ, the theologian helps people to get real.

The gospel is a reliable indicator of reality insofar as it reveals the nature and purpose, the source and destiny, of the whole created order. This, too, is public theology: to make known "the mystery hidden for ages and generations but now made manifest to his saints, . . . Christ in you" (Col. 1:25–27 RSV). Public theology is the setting forth in propositions and, more importantly, in *persons* the reality of new life in Christ. The church, the company of those who have been raised with Christ, is the vanguard of the new created order. The consummate pastor-theologian Jonathan Edwards says something very similar: the end of God's work of redemption, and thus the whole purpose of history, was to create a kingdom for his Son, a people that would be his special possession. Those who have been raised with Christ, the company of the redeemed, are but the firstfruits of this ultimate reality.

Metaphysics is the study of reality, or *what is*. A pastor-theologian may never use the word "metaphysics" in public, but it does not follow that metaphysics is unrelated to one's ministry. Every person has a metaphysic, a worldview and life view, beliefs and concomitant practices that, taken together, reveal what that person thinks is ultimately important, valuable, and real.[12] The theologian's task is to indicate *what is in Christ*.

First and foremost, what is in Christ is God: true deity, the Second Person of the Trinity, the divine Logos: "the Word [who] was God" (John 1:1). Christ is the "image of the invisible God" (Col. 1:15), the "exact representation of [God's] being" (Heb. 1:3 NIV). Everything that Jesus says, does, and is reveals God. What there is in Christ is true knowledge of God. Jesus is God in the indicative mood.

Second, what is in Christ is true humanity. Jesus Christ is the second Adam, the Son of Man, the true Israel, the exemplary covenant servant of the Lord, the loving son who resists temptation and displays filial obedience, thereby showing us the purpose for which God created human beings in the first place. What there is in Christ is the perfect image of God in human form (2 Cor. 4:4; Col. 1:15). The third aspect of what is in Christ is the whole created order: "all things were created through him and for him" (Col. 1:16); "in him all things hold together" (Col. 1:17). In Christ there is the wise care of God for the world.

Finally, in Christ there is the working out of the "plan for the fullness of time," a preview and taste of the renewed and restored created order: "to unite all things in him, things in heaven and things on earth" (Eph. 1:9–10). In Christ, there is the reconciliation of God and humanity: "in Christ God was reconciling the world to himself" (2 Cor. 5:19). In the person and work of Christ, there is God's love and freedom for humanity, expressed in the life and passion of Jesus, and there is humanity's love and freedom for God, expressed in praise and obedience. What there is in Christ is the fulfillment of the law (i.e., the command to love God and neighbor as oneself). What theologians are ultimately for is the joyful publication of the redemption that is in Christ: what we ultimately have in Christ is redemption: "Therefore, if anyone is in Christ, he is a new creation" (2 Cor. 5:17).

What we find in Christ is thus the life, light, and love of God: "all the treasures of wisdom and knowledge" (Col. 2:3). And if we look hard enough, we see ourselves buried and raised in Christ, adopted into the family of God, members of the reconciled people of God made one in Christ: Israel and the church, Jew and Greek, male and female, slave and free (Gal. 3:28). When theologians say what is and is to come in Christ Jesus, they fulfill their vocation as "stewards of the mysteries of God" (1 Cor. 4:1). To think theologically means understanding God, the world, and ourselves in relation to *what is in Christ*.

What we find in Christ is good news and joy: "Christ, being raised from the dead, will never die again; death no longer has dominion over him" (Rom. 6:9). That is why being-in-Christ is a matter of being-toward-resurrection. The God who raised Jesus "will also raise us up by his power" (1 Cor. 6:14). Indeed, God has already raised us up with him "and seated us with him in the heavenly places in Christ Jesus" (Eph. 2:6). It follows that in one sense we now know "the power of his resurrection" (Phil. 3:10), but in another sense the resurrection is something future, for which we continue to hope (Phil. 3:11; 1 Pet. 1:3). The challenge of indicating *what is in Christ* follows from the already/not-yet nature of the resurrection—what we might term the *eschatological "is."*

The "is" of *what is in Christ* is not a straightforward indicative. That is because statements like "You were buried with him in baptism" (Col. 2:12 RSV) and "God made [you] alive together with him" (Col. 2:13) are not the kind of claims one can verify by appealing to sense experience. No, it takes a sanctified imagination, the Spirit-enlightened eyes of the heart (Eph. 1:18), to see, with Paul, that "I have been crucified with Christ" so that "It is no longer I who live, but Christ who lives in me" (Gal. 2:20).

> *To think theologically means understanding God, the world, and ourselves in relation to* what is in Christ.

It is vitally important not to confuse the *is* of *what is in Christ* with *as if*. That we have been raised with Christ presents us with an *eschatological indicative*: something that states what is *already but not yet fully* the case. Disciples really do enjoy union with Christ *already*, thanks to the indwelling Holy Spirit, even though they have *not yet* attained to the full measure of Christlikeness. Doctrine that sets forth *what is in Christ* requires a robust eschatological imagining, a faith-based seeing that perceives what is *not yet* complete—our salvation—as *already* finished, because of our union with Christ. It is a matter of seeing what is present-partial as future-perfect.

Theologians minister this eschatological reality, the truth of being-in-Christ. Everything depends on getting this point right. We can attain wisdom only if we live along the created and re-created grain of reality. Theologians set forth in speech *what is in Christ* and therefore say how things are. The eschatological *is* raises the question of the nature of reality. Indicative statements in the past and present refer to what was and is. That works well for most kinds of ordinary things and events (I'm not sure about quantum physics). However, the gospel concerns not *ousia* (being in general) but *parousia* (the new reality that is coming into being in the person of Christ). The ministry of the reality of *what is in Christ* requires the further ministry of helping people grasp that reality. It is to that aspect of ministering the gospel that we now turn.

A Ministry of Understanding: The *Diakonia* of God's Word

Contrary to the popular conception, theology is not an arcane science or academic compartment, like the other -ologies, whose field a scholar progressively masters by processing more and more information (or by earning higher degrees). To know *what is in Christ* takes much more than adding a few items to one's storehouse of knowledge. Yes, theology concerns the knowledge of God, but what it yields is not more data but greater understanding—of God, and of everything else in relation to God.

A theologian is a minister of understanding, one who helps the church grasp the meaning of what God has done, is doing, and will do in Jesus Christ, as well as what we are to say and do in response. To grasp the meaning of something—whether it be a machine comprising metal pieces, a sentence composed of English words, or a story made up of persons and events—one must have more than a knowledge of each part; one must be able to see how they fit into a larger whole, a broader context. Theology deals with the broadest context of all: God's triune work of redemption, the engine that drives world history.

To minister understanding is to help people make connections: between the parts of the Bible and the overarching story; between the Bible and the world in which they live; between who they are and who God calls them to be. Pastors are called not to practice academic theology but to minister theological understanding, helping people to interpret the Scriptures, their cultures, and their own lives in relation to God's great work of redemption summed up *in Christ*.

It should now be apparent why we are describing theologians as public intellectuals. The New Testament apostle was "a witness to his resurrection" (Acts 1:22) and, to be sure, this was a kind of public knowledge (viz., eyewitness testimony).[13] The theologian is a different kind of witness to the resurrection, however: one who understands how this single event puts all other events, the "whole" of world history, into meaningful perspective. But this is precisely the task of the public intellectual: to speak about matters like the meaning of life, matters that pertain to things *in general*. The theologian is a generalist who speaks about things in general (the renewed created order) in relation to one thing in particular: the resurrection of Jesus Christ. From the perspective of Christian theology, the resurrection is the general truth about the world, and the pastor deals with particular lives in light of this central truth about the turning point of history. In other words, Jesus Christ is the "whole" in light of which all other particulars have meaning (cf. Eph. 1:10).

> *The theologian is a generalist who speaks about things in general (the renewed created order) in relation to one thing in particular: the resurrection of Jesus Christ.*

To understand all things in relation to the risen Christ requires more part-whole thinking. Specifically, it requires holistic reading of, and theological literacy in (1) God's Word, (2) the human world, and (3) human words about the human world.

Reading God's Word: Biblical Literacy

We can only understand *what is in Christ* in light of the divinely inspired prophetic and apostolic testimony, which Jesus claimed was ultimately about him (Luke 24:27). Theologians minister understanding of what is in Christ, at least in part, by helping others to understand Scripture. While pastor-theologians are to do more than interpret the Bible, they must certainly not do less. In the early church, the apostles delegated to deacons the important task of distributing food to widows: "It is not right that we should give up preaching the word of God to serve tables" (Acts 6:2). Theologians, like the apostles, must devote themselves to "the ministry of the word [*diakonia tou logou*]" (Acts 6:4). "Man shall not live by bread alone, but by every word that comes from the mouth of God" (Matt. 4:4). In light of Jesus's teaching, it is surely significant that Luke uses the same term for serving tables as he does for serving God's Word. Theologians wait tables, serving the Word to others so that they can more easily digest it.[14]

Scripture alone provides an authoritative account of *what is in Christ*. If we would follow Christ, we must follow the Scriptures that lead us to Christ, present Christ, and teach us Christ's way. If we would have the mind of Christ, we must be students of the Scriptures, able to relate the law and the prophets to the person and work of Jesus Christ, as Jesus did himself. Theology exercises its ministry of understanding in helping followers of Jesus to be better followers of Scripture, and that means grasping its overarching story.

Theological understanding requires biblical literacy. If Scripture is the soul of theology, then the biblical illiteracy that has swept over North American churches like an epidemic is a threat to understanding what is in Christ and is a glaring obstacle to having the mind of Christ. We can illustrate the problem by reference to E. D. Hirsch's *Cultural Literacy: What Every American Needs to Know*.[15] Hirsch wrote the book out of a concern that many Americans do not know what they need to know in order to be effective citizens. Cultural literacy is a prerequisite for participating in America's fundamental institutions and in the national conversation about what it means to be an American: "To be culturally literate is to possess the basic information needed to thrive in the modern world."[16] As we shall see in the next section, pastor-theologians need to be culturally literate too. Yet at the very heart of the pastor's work is the need to foster biblical literacy in the church. Biblical literacy is necessary if Christians are to understand their identity in Christ (i.e., what it means to be a saint) and if they are to be effective citizens of heaven on earth (Eph. 2:19; Phil. 3:20).

Theologians wait tables, serving the Word to others so that they can more easily digest it.

This is not the place to offer a full-scale account of biblical interpretation and hermeneutics, much as I would like to do so.[17] A few salient points will have to suffice. First, biblical literacy means canonical literacy. It is not enough to know facts about the Bible. What is needed is *canon sense*: the ability to interpret particular passages of Scripture in light of the whole Bible. Canon sense means knowing where we are in the flow of redemptive history. Canon sense means thinking not only about but *with* the Bible, to the point of being able to interpret one's own experience with biblical categories, in light of the overarching story line of Scripture. Jesus did this with his own person and history. No one had canon sense more than Jesus himself.

Second, biblical literacy means biblical theology, a way of following the story that acknowledges unity and diversity, yet views Old and New Testaments together. Again, this is less a matter of the specialist knowledge that is the focus of biblical scholarship than it is a grasp of the interpretive framework through which the biblical authors understood the story of Israel and the church (the formal principle of biblical theology)—and a matter of what Edwards called the triune work of redemption (the material principle of biblical theology).[18] In brief, biblical theology acknowledges that everything in the world was created so that "the eternal Son of God might obtain a spouse."[19] From beginning to end, the Bible tells the story of God preparing a people set apart to be his treasured possession—and his temple. Stated in simpler story terms: God meets (creates) world; God loses world; God gets world back; God and world live happily ever after.

Third, biblical literacy means being able to read one's own world, one's own historical situation and life, in light of the world of the biblical text. Typology is an excellent means of doing this. As members of the New Testament church understood themselves via the events of Israel's history, so members of the contemporary church must understand themselves as participants in the same ongoing drama of redemption. The historical and cultural scenery may have changed, but Christians today are in the same redemptive-historical context as the early Christians, poised in expectation between the first and second comings of Christ, still having to endure various kinds of opposition in the world.

Theologians are readers of God's Word. To repeat: this is not a matter of becoming a specialist in biblical studies. It is rather a matter of becoming a generalist, the proverbial hedgehog who knows "one big thing," namely, the big redemptive-historical picture: the way in which the Triune God has acted "to sum up all things in Christ" (Eph. 1:9–10 ASV).[20]

Reading the World: Cultural Literacy

In order to minister God's Word, pastor-theologians need to read not only the Bible but also the world to which God's Word is addressed, the world in which God's Word is to take root and be applied. Here I am thinking not of the natural but the human world, the everyday world of human culture: all the things that humans have made and do together. Culture is the world of meaning in which a people dwell, a world presented in various works of meaning (e.g., books, films, paintings, ads, songs, fashion, cars, sports, buildings, meals, games) that communicate a society's beliefs and values. In short: a culture is a society's software, a program for cultivating humanity and shaping its freedom.

Pastor-theologians must educate their people about culture, for culture is in the full-time business of educating people and forming their humanity (culture cultivates!). Culture educates by programming certain types of behavior (e.g., consumerism) and by inculcating certain beliefs and values (e.g., patriotism). We can go further: culture is in the full-time business of spiritual formation, cultivating humanity. Culture ultimately educates not minds but hearts.[21] A materialist culture is geared in such a way as to form materialists, people with hearts who desire material goods in the misbegotten hope that they will make the emptiness go away. They won't fill the emptiness. Only love of God can satisfy the human heart, for our hearts were created to desire God.

The best pastor-theologians have always been aware of the formative influences of culture. Augustine was doing public theology when he urged his congregation not to attend public spectacles. Augustine (and Tertullian) believed that the Roman theater was so rooted in pagan religion that Christians ought not support it, not least because it encouraged immorality. Contemporary culture is subtler in its influence. Every Christian needs to see the PBS *Frontline* documentary "The Persuaders," a brilliant exposé of the way marketing gurus seek to influence public opinion, and behavior, in ways that make more profits for their clients.

The so-called "culture wars" are really only a symptom of a deeper problem: the fact that Christians struggle not against flesh and blood, nor against food and film, but against the powers and principalities that seek to capture our minds and hearts. Cultural literacy is the ability to "read" or make sense of what is happening in our contemporary situation. It is especially important to be able to make sense of cultural trends. Culture itself is not the problem; there are many aspects of culture that reflect the image of God and common grace. At the same time, other cultural currents provide media for socially transmitted diseases, including MTD (moralistic therapeutic deism)—perhaps the default cultural theology of our time.[22]

Over a generation ago Carl F. H. Henry was appealing for cultural literacy when he identified an important (post)modern trend: "No fact of contemporary Western life is more evident than its growing distrust of final truth and its implacable questioning of any sure word."[23] As we read contemporary culture, we can perceive that this ideological cancer has progressed to the point of regarding all institutions and authority with systemic distrust and cynicism.

Cultural literacy is the ability to make sense of what is happening in contemporary society, the ability to read cultural texts and make sense of cultural trends. The purpose of cultural literacy is to achieve understanding, and we need rightly to understand what is happening in order to know how those whose citizenship is in heaven ought rightly to respond. Cultural literacy is part and parcel of a Christian's dual citizenship, being in the world (being-toward-death) but not of it (being-toward-resurrection). The church as a community of the resurrection seeks to live out or perform its discipleship to the living Christ, and to do so we need to know what kind of cultural scene we're playing. The purpose of cultural literacy is thus to ensure that members of the church will be cultural agents: persons who are not merely passive consumers of the cultural fare but also persons able to leave their own mark on culture, the mark of cross and resurrection.

Cultural literacy refers to what Christians need to know about their everyday culture in order to be effective cultural agents for Christ's kingdom.[24]

Cultural literacy refers to what Christians need to know about their everyday culture in order to be effective cultural agents for Christ's kingdom.

Many—too many!—books have been written examining culture from various disciplinary perspectives: sociology, economics, social psychology, and cultural studies, to name but a few. Clearly, pastor-theologians do not have the time to process all this material. There are helpful shortcuts: for example, a periodical like *Books and Culture* is a good source of secondhand knowledge, thanks to its reviews of important books in a number of different academic areas. As people who are both in but not of the surrounding culture, pastor-theologians will also have firsthand knowledge of what is happening. As organic intellectuals who minister understanding, however, their main service will be to help the church to read the world situation in light of God's Word.

To understand culture one must be aware of it, yet culture often goes unnoticed because it, like air, is the atmosphere we breathe on a daily basis. The most important task of the pastor-theologian is thus to ensure that the congregation wakes up and stays awake, becoming aware of culture and what it is trying to cultivate in our hearts and minds. Jesus encourages his disciples, "Keep awake and pray" (Mark 14:38 NRSV): prayer wakes us up by focusing our attention on the presence and activity of God, and on God's purpose for our world.[25] Cultural spin doctors, those who lead marketing and political campaigns, may create compelling images and tell compelling stories, but prayerful theology focuses on what is in Christ, and he who is the light of the world lifts the fogs of cultural confusion. Pastor-theologians minister understanding (and build bridges between biblical and cultural literacy) when they read the world in light of Scripture and direct their congregations in ways of wisdom and human flourishing.

Reading Fiction: Human Literacy

The pastor is a public theologian who ministers understanding to the people of God in order to build them up into Christ. It therefore stands to reason that "pastors must ever grow in their knowledge and understanding of people."[26] The best way to know people is to live among them, to share their sorrows, joys, challenges, and frustrations. People come in many shapes and sizes, however, and there is not enough time to become acquainted with every individual one meets—hence the importance of becoming acquainted with literature, the laboratory of the human condition.[27] But why should we imaginatively enter into stories that never happened and into experiences that we would not want to go through ourselves? C. S. Lewis puts it best when he speaks of the "enlargement of our being": "In reading great literature I become a thousand men and yet remain myself."[28]

Lewis raises a crucial point for the pastor-theologian. It is most important that pastor-theologians get out of themselves and learn to see things from other points of view. To love others, we must be able to put ourselves in their place. Is this not what God does for us in Jesus Christ? He identifies with us not merely imaginatively but incarnationally. I am neither black nor female, nor was I sexually violated as a child, but I come to know something of what it is like to be that person through reading Maya Angelou's I Know Why the Caged Bird Sings. Reading fiction helps us understand, and identify with, those who are not like us. That is the first reason why pastor-theologians ought to read fiction: to become literate in and sympathetic to humanity, in all its unity and diversity.

A second reason to read fiction is that the great poets and storytellers often write about universal themes: quests for happiness, tragic loss, love in all its permutations, and so forth. Flannery O'Connor's short stories teach us to look for grace in unexpected places (e.g., the grotesque). Dostoevsky's The

Brothers Karamazov contains an insightful probing of the problem of evil. Many contemporary novels—again, too many!—communicate what life is like *apart from Christ*. It is one thing to know intellectually that some people are not saved; it is quite another vicariously to know with one's whole being what that feels like. Fiction affords us the opportunity to understand what we have not personally experienced.

A third reason to read is to understand the special privileges, opportunities, and challenges of being a minister of God's Word. I have already mentioned Sinclair Lewis's cautionary tale of *Elmer Gantry* and the ever-present temptation to make one's own name great rather than Christ's. Another book, with a more positive role model, is Marilynne Robinson's Pulitzer Prize–winning novel *Gilead* (2004), which I read twice with groups of seminary students. I would be willing to argue that more could be learned about the life of a pastor from reading *Gilead* than from many books on pastoral theology.

A fourth and final reason for pastor-theologians to make reading fiction a priority relates to what we said earlier about cultural literacy. Works of fiction open up not only the lives of individuals but also whole cultures. Before I met her parents, my wife, Sylvie, insisted that I read Marcel Pagnol's novels *Jean de Florette* and *Manon des Sources*. These books perfectly captured the distinct culture of the lower classes in Provence in the mid-twentieth century, the peasant world in which Sylvie's parents grew up. When I finally met them, it was as if I already knew them, so closely did they resemble the characters in Pagnol's books. It occurred to me that missionaries to foreign countries ought to make as much effort to get to know the literature of a culture as its language.

Of course, as Newbigin has rightly observed, our own Western culture has now become a mission field.[29] Accordingly, pastor-theologians ought to read some contemporary fiction in order to get to know the culture in and to which they are ministering. At the time of this writing, for example, one of the best-selling fiction books at Amazon.com (also the number 2 best seller in the category "Spirituality, personal transformation") is Paulo Coelho's 1993 novel *The Alchemist*, which has sold over 150 million copies worldwide. Its partly autobiographical story is about a shepherd boy who travels from Spain to Egypt in order to follow his Personal Legend. He learns that the "world's greatest lie" is that we lose control of what is happening to us. The truth, according to this New Age gospel, is that the Soul of the World wants everyone to be happy: "To realize one's destiny is a person's only real obligation," and

the universe "conspires" to help us succeed. According to the novel, spirituality means being true to oneself and taking risks, not taking up one's cross to
become like Christ. It's not MTD (moralistic therapeutic deism) but what
we might term HQP (humanistic quixotic pantheism). In any case, reading it helps theologians to better understand large swaths of contemporary
culture.

I know, I know: pastor-theologians are busy—but too busy to read fiction?
I suspect that a cost-benefit analysis might well indicate that whatever time
pastors spend in reading fiction pays inordinate dividends. It is hard to put
a price on wisdom and understanding. Here, too, there are shortcuts. I recommend dropping in at www.goodreads.com from time to time, or "Arts &
Letters Daily" (www.aldaily.com). Neal Plantinga encourages newcomers to
start small: one novel a year.[30] Four books per year is even better, one for each
of the aforementioned reasons for reading.

Reading takes us only so far, of course. Theological understanding is not
merely theoretical. It involves more than head knowledge. Church towers
ought not to be made of ivory. Understanding is also practical. When we
truly understand our situation, we are able to *do* something about it. Gaining
understanding produces know-how, as in knowing *how to act out knowledge
in everyday life*. And this is the goal of understanding: to embody the mind
of Christ by acting out what is in Christ. We therefore turn our attention to
this final way of ministering Christ.

A Ministry of (New) Life: Theology in the Imperative Mood

The gospel is in the indicative mood. Preaching the good news involves saying
what has happened and what is the case: Jesus has died for our sins; God raised
Jesus from the dead; Jesus is now the living Lord, to whom the Spirit unites
us in faith. Yet the gospel indicative—what is in Christ—also contains a tacit
imperative, a demand actively to conform to *what is* and joyfully participate in
what is. And insofar as living into the reality of Christ is a corporate project,
we could also speak of the cohortative mood (from Latin *co*, "together" +
hortari, "encourage"), whose telltale "Let us" signals that pastors must heed
their own exhortations: "*Let us* pursue what makes for peace and for mutual
upbuilding" (Rom. 14:19). "*Let us* leave the elementary doctrine of Christ and
go on to maturity" (Heb. 6:1). "*Let us* love one another" (1 John 4:7). Living

to God, living into Christ, living through the Spirit, with others—this is the essence of theology.

The pastor-theologian walks a fine line, reminding Christians of what God has already done yet also encouraging them to make their lives correspond to this reality. Being in Christ is both gift and task, privilege and responsibility. Exaggerate the gift, and you risk antinomian complacency; exaggerate the responsibility, and you risk legalistic anxiety. The apostle Paul walks this fine line in his epistles, many of which begin by reminding readers of the great indicative (Jesus died and was raised for our justification) and then go on to exhort readers to live into this reality. In Colossians, for example, Paul first summarizes what God has done, "If then you have been raised with Christ," and only then drops the imperative, "seek the things that are above, where Christ is" (Col. 3:1).[31]

Living to God, living into Christ, living through the Spirit, with others—this is the essence of theology.

Some may object to my associating the gospel with imperatives. What has gospel to do with law? Interestingly enough, the idea of obeying the gospel is a thoroughly biblical idea. It is possible to hear the gospel but not obey it (Rom. 10:16). The consequence of not obeying the gospel is eternal destruction: existence "away from the presence of the Lord" (2 Thess. 1:9; cf. 1 Pet. 4:17). Obeying the gospel is not a burden for those whom the Spirit has joined to Christ, however, for Christ lives in them. At the same time, the imperatival mood of theology matters: God saves us by grace through faith, but we must nevertheless work out our own being-toward-resurrection "with fear and trembling" (Phil. 2:12). Richard Gaffin rightly captures the tension: "Where the indicative is present, a reality, there concern for the imperative must and will be a reality that comes to expression, however imperfectly, minimally or inadequately."[32]

Theology is the project of corresponding to what is in Christ in word and deed. To be or not to be *in Christ*: that is the only question for the disciple. In making explicit *what is in Christ*, Christian doctrine

To be or not to be in Christ: that is the only question for the disciple.

implicitly gives disciples their marching orders: correspond to what is. When disciples live into the reality of the resurrection—which is to say, the renewed created order—they participate in the truth, goodness, and beauty of Jesus Christ.

"Get Wisdom"

"Get wisdom, get understanding." (Prov. 4:5 NIV)

The Gospels tell us only a fraction of what Jesus said and did (John 20:30; 21:25), but what is written is all that is necessary for faith and life (20:31). Similarly, Paul is not interested in all truth (e.g., the arts, agriculture), but rather only in "the truth that accords with godliness" (Titus 1:1 altered). Moreover, this truth that accords or leads to godliness is based on "the hope of eternal life" (1:2), which is to say, our participation in Jesus's resurrection. The thrust of Paul's epistle on pastoral theology is that pastors are to help the church to live into God's plan of salvation, the mystery now revealed in the cross and resurrection of Jesus Christ.

That gospel truth "accords with godliness" (*kat' eusebeian*) deserves special attention: if we can understand this, we will be able to see why the evangelical mood involves both indicatives and imperatives. Paul is here describing Christian existence, which integrates the knowledge of God with the godly life that is consequent upon this knowledge. The purpose of knowing God is to produce godliness in the knower: we must act out what we know.[33] "Godliness" best corresponds to what in the Old Testament is called the "fear of the LORD," and again the emphasis is on the essential connection between knowing God and godly living.[34] Believers must do what they know to be true.

Gospel truth leads to godliness, and godliness corresponds to gospel truth. By way of contrast, unbelievers deny the truth, and their knowledge of it, by their disobedience (Titus 1:16). "The fear of the LORD [godliness] is the beginning of wisdom" (Prov. 9:10). Wisdom is the operative term, for wisdom is applied knowledge, knowledge lived out and put into practice. And this is the purpose of theology: to help believers grow in the wisdom of Jesus Christ. The wise person does the truth. This is why the wise person flourishes: to live out the truth is to go with rather than against the grain of reality. The fool seeks to live against the grain of reality, a lost cause if there ever was one.

Pastor-theologians speak in the imperative mood whenever they urge Christians to become what they are in Christ. Theology cultivates wisdom to the extent that it directs disciples in their particular contexts to correspond to the renewed created order in Christ. Doctrine not only tells us *what is* and *how things are*; it also asks us to trust that *this is how things are* to the point of staking one's life on it. Faith lays hold of what is in Christ and seeks to live into it, or rather to live it out in godly action.

"Work Love"

"Put on love." (Col. 3:14)

"God was in Christ" (2 Cor. 5:19 KJV) and "God is love" (1 John 4:8). What is in Christ is essentially the love of God for the world. In Christ we perceive the end of all creation: "In the resurrection of Christ creation is restored and the kingdom of God dawns."[35] Christian wisdom means living according to the new order inaugurated by the resurrection of Jesus, something we can do only because we have the freedom of the Spirit, which is the freedom to conform to what is in Christ (2 Cor. 3:17). Evangelical theology in the imperative mood has everything to do with the shape this freedom in Christ takes.

In Christ there is "only faith working through love" (Gal. 5:6): "Love is the overall shape of Christian ethics, the form of the human participation in the created order."[36] Love is the principal fruit of the Holy Spirit (Gal. 5:22; cf. 1 Cor. 13:13), our foretaste and down payment (2 Cor. 1:22) of our new being in Christ. Pastor-theologians minister new life in Christ as they help the church to rightly order its loves. We rightly order our loves when we act in ways that correspond to the order of the new creation, to ultimate reality.

The imperative (i.e., "work love") presupposes indicative knowledge (i.e., "this is how things are"). Our works of love are rightly ordered only when they correspond to the new order of things given in reality, *what is* in Christ: "In the ordering of love it is truthfulness that is at stake: whether our love recognizes what the neighbor is, what God is, and what the true ordering of creature to Creator must be."[37] We love our fellow believers as ourselves when we see them for what they are: saints, like us, who have been raised with and united to Christ. Paul's imperative "Put on love, which binds everything together in perfect harmony" (Col. 3:14) only makes sense against an indicative background, namely, that God has raised Jesus from the dead, making good on his plan "to unite all things in him" (Eph. 1:10). New life in Christ means loving what is in Christ, and that means each member of his body. Indeed, if husbands are to "love their wives as their own bodies" (Eph. 5:28), how much more should pastors love their churches, not because they are their own bodies, but because congregations are the body of Christ.

"Imitate Christ"

"Put on the Lord Jesus Christ." (Rom. 13:14)

The company of faith has been made new in Christ (2 Cor. 5:17). This is the prime indicative: God has raised us up with Christ in anticipation of the end of creation. Pastor-theologians teach the truth by saying and showing what is in Christ, and the church gains understanding and works love as it seeks to correspond and live into that reality. The final imperative, however, is the most paradoxical of all: "Put on Christ—the new self, with resurrection practices" (see Col. 3:9–14). Those who bear his name must not only correspond to what is in Christ but also recognize, and let blossom, the reality that is Christ in us. Paul speaks of "the riches of the glory of this mystery, which is Christ in you, the hope of glory" (Col. 1:27).

The hope of glory turns out to be the plan of salvation conceived "before the foundation of the world" (Eph. 1:4). Here is what C. S. Lewis has to say about the end of creation and the purpose of the church: "The Church exists for nothing else but to draw men into Christ, to make them little Christs. If they are not doing that, all the cathedrals, clergy, missions, sermons, even the Bible itself, are simply a waste of time. God became Man for no other purpose. It is even doubtful, you know, whether the whole universe was created for any other purpose."[38]

The peculiar vocation of pastor-theologians is to assist Christians to walk the way of Jesus Christ, the way of truth and life (John 14:6), not least by demonstrating it themselves. The way to follow Christ is to do—to *be*—like him.[39] Pastor-theologians are representatives of the new order in Christ. Ideally, they should be able to say, with Paul, "Be imitators of me, as I am of Christ" (1 Cor. 11:1). As organic intellectuals in the body of Christ, pastor-theologians must above all exhibit the mind or attitude of Christ, which Paul characterizes in terms of humility (Phil. 2:5–11). Imitating Christ is not a matter of being morally perfect, but rather of dying daily to the old self (1 Cor. 15:31; cf. Luke 9:23). It is the cruciform pattern of Jesus's life, a pattern of self-giving love, that pastor-theologians must cultivate, in themselves and in their charges.

To put on or imitate Christ is not about pretending to be something one is not by trying as hard as one can. On the contrary, it is about letting the Spirit realize in us the reality that we are: "If anyone is in Christ, he *is* a new creation" (2 Cor. 5:17).[40] Ethics (the domain of the imperative) is not about struggling to act like Jesus, as if Jesus were an external ideal; it is rather about acting Jesus out, because our life participates in his. Dietrich Bonhoeffer puts it well: "The place that in all other ethics is marked by the antithesis between ought and is . . . is occupied in Christian ethics by the relation between reality and becoming real, . . . the relation between Jesus Christ and the Holy Spirit."[41] Christ now reigns, and it is the disciple's privilege and responsibility to participate in this reign by acting out or *actualizing* what Christ has made real, and therefore really possible: "[Christ] is the 'is' and, in the Spirit, the 'ought.'"[42]

> *The real work of theology is the work of getting real—conforming people's speech, thoughts, and actions to the mind and heart of Jesus Christ.*

What are theologians for? What is the distinct service of the pastor-theologian? We reply: for confessing, comprehending, celebrating, communicating, commending, and conforming themselves and others to what is in Christ. Theology serves the church to the extent that it helps disciples fulfill their vocation to put on Christ and to grow into "the measure of the stature of the fullness of Christ" (Eph. 4:13). The real work of theology is indeed public: growing persons, cultivating a people. It is about helping individuals and communities to grow into the fullness of Christ. In sum: the real work of theology is the work of *getting real*—conforming people's speech, thoughts, and actions to the mind and heart of Jesus Christ, the source and standard of all truth, goodness, and beauty.[43]

The Goods of Theology: What Are Seminaries For?

The purpose of the pastor-theologian has everything to do with a seminary inasmuch as seminaries exist to train pastor-theologians. This is not the place for a wholesale examination of the state of the seminary. We have time for a brief excursus only (the proverbial three-point sermon). It is nevertheless fitting to say something here, in this chapter, as we transition from thinking about the purpose of pastor-theologians to the practices of pastor-theologians in the next. How can seminaries best form pastor-theologians to be farmers of men, women, and children whose aim is to prepare the bride of Christ by making the church wise unto salvation in Christ?

1. *Seminaries exist to foster biblical and theological literacy for the sake of understanding and living out what is in Christ.* The seminary is not *primarily* a place for acquiring skills or knowledge that could be acquired equally well in other institutions: public-speaking skills, pedagogical skills, counseling skills, or for that matter, philosophy, history, or even religion. The seminary is not *primarily* a place for conveying information but rather for educating and forming the church's organic intellectuals, leaders who embody the intellectual love of God. The seminary should *primarily* be a place where theology is not merely taught but actually learned and, to the extent that it is possible in a nonresidential campus, lived in community.

The seminary's special vocation is to cultivate in students the knowledge and wisdom required rightly to handle God's Word (Scripture, the gospel) and to form students into persons in whom the word of Christ will dwell richly (Col. 3:16). The word dwells richly when it permeates a person's thinking, doing, and being. This is only fitting, for the seminary's primary task is to form the mind of Christ in its students.

Fostering theological literacy means grounding students in theological tradition. From the very beginning, pastors and teachers passed on what they had received from others. While there are still many issues that require further reflection, the first responsibility of seminaries is to root students in the understanding of the gospel that the whole church has already attained: orthodoxy.

Many evangelical seminaries are nondenominational. This can be both a strength and a weakness. The strength is that it exposes students to the best of several traditions. The weakness is that it increases the likelihood that students will graduate without a coherent theology. In an age where both traditions and denominations are being abandoned, it is vital that evangelical seminaries communicate a sense of identity to their students by revisiting their evangelical heritage. No doubt some will object: what evangelical heritage? Which theological tradition? Are evangelicals of a Wesley stripe or a Westminster type, Arminian or Reformed? Yes.

Evangelicalism arose as a renewal movement of confessional Protestantism; Protestantism emerged as a reform movement of Roman Catholicism. The point is that evangelicals are Protestant and that Protestants are reformed (not

Roman) catholics. To be evangelically literate is thus to know the catholic tradition. Wallace Alston has rightly drawn attention to the pastor's vocation as "traditioning the church": "The traditioning task of the pastor, whereby the centuries of Christian thoughtfulness and belief are delivered into the hands of succeeding generations, has been displaced by indicators of success and replaced by the various guarantors of pastoral longevity."[44] How can pastor-theologians tradition others unless they have been traditioned?

2. *Seminaries exist not to reinforce but rather to transcend the typical compartmentalization of "biblical," "systematic," and "practical" theology for the sake of interdisciplinary pastoral-theological wisdom.* Too often practical theology is treated, not least by students intending to continue their studies, as the not-so-bright stepbrother in the family of seminary departments. These bright students complain about the various ministry hoops through which they have to jump to fulfill their degree requirements. Conversely, students keen on learning how to minister often lament having to take heavy-duty intellectual fare, the kind that systematic theology typically serves up. This theoretical/practical system of theological apartheid serves no one; indeed, it sets pastors up for failure in the church.

The "bright" students who opt for doctoral studies typically find themselves having to choose between church history, biblical studies, or theology. "Practical" theology is not on the menu (Want to be practical? Get a DMin or PsyD), and this is one of the main reasons intellectuals in the church have a reputation for being abstract and theoretical rather than organic and practical. It is a real shame for, as we have argued throughout the present work, the work of the pastor-theologian is intellectually demanding, requiring wisdom and understanding—the ability to relate knowledge to on-the-ground problems and issues—which is often more than is required in the academy, where doctoral work is easily disconnected from the rough-and-tumble of everyday life.

The thrust of the previous section is that practical theology (the gospel in the imperative mood) is largely an implication of doctrinal theology (the gospel in the indicative mood). And doctrinal theology, at its best, is always practical to the extent that real-life questions about Scripture and the Christian life are the impetus to faith's search for understanding. What is called practical theology is simply the outworking, in every life, of the theologian's attempt to understand what is in Christ and how what is in Christ bears on practical situations (e.g., parent-child relationships, employer-employee relationships) and contemporary issues (e.g., social justice, sexuality).[45]

The pastor-theologian does not have a unique professional or clinical skill but is rather the theological conscience of the church and thus understands everything in biblical-theological context and in relation to what God is doing in Jesus Christ. Practical theology is not so much a distinct subject, then, as it is the center of the seminary's task to cultivate understanding: "Pastoral care is an opportunity to communicate, verbally or non-verbally, directly or indirectly, the faith of the church."[46] It remains an open question whether this means that practical theology should cease being a separate department in the seminary and instead become the glue that holds everything else together.[47]

3. *Seminaries exist to foster a particular kind of generalist: one who understands all things in the light of the biblical testimony to what is in Christ, keeps company with Christ, acts out the eschatological reality of being raised with Christ, and helps others to do the same.* It is bad enough that evangelical students leave seminary with a theological identity crisis. Even worse is the challenge of relating what they have learned in different departments. What holds the MDiv curriculum together and makes of it something more than a disparate collection of degree requirements? To raise this question is to inquire into what integrates the curriculum or, more pointedly, what gives the seminary integrity.

> *Seminaries exist to foster a particular kind of generalist: one who understands all things in the light of the biblical testimony to what is in Christ.*

What makes this question especially challenging is the unique nature of the church's organic intellectual, which, as we have seen, is not a function of specialized skills or knowledge: "If pastoral theology has any legitimate identity, it is the identity of a disciple that serves to pull all of the other branches of theological study into the center, to the place where ministry must happen in care for God's people. As such, pastoral theology has the special virtue and grace of being a generalist discipline."[48] Yes, but what kind of generalist? The short answer: the kind of generalist who thinks about everything in life in relation to its summation in Jesus Christ (Eph. 1:9–10).

The point of seminary curricular integration should therefore be pastoral wisdom, which demands literacy, competency, and excellence alike. By literacy, I mean everything pastors need to *know* in order to carry out their vocation of becoming a shepherd like Christ. By competence, I mean capacities a pastor must acquire in order to *do* ministry effectively and put literacy to good use;

pastor-theologians must be generalists not only as pertains to knowledge but also to skills. By excellence, I mean all the personal qualities a pastor needs to have in order to *be* one who rightly ministers Christ—the way, truth, and life—to others.

To minister Christ, one needs to know Jesus Christ, and for this we need the testimony of the Old and New Testaments, the tradition of the church's sustained reflection on this testimony, and personal experience of Christ's presence and activity. Learning Christ—with heart, soul, strength, and mind alike—must be the beginning and end, the center and circumference, the energy and matter of the seminary curriculum. Let seminaries resolve "to know nothing . . . except Jesus Christ and him crucified" and resurrected (1 Cor. 2:2; 15): the Christ, the whole Christ, and nothing but the Christ.

On Death

DAVID GIBSON

> A good name is better than fine perfume,
> and the day of death better than the day of birth.
>
> Ecclesiastes 7:1 NIV

The place of the pastor in the realm of death is well known. The pastor is there to comfort the grieving when death visits; the pastor is there to disturb the comfortable when death has been gone awhile. The vistas of present loss and future judgment seem to govern the contours of death in pastoral ministry, whether it is encountered as personal counselor or biblical expositor.

In compact form, I wish to suggest another horizon. Death gives life. *The day of death is better than the day of birth.*

The pastoral charge engages in the degodding of our fabricated gods, and it is a cultural mistake to ever think the heat of the battle is with the idols of money, sex, and power. Such things receive homage only because of the more deep-seated idol of the self. The desire to be an immortal creature apart from God is the primary sin—*pride*—and God's dismantling tool is death. That death, when received as the appropriate marker of finitude this side of the fall, can be the source of a life well lived, the true destroyer of our deceitful deities.

131

Death creates as well as kills. It can shape and mold as well as tear and shatter. This is because the curse is a *performative* speech-act: it communicates the divine displeasure at the creature's usurping the Throne and so enacts the limited boundaries of human existence that must be respected. Transgress the boundaries, and disintegration ensues. Expect more for yourself than has been promised, and behold! Eden regained? Two handfuls of mist. Seventy years of vapor vanishing from the ever-rotating earth. More than a sentry posted at border control, death does not simply patrol the boundary; it is itself the boundary, a marker to define and delimit the whole project of being human this side of the fall.

Here is the betterness of death. Qoheleth's words in Ecclesiastes 7:1 are doubtless open to different interpretations, but my suggestion is that we are being invited to see death as homiletician par excellence. Death is a Teacher. The day of death is better than the day of birth—not because death is better than life, *but because a coffin preaches better sermons than a crib*. "It is better to go to a house of mourning than to go to a house of feasting, for death comes to us all, and the living should take this to heart" (7:2 NIV altered). "The heart of the wise is in the house of mourning, but the heart of fools is in the house of pleasure" (7:4 NIV).

Qoheleth has studied two types of people at a funeral. The fools, who shift in their seats, desperate to be outside in the sunshine and back to what they were doing; and the wise, who stare at the coffin and realize that one day it will be their turn. Such inattention or attention to death paves two very different roads through life.

Observe the fat cat at the top of the pile, seated at the best table in the exclusive restaurant. He has done it all, made it all, and he eats all alone in his discontent (4:7–8). Proud? Selfish? Perhaps—but why? It is because he does not believe he is going to die. He has never met death's gaze with a steady eye. He has not met his death in advance and watched it pry open his hands and operate on his heart.

The wise, seated in the crematorium and riveted anew to their mortality, say to themselves: "If I am going to die, how then shall I live?" They rise, reborn by death's answer: wine and work, sex and food, love and laughter, beauty and truth, and lots of each—that will do for starters (9:7–9). Death makes pleasure-seekers, not doom-dwellers or naysayers. The list of wise pursuits in 9:7–9 is representative, not exhaustive. May we paraphrase? Ride a bike, see the Grand Canyon, go to the theater, learn to make music, visit the sick, care for the dying, cook a meal, feed the hungry, watch a film, read a book, laugh with some friends until it makes you cry, play football, run a marathon, snorkel in the ocean, listen to Mozart, talk to your parents on the phone, write a letter, play with your kids, spend your money, learn a language, plant a church, start a school, speak about Christ, travel to somewhere you've never been, adopt a child, give away your fortune and then some, shape someone else's life by laying down your own.[1]

One day, working and planning and knowledge and wisdom will cease, so do them now while you can. Whatever your hand finds to do, do it with all you have. Dying people, who truly know they are dying, are among all people the most alive. They are not here to live forever. They are here to live for now, for today—and most of all they are here to live for others. "Two are better than one" (4:9). "A cord of three strands is not quickly broken" (4:12 NIV). Think how strong four would be, or five.

Has the rumor of a coming banquet reached even Qoheleth, of all people? Is he spreading the rumor or keeping his lips sealed? Whatever he knew, we know these things should flow from our pulpits as the very content of our public theology of death. While it is a truism that nothing is as certain as death and taxes, it is also true that death does everything it can to escape public notice. Ernest Becker has compellingly shown us that denying death is the mainspring of much human activity.[2] Too terrible to face, we ignore it or euphemize it in respectable discourse, and we relegate it as the thing that happens to others. How different for Qoheleth and the disciples he instructs. When the creature sees itself as *creature,* finitude need not produce crushing fear and despair that we have to ornament with illusion. Facing death is the mainspring of fruitful human life. For death is the vital ingredient in being wonderfully fascinated with what comes before it—*life.* When we prepare to die, we learn how to live.

Death trades in humility. It punctures the futile project of trying to be God. Death teaches the young to lose their life for something greater than life, and to risk all for Christ and his kingdom; it teaches the old why God beyond the grave is the hope of a world reborn in righteousness and equity. Death crafts a worldview dedicated not to the pursuit of gain, but to generosity and contentment. "Better one handful with tranquility than two handfuls with toil" (4:6 NIV). Death gives perspective in pain. It helps us lose, for one day God will put everything right.

Spend your death on living.

Preaching the Doctrine of the Gospel
as Truth, Goodness, and Beauty

BILL KYNES

As a pastor, I am called to be a herald of the truth of the gospel as it is revealed in the pages of Scripture. That gospel truth is called doctrine, and when I expound this doctrine, I appeal to the minds of my hearers, seeking to explain with clarity what God—through the life, death, and resurrection of Christ—has done in real human history to reconcile us to himself and to restore us in the image of Christ for God's glory. I set forth the grand story of creation, fall, redemption, and restoration, pointing to the ways in which this story best makes sense of the cosmos and of our own consciousness. In declaring that we are created in God's image, the Bible explains why we as human beings have such dignity but can be so depraved, why we are both a part of nature but are also above nature, and why we so desperately long for meaning, purpose, and significance in our lives. In my preaching I address human reason and call people to put their faith in the gospel of Christ because it is true.

But the doctrine that is the gospel is more than merely rational; it is also moral. In expounding the teaching of the Scripture, I also appeal to my listeners' consciences. I set before them the holiness of our great God and the standards of his law. I seek to unmask their self-justifications, hypocrisies, and foolish idolatries and to confront them with the Judge of all the earth, who knows unerringly the thoughts and intentions of their hearts. We are truly guilty as we stand before a holy God. Yet this same Bible doctrine also reveals a God of mercy and compassion, who has acted in grace to take away our sin. Through the atoning blood of Christ, the gospel offers forgiveness and a moral cleansing from within. The message I am called to proclaim is not only true; it is also good. The gospel not only satisfies the mind; it also soothes the conscience and compels the believer to live in Christlike righteousness. In my preaching I call people to put their faith in the gospel of Christ because it is good.

Yet there is more. The gospel and the new life it engenders are not only true and good; they are also beautiful. As Christian doctrine declares, in that ugly Roman cross we actually behold an act of unmatched beauty—a sacrificial, forgiving love poured out to save those who deserved nothing but divine wrath.

And from that cross flows an appealing quality of life: "the unfading beauty of a gentle and quiet spirit" (1 Pet. 3:4 NIV), humble and compassionate, not self-promoting, but purposeful, contented, and full of a simple joy. Followers of Christ forsake the vain pursuit of money and worldly fame and lay hold of something far more satisfying. In relationships of love and care, the community that Christ creates by his Spirit at times displays glimpses of its future glory, when it will be "a bride [beautifully] adorned for her husband" (Rev. 21:2). When I expound the truth of the gospel with all its moral force, I appeal not only to the mind and to the conscience, but also to the heart—to that aesthetic sense that is drawn to what is attractive, desirable, and pleasurable, even glorious. I call people to put their faith in the gospel of Christ because it is beautiful.

I declare the gospel in all its truth, goodness, and beauty. I am encouraged in this approach to preaching by the apostle Paul's example in his Letter to Titus. In the opening verse he speaks of the "knowledge of the truth that leads to godliness" (1:1 NIV); that connection of truth and moral goodness forms a major theme of the epistle. Christian leaders, Paul says, are to "hold firmly to the trustworthy message as it has been taught," and they are to "encourage others by sound doctrine" (1:9 NIV). He urges Titus, "You must teach what accords with sound doctrine" (2:1), and then Paul immediately instructs Titus in the way of life that is to characterize Christian believers—as older men, older women, younger women, young men, and slaves. They are to live lives of reverence, self-control, purity, humility, and godliness (2:2–3:1). And what Paul says to slaves can equally be said to all: they are to live in such a way that "they may adorn the doctrine of God our Savior" (2:10), or as translated by the NIV, that "they will make the teaching about God our Savior attractive." The moral goodness that ought to flow from the truth of sound doctrine is to display a beauty that will be attractive.

And shouldn't we expect just this connection? For Christian doctrine is teaching about the gospel. And the gospel is a revelation of the character of God. And Christian theology asserts that all three of these—truth, goodness, and beauty—are united in God himself. In a sense, they are just three different ways of speaking about who God is as perfect truth, infinite goodness, and pure beauty—a beauty that is utterly glorious. These three cannot be separated into different compartments, for God's truth is good, his goodness is beautiful, and his beauty is true. God is the source of all truth, goodness, and beauty; hence all that is true, good, or beautiful in this world ultimately points to God. Thus sound doctrine—that is, faithful teaching of God's gospel—will embody all three: the good way of life that flows from the truth of the gospel is a thing of beauty.

In my desire to be faithful to my calling as a pastor, I seek to proclaim the gospel in all its truth, goodness, and beauty, appealing to the mind, the conscience, and the heart. It is my prayer that the Spirit of God will then use what I preach to move the will of the listener to respond to this gospel doctrine in repentance, faith, and loving obedience.

Reading for Preaching

CORNELIUS PLANTINGA JR.

Preachers undertake a program of general reading for various reasons, including sheer or guilty pleasure, but most of the reasons have to do with respect for listeners. Respectful preachers do not assume that their own life experience is rich-enough soil for growing a sermon, and so they import nutrients from others. Preachers read poetry, for instance, to tune their ear for language, their first tool. They also read biography to acquire good judgment, especially of human character. Meanwhile, journalism strengthens the preacher's grasp of contemporary trends and events. Essays teach preachers to focus their thought (many of George Orwell's essays are about exactly one thing). And children's literature ("They say Aslan is on the move" [C. S. Lewis]) gives the preacher a model of prose style, one that could be described as "noble simplicity."

Preachers do not undertake this program to make sermons pretty or lush. Not every congregant wants to hear that "the sky was blushing pink behind the hills of Moab." Or that "the apostle's wings were furled as his feet paced the beaten causeway of life." After all, who talks like that? In general, highly literary preachers, whether employing their own language or someone else's, can sound effete.

Still, there are mighty reasons for the preacher to read fiction and to paraphrase or even quote it occasionally. For one thing, preachers are always on the prowl for illustrations. So the preacher pondering Paul's glad counsel, "Clothe yourselves with . . . humility" (Col. 3:12 NIV), wants to know Marilynne

Robinson's preacher John Ames in *Gilead*, who incarnates genial self-irony, an appealing species of humility. Ames tells us one of his dreams: "I was preaching to Jesus Himself, saying any foolish thing I could think of, and He was sitting there in his white, white robe looking patient and sad and amazed." The preacher of patience will remember Ma Joad from *The Grapes of Wrath*, a woman of immense capacity for absorbing irritants, even injustices, without becoming paralyzed by them.

Where successful illustrations from fiction are concerned, much depends on the preacher's judgment. How apt is this illustration? How fancy? How tight is the fit between it and what it illustrates? How useful would this illustration be to a general audience?

But no veteran preacher reads fiction just for its ability to illustrate pre-established themes. For one thing, reading merely for illustrations is too much like work. For another, reading with so narrow an aim distracts the preacher from a bigger and more general advantage, namely, that a well-chosen program of reading tends to make the preacher wise. After all, good writing abounds in revealing incidents, images, character sketches, phrases, and observations about everything under the sun, including life, death, sin, grace, pilgrimage, patience, God, aging, rejoicing, longing, going home, and reaping what you sow. Preachers address the same themes in Scripture; they have an advantage if they do so with minds already rich in understanding such themes.

Take one example out of thousands. In Steinbeck's *East of Eden*, Samuel and Liza Hamilton, husband and wife, lose their eldest daughter, Una. In telling us of this loss, Steinbeck makes us see how death is differently received by one human soul than by another:

> Una's death cut the earth from under Samuel's feet and opened his defended keep and let in old age. On the other hand Liza, who surely loved her family as deeply as did her husband, was not destroyed or warped. Her life continued evenly. She felt sorrow but she survived it.[3]

Why such difference? Samuel didn't really believe in death. To him, it was "an outrage, a denial of the immortality he deeply felt." But in Liza's world death is inevitable: "She did not like death, but she knew it existed, and when it came it did not surprise her."

The thoughtful preacher will ponder this difference and compare it to biblical attitudes toward death. Is death an outrage ("the last enemy to be overcome" [cf. 1 Cor. 15:26]), a phenomenon that should never have entered our world? Or is death a natural part of the rhythm of life, in which there is "a time to be born, and a time to die" (Eccles. 3:2)? Or both?

The preacher's gift and calling is wisdom. Without it, who could stand under the Sunday assignment to teach, caution, inspire, and encourage a congregation? With it, the preacher may at least hope that the congregation will not sit there looking "patient and sad and amazed." Preachers know that with just a few shelves of novels, they have a hundred possible worlds to enter and dwell in for a time, each a revelation. Inside one of these worlds, preachers store up "middle wisdom," the insights that range in the center of the spectrum from trivia to profundity. Here are some sample insights:

- Human compassion is often just under the surface, and if a tough guy shows it first, it becomes contagious as others take permission.
- But compassion can feel less like a gift than a load when the compassionate person wants to be good to you on *his* terms.
- Anger can destroy and corrupt, but when it is aimed at injustice, anger can quicken people and make them purposeful.
- Silence is the natural context from which to speak, and it is the natural context from which to listen. The rhythm of silence, sound, and silence is built into creation by God; and when we break the rhythm, we become disoriented.
- Under the pressure of sin, love can take unthinkable forms, even ones that look like betrayal.

Wise preachers read to become wiser. After all, they have a high hill to climb every week. Where else in human life is a person called forward to address a significantly mixed audience on the world's most magnificent topics—God, glory, salvation, resurrection, memory, hope—and to do so in a way that really engages the listeners? The preacher has to be a little crazy to climb this hill. Or else expectant that, once again, the Holy Spirit might blow the sermon home to listeners.

4

Artisans in the House of God

The Practices of the Pastor-Theologian

KEVIN J. VANHOOZER

> For we are fellow workers for God; you are God's field,
> God's building. (1 Cor. 3:9 RSV)

Theology is not an end in itself. Unlike institutions that seek to perpetuate their own existence, theology has a higher aim than mere self-preservation. The ultimate end of theology, as with all things human, is the glory of God. However, theology's proximate end is to build up the people of God, equipping them to realize their ultimate end: glorifying God in everything that they do, say, and suffer. The mission of theology has everything to do with participating in God's own mission to the world. Everything in theology eventually returns to this starting point: the Father's creating and embracing all things with his two "hands," the Son and Spirit.

In this chapter we survey a number of the concrete practices by which pastor-theologians engage in Christian ministry, which is to say, *God's* mission. The point is so obvious that it is easily missed. Indeed, the present book opened by sounding an alarm, namely, that many congregations and pastors have secularized understandings of the Christian ministry. Just as the biggest mistake we can make as Christians is to think that God is there for us, a supporting actor in our life stories (rather than we being the bit players in God's story), so the biggest mistake a pastor can make is to think that the ministry is first and foremost a human work, supported by God. On the contrary: God has been active in building his church since before the foundation of the world (Eph. 1:4; Rev. 13:8). The pastor is simply a St. Johnny-come-lately to the cause.

Pastors can minister what is in Christ authentically only if they themselves are in Christ.

We can be more specific. Although the church is a work of the Triune God, the pastor participates in the Son's work in particular. Jesus Christ is the supreme prophet who not only speaks but is the Word of God directed to humanity. Jesus Christ is the supreme priest insofar as he both offers and is the bloody sacrifice that alone removes sin. As God-man, Jesus Christ is the unique mediator who represents God to others and others to God. Jesus is both God's royal word and humanity's wise and obedient response.

Pastors participate in Jesus's own ministry, thanks to their union with Christ. Like all believers, pastors are united to the person of Jesus Christ, the risen Son of God, who now reigns at the right hand of the Father. In addition, though to some extent all believers share in the Son's ongoing work, pastors have been set apart to participate in a distinct way in Christ's office as the Great Shepherd: "It is the bold intention of Christ's ministry to combine the prophetic and priestly ministries into a single, unified ministry of word and sacrament in which one person serves both the priestly office of conducting public worship and the prophetic office of providing religious instruction, exegesis, and proclamation of the word of God."[1] The pastor therefore represents and participates in Jesus Christ's own ministry.

It is important to keep in mind that the pastoral ministry is primarily the work of Jesus Christ and only secondarily of human pastors. Pastors can minister what is in Christ authentically only if they themselves are in Christ.[2] And because they are in Christ, Christ is also in them, communicating himself, together with his benefits, through his Spirit: "Through our union with Christ we share in the ministry of Jesus Christ with, to, and for us, through the Holy Spirit, to the glory of the Father."[3] The practices that constitute the work of the pastor-theologian may encompass the specialized skills of the so-called helping professions, but ultimately what makes them theological practices is that they are ways of communicating *what is in Christ*.[4]

The present chapter begins by examining what we are calling the Great Pastoral Commission: to "make disciples" and to "build God's house." The latter image is of special interest, especially in light of its development in Ezra-Nehemiah and Ephesians. The rest of the chapter examines four pastoral practices, each in its own way a correlate to the Greatest Commandment (Mark 12:30). To anticipate: pastor-theologians love God and the people of God with all their soul, mind, heart, and strength when they proclaim, teach, celebrate/administer, and demonstrate *what is in Christ*.

The Great Pastoral Commission: "Make Disciples"; "Build God's House"

Jesus uses the term "church" (Gk. *ekklēsia*, "gathered assembly") only three times, all in the Gospel of Matthew (16:18; 18:17 [2x]). Yet elsewhere Jesus had much to say about God's plan for a set-apart people, depicting them alternately as a flock, a harvest of grain, fish gathered in a net, and as wedding guests. For example, Jesus said he was sent "to the lost sheep of the house of Israel" (Matt. 15:24), yet he also acknowledged that "I have other sheep that are not of this fold" (John 10:16). It is therefore significant that Jesus's last words to his disciples after his resurrection, which are also the last words in Matthew's Gospel, pertain to provisions for his set-apart people: "Go therefore and make disciples of all nations, baptizing them in the name of the Father and of the Son and of the Holy Spirit, teaching them to observe all that I have commanded you. And behold, I am with you always, to the end of the age" (Matt. 28:19–20).

We can also view this Great Commission as a Great Pastoral Commission. For, while all Christians must bear witness to their life in Christ, it is the special privilege and responsibility of pastors to baptize and teach disciples.[5] The Great Pastoral Commission is about forming, out of many nations, a holy nation (1 Pet. 2:9; cf. Exod. 19:6). Or, to use a related image: the church is an *eschatological embassy*, "an institution that represents one nation [i.e., the kingdom of God] inside another nation."[6] It is one thing to administer earthly institutions but quite another to administer an eschatological reality, which is precisely why pastors need to be theologians.

Pastors are public theologians because they work with *people* (the gathered assembly as an eschatological [otherworldly] public amid a secular [worldly] public) on *God's* behalf. The particular vocation of the pastor-theologian is to build up Christians in Christ: "And his gifts were that some should be apostles, some prophets, some evangelists, some pastors and teachers, for the equipment of the saints, for the work of ministry, for building up the body of Christ, until we all attain to the unity of the faith and of the knowledge of the Son of God, to mature manhood, to the measure of the stature of the fullness of Christ" (Eph. 4:11–13 RSV).

Pastors exist to edify people in Christ. Indeed, everything that happens in the church ought to edify people. To "edify" (Gk. *oikodomeō*) is to build up (Rom. 14:19; 1 Cor. 14:3, 12; 2 Cor. 10:8; 12:19; Eph. 4:12, 29). The New Testament uses two different images for edification: one is organic and the other inorganic. The organic image pertains to growing living things (e.g., crops in a field). Jesus instructs Peter: "Feed my sheep" (John 21:17). Here growth is a matter of nutrition and nurture, of administering first the milk of the word of God and then the meat and potatoes (i.e., "solid food," Heb. 5:14). The inorganic image is that of a building. Paul mentions both images in the same breath in 1 Corinthians 3:9: "You are God's field, God's building." The point is that pastor-theologians are essentially church cultivators, church builders—where "church" refers not to a literal building but to an edifice made up of people. This is the idea the present chapter highlights with its leading image of the pastor-theologian as an artisan in God's house.

"Upon This Rock": Which Rock? Whose Foundation?

Before we turn to examine the ways in which pastor-theologians build up disciples, however, we need to consider another image that stands somewhere between fields and buildings: rocks. Rocks are taken from fields but then incorporated into buildings. Perhaps this is why Jesus appealed to this image in his first, and arguably most famous, reference to the church: "And I tell you, you are Peter, and on this rock I will build my church" (Matt. 16:18). There are several things to notice in this controversial passage—controversial largely because it is the major sticking point in the debate between Roman Catholics and Protestants over the role of the pope and his "Petrine" office.

First and foremost, it is abundantly clear that Jesus here promises to build the church himself: it is *his* church ("my"), and *he* is the principal agent of its construction ("I will build"). This follows from Jesus's resurrection, ascension, and heavenly session, and from his sending his Holy Spirit to equip various people in the church for various kinds of edifying work. To repeat: Jesus is the prime minister (i.e., the principal operative agency) of the church.

The second point is more contentious: what, or who, is the rock? There are three main interpretive possibilities: Christ himself (e.g., Augustine); Peter himself (e.g., Roman Catholics); Peter's confession of Christ (e.g., many Protestants; see Matt. 16:16–17). Other relevant texts include 1 Corinthians 3:11 ("For no one can lay a foundation other than that which is laid, which is Jesus Christ"), which identifies Jesus Christ as the foundation (*themelios*) of the church; and Ephesians 2:20, which identifies the apostles and prophets as the foundation (*themelios*, again) and Christ Jesus as the "cornerstone." Grant Osborne attempts to bring lapidary clarity into the discussion: "Jesus is the builder and cornerstone, but Peter is the first leader/rock/foundation on whom Jesus erects the superstructure."[7] Peter is the rock, Osborne thinks, though in context "it is certainly the Peter who confesses Christ."[8]

We belabor the point because, if pastor-theologians are charged with building God's house, it is important to know on what foundation they should build. Robert Gundry notes that *petros* ("Peter") in Greek could be translated "loose stone"—hardly the thing for the church's foundation. By way of contrast, "this rock" (*petra*) is bedrock. Matthew uses *petra* earlier, in 7:24, when Jesus says, "Everyone . . . who hears these words of mine and does them will be like a wise man who built his house on the rock [*petra* in the accusative]." According to Gundry, "this rock" therefore means "the words of Jesus, his teaching."[9]

The words of Jesus matter only because Jesus is himself God's Word. Peter's confession of Jesus as the Christ in Matthew 16:16–18 goes hand in hand with his other confession, recorded in John's Gospel, where he says to Jesus "You have the words of eternal life" (John 6:68). *The church is built on both the form and content of Peter's twin confessions: the verbal profession of faith in both Jesus and his words as the source of eternal life.*[10] Jesus will build his church on confessors and their confessions.[11]

Jesus is the master builder who will build his church on the rock of confessors and confessions. Pastor-theologians have a special role in serving as authorized representatives of Jesus, charged with preserving the integrity of these confessions. A confession is a self-involving affirmation, one of the principal ways of communicating Christ in the indicative mood. The present chapter examines the many ways in which pastor-theologians confess or communicate Christ:

proclaiming, teaching, celebrating, and demonstrating. Pastor-theologians confess Christ in many ways, especially (but not exclusively) with words, as did Jesus himself.

Growing Disciples: God's Field

Pastors are public theologians who work with people to build Christ's church. Much of the work is public in the sense of nurturing people in general, in open view; yet there is also an important place for working with people as individuals. "Feed my sheep." People are persons: a flock is composed of individual sheep, and one can only feed a flock by ensuring that each individual sheep is eating. The pastor-theologian works with people but must also be able to work with (i.e., minister to) individuals. There is no single formula or shortcut for making disciples, though there is a template: Jesus Christ, the Good Shepherd (John 10:14).

There is no single formula or shortcut for making disciples, though there is a template: Jesus Christ, the Good Shepherd.

What there is in Christ is a model for all subsequent pastor-theologians. Even if shepherd is not the overarching image, it is nevertheless instructive. Peter describes Jesus as "the Shepherd and Overseer of your souls" (1 Pet. 2:25). Jesus is an overseer (Gk. *episkopos*) who guards or looks after souls, that is, a person's self or inner life. Jesus is the "chief shepherd [*archipoimenos*]" (5:4), but pastor-theologians participate in this shepherding task (5:2) as his appointed representatives ("undershepherds"). Indeed, Paul exhorts the elders of the church at Ephesus, "Pay careful attention to yourselves and to all the flock, in which the Holy Spirit has made you overseers, to care for the church of God" (Acts 20:28).

It is important not to confuse "overseeing" with "lording it over." Peter explicitly cautions church leaders against imitating worldly leaders who abuse their power or role (1 Pet. 5:3). The chief shepherd himself explains "the good shepherd lays down his life for the sheep" (John 10:11): "The leaders of God's people possess only one kind of authentic authority—the authority of serving the flock by giving their lives for it."[12] Pastor-theologians here communicate what it is in Christ with more than words.

Pastor-theologians tend to the flock and cultivate God's field when they oversee or (to use the traditional term) "cure" souls. The cure of souls means caring for a person's deepest self: the orientation of the heart toward other persons and especially toward God. There is nothing more fundamental than a person's relationship to God, no other gospel for curing what ails us in the depths of our being than the gospel of Jesus Christ. The care or cure of souls refers to the cultivation of Christlikeness in the field of human flesh, and hence the transformation of the individual into a person who more faithfully images God.

Overseeing souls is what Eugene Peterson calls the pastor's "work of the week."[13] This work cannot be done during the Sunday worship service because it requires attending to the state of individual persons. It is a matter of discerning, and helping individuals to discern, the presence and activity of God in a person's life. To do that, pastor-theologians need to know both the character of God and the character of the soul being cared for. Peterson insists that soul care is not a specialized form of ministry but a way of describing the whole pastoral task: to make disciples by building up individual persons into Christ and Christlikeness, one soul at a time. This too is public theology, but it describes only part of the pastor-theologian's task in building the church.

Building Temples: God's Building

We have already mentioned Jonathan Edwards's belief that God created the world in order to procure a spouse for his Son. Hugh of St. Victor said something similar centuries earlier, something that serves as a point of transition from thinking about individual souls to the church as a corporate entity. For Hugh, the primary pastoral-theological task was to re-form the soul into a proper dwelling place—a bridal chamber!—for the divine presence. One scholar suggests that Hugh took his cue regarding "soul construction" from the impressive way gothic cathedrals were being built at the time (twelfth century).[14] Hugh believed that soul care is actually soul *repair*: a matter of receiving again the form of wisdom, namely, Christ, the true image of God. The pastor's goal is "to re-form the soul in the image of God, such that the soul and the church become dwelling places, houses, temples for God."[15]

In at least one place the apostle Paul refers to the bodies of individuals as "temples" of the Holy Spirit (1 Cor. 6:19). Most of the time when Paul uses temple imagery, however, he has in mind not an individual but a corporate body: the whole church. The church, not a collection of individual persons but a people organically united in Christ, is the end for which God created the world. Pastor-theologians are thus charged not only with ministering to individuals but also with keeping the house of God—the church as living temple composed of stones from many quarries—in good repair.

It is not the first time that the house of God has stood in need of repair and in need of people to lead the work of repair. The progress of redemption is not always a steady process. Jonathan Edwards likened the history of the church to "a building that slowly rises to completion, though its construction may be intermittent."[16] The Babylonians destroyed Solomon's temple, and for decades the temple site lay in ruins. Pastor-theologians can perhaps learn something from those predecessors who were involved in rebuilding God's house in Jerusalem and whose story is told in Ezra-Nehemiah. Indeed, Ezra-Nehemiah provides biblical precedent for our leading image of pastor-theologians as artisans of God's house.

Ezra-Nehemiah: Rebuilding and Reform

We are the servants of the God of heaven and earth, and we are rebuilding the house that was built many years ago. (Ezra 5:11)

Ezra-Nehemiah tells the story of three builders and building projects: Zerubbabel and the reconstruction of the Jerusalem temple (Ezra 1:1–6:15); Ezra and the reconstruction of the Jerusalem community (Ezra 7–10); Nehemiah and the reconstruction of Jerusalem's walls (Neh. 1:1–12:26). In each case there is opposition to the building, yet each leader accomplishes his respective mission and then oversees an assembly of exiles that gathers to mark the occasion (Ezra 6:16–22; Neh. 9–10; Neh. 12:27–13:3).

The church too is a holy nation of exiles, resident aliens (cf. 1 Pet. 1:1; 2:11) who are trying to build a house for God under what are often less than ideal circumstances. In appealing to the construction of the Second Temple, I am not allegorizing the text; rather, I am noting a redemptive-historical continuity between Israel's struggle to live out their covenant with God faithfully and the church's struggle to do the same thing today. Ezra-Nehemiah is an encouraging word to pastor-theologians charged with reconstructing the house of God. Like Ezra and Nehemiah, church leaders have to overcome opposition from without and within as they struggle toward but never reach the consummation—a fittingly holy dwelling place for God—for the people are still in the process of becoming holy. Like Ezra and Nehemiah, the problem "is not so much one of continuing exile but of incomplete restoration."[17] Like Ezra and Nehemiah, church leaders today find themselves struggling to be faithful to God while living in occupied territory, as it were (amid a surrounding secular culture).[18] Interestingly enough, the first commentary on Ezra-Nehemiah is that of the Venerable Bede in the eighth century, and according to him the text "designates the Lord Himself and His temple and city, which we [Christians] are."[19]

There are twenty-six references to the "house of God" (*bêt hāĕlōhîm*) in Ezra-Nehemiah. Ezra 1–6 recounts the exiles' return to Jerusalem and their reconstruction of the temple, the physical sign of God's covenant presence with his people. Though the people have to do the work, it is clear that divine agency is the real impetus behind the project, for it is the Lord who stirs up the spirit of Cyrus, king of Persia, to see that the Jews rebuild God's house (Ezra 1:1–3).[20] But the rebuilding of the temple is only the beginning of the story. The real challenge, and the heart of Ezra's concern, is with the restoration of a holy *people*. This is why Ezra may well be the quintessential public theologian in the Old Testament.

Ezra is introduced as a priest (Ezra 7:11) and a "scribe skilled in the Law of Moses" (7:6), and this means "a student and expositor of God's written word."[21] Ezra was a student who "had set his heart to study the Law of the LORD, and to do it and to teach his statutes" (7:10). Note the progression: one cannot say about Ezra, "Those who can, do; those who can't, teach." On the contrary, for Ezra, study leads to doing, and only then to teaching: "[Ezra] is a model reformer in that what he taught he had first lived, and what he lived he had first made sure of in the Scriptures."[22] In sum: Ezra threw himself into the task of ministering and communicating God's word with all his soul, mind, heart, and strength.

Ezra 7–10 relates the story of Ezra's return to Jerusalem to reconstruct not the temple but the community, hence its relevance for our concern with how pastor-theologians build the church. Ezra-Nehemiah is not simply a historical account of what happened in a world far away. Rather, it is a narrative of religious reform under the word of God and, for this reason, is of striking contemporary significance. The heart of the story is Ezra's use of God's word to reform the people of God. It is a narrative about public theology. Bede shrewdly notes that it was only fitting that Ezra, having repaired the destroyed buildings, turn his attention to the inward restoration of the people's faith and love.[23]

When Ezra arrives in Jerusalem, he is appalled at the news that the people have intermarried with non-Jews, thereby failing to set themselves apart from "the peoples of the lands" (Ezra 9:1–4). His public prayer of confession helps the people who have gathered to him grasp the extent of their unfaithfulness (9:6–10:1). Ezra reforms the people by using the word of God as a lens through which the people see themselves as they are: idolaters who, by marrying foreign wives who worship foreign gods, are living outside God's law—covenant outlaws. Even a rebuilt temple is no good as a dwelling place for a holy God if it stands in the midst of an unholy people.

The book of Ezra ends with the community's heartfelt response, which involved both confessing sin and changing their ways: "Therefore let us make a covenant with our God to put away all these wives" (10:3). The point of the passage is not about divorce, much less racism, but rather about community reformation and renewal.[24] Interestingly, the Mosaic law itself gave no direct guidance on this particular problem (viz., foreign wives), so Ezra improvises an interpretation that accords with the spirit of the law.[25] Bede believes the foreign wives "stand for the heresies and superstitious sects of philosophers."[26] Similarly, pastor-theologians need to think hard about what dynamic equivalents of foreign wives or idols the church harbors today (1 John 5:21).

The book of Nehemiah continues the story, with Nehemiah returning to Jerusalem to rebuild its walls. Repairing the walls was necessary not only to defend the community but also to restore its essential unity.[27] Nehemiah organizes the work so that each household would be responsible for that part of the wall closest to it (Neh. 3:28–30). Bede sees this as a type of the community that is building the new Jerusalem, although he may go further than is exegetically warranted when he suggests that those who build the city gates are none other than prophets, apostles, and evangelists![28] What is warranted is the inference that those, like Nehemiah, who build God's house in the present, will be subject to various kinds of internal and external opposition (Neh. 6).

Nehemiah 7–13 once again features Ezra, the public theologian. It is not enough to have the right externals, like walls, in place; what counts is having the word of God in receptive and obedient human hearts, which is why Ezra-Nehemiah again focuses on the reform of the community. This final section features Ezra's reading/explanation of God's law and the people's enthusiastic response.[29] Especially noteworthy is the repeated emphasis on the people's "understanding" (Neh. 8:2, 3, 7, 8, 12). Equally noteworthy is the people's joyous response, *because* they had understood the words spoken (Neh. 8:12). If this is true of the word of the law, how much more should it be so with the proclamation of the gospel? If only the church would commit itself joyfully in the same way to the revitalization of its community and say, with the assembly gathered around Ezra, "We will not neglect the house of our God" (Neh. 10:39).

Ephesians: The Church as Living Temple

The apostle Paul, like Ezra, was also a public theologian, ministering the word through the Spirit in order to build up God's people into God's house. Recall the opening quote with which we began the chapter: "You are . . . God's building" (1 Cor. 3:9). This is hardly an isolated image, either in Paul or the rest of the New Testament.

The Gospel of John presents Jesus himself as the true temple, who is and does everything the earthly temple was supposed to be and do. The crucial text is John 1:14: "And the Word became flesh and dwelt [lit., "pitched its tent"] among us, and we have seen his glory." The clear allusion is to the wilderness tabernacle constructed by Moses and to the glory cloud representing God's presence, which settled first on that ancient tent (Exod. 40:34–38) and then, later, on the temple at Jerusalem (1 Kings 8:10–13). That glory was absent from the reconstructed Jerusalem temple, but it was present in the temple of the body of Jesus (John 2:19–22; cf. 13:31–32). Jesus's body is the holy of holies, the special dwelling place of God on earth and the place where atonement would be made and reconciliation accomplished.

In light of our previous discussion about the rock on which Jesus would build his church, it is interesting that Peter is the one who identifies Jesus as the precious "living stone" that has become the cornerstone of "a spiritual house" (1 Pet. 2:4–5; cf. Isa. 28:16). Peter does not identify this house as a temple, or connect "spiritual" to the Holy Spirit, but he might as well have, for he goes on to describe the spiritual house as "a holy priesthood" that exists "to offer spiritual sacrifices acceptable to God" (1 Pet. 2:5). Elsewhere "house of God" refers explicitly to the temple (Matt. 12:4; Heb. 10:21). What is most striking, however, is that now it is God building his people into a spiritual house (cf. 1 Pet. 4:17) composed of living stones (because of their union with Christ, the chief living stone), with Jesus as the cornerstone. Pastor-theologians, coworkers in this triune building project, work not simply on individuals but also on a corporate entity: a local community that keeps company with Christ: "The 'spiritual sacrifice' that this corporate priesthood and temple offers is its holy, cruciform life as a godly people in the midst of the nations, and for their sake."[30]

Paul clearly states that the church is "the temple of the living God" (2 Cor. 6:16). He is equally explicit that the church, and thus the living temple, is made up of Jews and Gentiles alike—a striking difference from the Jerusalem temple, to whose inner courts Gentiles were forbidden entrance. The church—that is, the people—embody the gospel because they are living proof that, in Christ, God has transformed a divided humanity into a united people. It is of this church, in which there is no longer Jew or Greek, that Paul likens himself to a "skilled master builder" (1 Cor. 3:10).

The church is a triune building project, centered in and on the person and work of Jesus Christ. The ministry of reconciliation is the work of the Son through the Spirit for the Father. The Gentiles are therefore "no longer strangers and exiles" but "members of the household of God, built on the foundation of the apostles and prophets, Christ Jesus himself being the cornerstone" (Eph. 2:18–20). To be members of God's house is to be a people set apart for the project of "living to God." Paul conceives of the church as the house or temple of God, with members as stones that have been incorporated into Christ. Pastor-theologians exist to minister *what is in Christ*, and in Ephesians 2:21–22 Paul begins to unfold this reality. In Christ "the whole structure, being joined together, grows into a holy temple in the Lord" (2:21); in Christ "you also are being built together into a dwelling place for God by the Spirit" (2:22).

> *The church—that is, the people—embody the gospel because they are living proof that, in Christ, God has transformed a divided humanity into a united people.*

The pastor-theologian participates in what is essentially an ongoing building project. The foundation has been laid—Christ's atoning work is finished—yet the structure is "growing" into a holy temple. Peter O'Brien highlights the mixture of building (inorganic) and growing (organic) images: "The building being *joined together* refers not simply to the union of one stone with another, but also to the union of the whole structure with (and in) the cornerstone."[31] The people are in Christ, *and* they are growing further into Christ and Christ-likeness (i.e., holiness). Whereas Paul elsewhere associates the temple with a local congregation (1 Cor. 3:16–17), here in Ephesians 2:21 the temple refers to all who are now in Christ, blessed "with every spiritual blessing in the heavenly places" (Eph. 1:3). In short, the church, the people joined together "in Christ," is a temple because the Holy Spirit, the Spirit of the risen Lord, indwells it (2:22).

The church, then, is no ordinary building. It is rather a heavenly temple, a place where God's will is being done on earth as it is in heaven. The church, the people joined together in Christ, is the place where God's life, light, and love becomes lived out in space and time. Whereas the Fourth Gospel identifies Jesus's physical body as the place where God dwells, Ephesians 2 provides an updated account: thanks to Christ's death and resurrection, the church is now the place where Christ lives by his Spirit: "Believers on earth, recipients of this circular letter, are linked with the heavenly realm in and through the Spirit of the risen Lord."[32]

A number of commentators connect what is happening in Ephesians 2 to the practice of ancient Near Eastern kings to build temples commemorating victory in battle. Yahweh does something similar, creating a garden temple in Eden after subduing the watery chaos and then providing the Jerusalem temple to mark the conquest of the promised land. Indeed, G. K. Beale believes that God building a fit dwelling place is the theme of the entire Bible: the temple is "a small model of the entire cosmos" and so points forward to a cosmic temple where God's presence will be all in all.[33] When viewed against this backdrop, the church, a living temple, is what God builds to commemorate his victory over the powers and principalities that have enslaved God's creation: "God is building the multiracial, multiethnic, multigenerational church of Jesus Christ, which stands as a monument to his triumph over the powers of darkness."[34] The church, we can say, *is* the victory of God: "These realities—that the temple is a symbol of the cosmos, and that the church is the temple of the Spirit—mean that the church is to be a preview of what the world is going to become."[35]

Paul views his pastoral task as nothing less than cultivating a new humanity in Christ. To "learn Christ" (Eph. 4:20) is to put off the old self in order "to put on the new self" (4:24). This is more than just a metaphor, though pastor-theologians will need to exercise care in communicating what it means and what practical changes it requires. Paul anticipates the need and lists a number of activities and patterns of life that Christians must avoid and others that they must adopt. Pastoral ministry is less about meeting felt needs than it is about conforming disciples to the truth that is in Jesus (Eph. 4:21). Of special importance are speech practices: "Let no corrupting talk come out of your mouths, but only such as is good for building up" (Eph. 4:29). Here too, we say that pastors and laypeople alike participate in a ministry of edification via words.

Pastor-theologians are engaged in a far more ambitious building project than any church committee ever proposed. Pastor-theologians are in the vanguard of a victory procession celebrating God's triumph over death, destruction, and disintegration, a procession enlivened by the "procession" of the Holy Spirit from the Father and his risen Son. The church is but the spearhead of a work not merely of urban but also *cosmic* renewal, anticipating in its reconciling practices the reconciliation of all things. To confess with the saints across space and through time "I believe . . . in the church" is to confess that the church is the harbinger of the new heavens and the new earth. It is the privilege and responsibility of pastor-theologians to oversee and encourage the church's understanding of and participation in these firstfruits of the new reality "in Christ."

> *The church is but the spear-head of a work not merely of urban but also* cosmic *renewal, anticipating in its reconciling practices the reconciliation of all things.*

Evangelist: Proclaiming What Is in Christ

Christian theology, we have suggested, involves setting forth in speech and life *what is in Christ*. Pastor-theologians minister (i.e., communicate) this eschatological reality in their words, deeds, and general (joyful) being-toward-resurrection. The pastor-theologian works largely in the indicative mood, proclaiming the gospel and, whenever possible, using words to do so: Jesus's own words and words about Jesus.

Pastor-theologians are ministers of God's word, aiming to get the word of God to dwell richly in disciples (Col. 3:16). The word of God is largely the gospel, the proclamation of the new reality inaugurated in Jesus Christ. This is the word that needs to get out: "Did you hear? All things have been made new in Jesus Christ. There is therefore no condemnation for those who are in Christ Jesus, for God is reconciling all things to himself in Christ. Did you hear? Do you grasp the significance of what this means?"

Of course, the way we live fills out the meaning of our words. What does "love" really mean? Jesus tells and shows us: "Greater love has no one than this, that someone lay down his life for his friends" (John 15:13). Pastor-theologians can only minister understanding of the gospel if their form of life corresponds to their words. One cannot say "He is risen" with a long face without betraying the content.[36] In the same way, it would be a performative contradiction to preach on the story of the Good Samaritan and then turn a blind eye to the bleeding stranger at the church doorstep on your way out. The word of God must become flesh, again and again.

Yet, as we have seen, pastor-theologians have been given a special commission to minister the word (Acts 6:4), and to do so largely with words, backed up, of course, with fitting actions. This is a wonder: pastors can, and must, feed the sheep and build the church with words. Why? Because faith (and understanding) comes from hearing the gospel (Rom. 10:17). Jesus is a person, not a proposition; however, language is the means the Spirit uses to enable the gospel to become the all-encompassing framework that allows disciples not only to think but also to situate themselves in relation to the truth, goodness, and beauty of what is in Christ. Language is the means the Spirit uses to introduce people to the living Christ. Words present Jesus. Words mediate a disciple's relationship to her Lord. Words do not merely inform but also communicate an orientation to the whole of life, coloring experience and directing action. The stuff of pastoral ministry is not the blood of sheep and goats, but words and people (the only thing that occasionally is slaughtered during the regular worship service is the biblical text). Pastor-theologians are evangelists in a broad sense: in proclaiming the gospel, they use words not only to get the Word of God to dwell richly in disciples but also to enable disciples to indwell the strange new world of the gospel.

Counsel: The Pastoral Ministry of the Word

It is a mistake to limit the ministry of the word to formal sermons. When Paul elaborates on what he means by "Let the word of Christ dwell in you richly," he mentions not only teaching but also admonishing and singing too (Eph. 5:19; Col. 3:16). That is significant: pastors minister words not only to heads but also to wills and hearts—to the whole person. To care for whole persons—souls—is to attend to a person's inner as well as external life. Circumstances matter, to be sure, but it is the heart, the willing and desiring center of existential operations, from which all doing springs.

Other people care for us, but the pastor cares in a special way: as one appointed by Christ to minister the truth, goodness, and beauty of the gospel to every person in the church. This is what makes the pastor's care different:

it concerns Jesus Christ and is exercised on his behalf. Pastors cannot always help to change painful circumstances, but this is not what building people up in Christ means. What is different about disciples is not that they suffer less, but rather how they respond to God's presence and activity in the midst of suffering. The pastor helps people to process their experiences in light of the gospel and in relationship to the living Christ, assisting them to respond to everything, including adversity, in faith, hope, and love. One way that pastor-theologians care for souls, then, is by changing the picture by which many relate to God. We could put it this way (with apologies to John F. Kennedy): "Ask not what God can do for you but what you can do (and suffer) for God and his country (i.e., heaven)."

The ministry of the word involves not only teaching (see below) and admonition but also consolation. There is, of course, a time to speak *and* a time to be silent, when pastors have simply to keep watch over the flock during the dark night of the soul. There are, nevertheless, certain consolations of theology even during these long dark nights: God does not directly will suffering. God's wisdom can draw good out of any evil. God has defeated evil and will defeat it again. God will never leave us or forsake us. These truths are more powerful when the church functions as the body of Christ, bearing one another's burdens and weeping with those who weep.

Pastors should not wait for crises to develop before they offer counsel: "Pastoral care has as its purpose not only the giving of comfort but also the redirection of life."[37] To do this well, pastors must learn to know people, and this takes time—mainly to listen. It may seem odd that listening is part and parcel of the ministry of the word, but such is the case. Only by listening can a pastor take the measure of a person's spiritual state. Only by listening to a person's story can a pastor find ways to integrate that story into the gospel story.

The pastor-theologian's counsel is not a mere subset of psychotherapy. This way MTD (moralistic therapeutic deism) lies. The ultimate goal is not "helping people" if this means simply "making people feel better." These are, at best, by-products of the ministry of the word, not its raison d'être. No, what pastor-theologians have to offer is not simply good feelings but really good news, and the abundant comfort that is available only in Christ (2 Cor. 1:3–7). William Willimon puts it well: "Perhaps our overarching goal in our pastoral counseling ought to be contributing to our people's maturity in Christ, rather than to their health."[38] Or, to put it in terms of the present book, the goal should be to conform our people, hearts and heads, to *what is in Christ.* And an important part of what is in Christ is consolation, from the "God of all comfort" (2 Cor. 1:3). The pastor who cares for souls acts as a midwife concerned with the birth and nurture of the mind of Christ in his disciples: *"For Paul, Christ's exemplification of the attitudes and actions appropriate to God's kingdom provides the defining standard of what it means to be mature."*[39]

Visitation: The Embodied Ministry of the Word

The full-bodied ministry of the word is an embodied pastoral practice. Though circumstances may on occasion require letters, telegrams, or emails, the default mode for ministering the word is in person. Scripture records several divine visitations: Joseph promised his brothers that God would "visit" them and bring them out of Egypt (Gen. 50:24). For God to visit is for God to be present and active—to be all that he is—in salvation or judgment, depending on who it is God comes to see.

Jesus Christ, the Word "made flesh," is of course the climactic divine visitation (John 1:14 KJV). When Jesus healed the widow's son, the people said, "God has visited his people!" (Luke 7:16). Interestingly, the Greek term for "visit," both in the Old Testament (LXX) and New Testament, is *episketomai* (from *epi* + *skopos*), the root for the term *episkopos* ("overseer"). To visit is not to "oversee," however, but to "go and see." Jesus himself visited people in their homes. Moreover, when pastors go and see those who might otherwise be out of congregational sight and mind, they steer clear of Jesus's warning to those who minister in his name with words only: "I was naked and you clothed me,

> No church should be so large as to harbor anonymous Christians.

I was sick and you visited me, I was in prison and you came to me" (Matt. 25:36; cf. James 1:27). Visitation is one way that pastors can participate in Jesus's ministry to the poor, sick, dejected, struggling, and lost.

The purpose of visitation, like all other forms of the ministry of the word, is to communicate the gospel by embodying Christ, God's love for the world. To love the people of God means going to see how they are getting on. Only when pastors come to see the context of a person's life, at particular times and places, can they minister the word in the particular ways that direct people in the way of Jesus Christ. Pastor-theologians therefore build the house of God one human household at a time. If Tom Oden is correct in thinking that the duty to "visit from house to house" is intrinsic to the pastoral office, then we perhaps gain some sense of how large churches should be.[40] If pastors themselves cannot visit every household, then they should at least train elders who can. No church should be so large as to harbor anonymous Christians.

Sermon: The Preaching Ministry of the Word

The sermon is not the exclusive form of one's ministry of the word, but preaching is nevertheless the pastor-theologian's most characteristic practice, and one of the most important. Preaching is not the whole of pastoral ministry, but it is its microcosm: as the sermon goes, so goes the (holy) nation.

Preaching "is the most public of pastoral acts."[41] Glossophobia—the fear of speaking in public—regularly appears in opinion polls as the number one fear in America (the fear of death is the second greatest fear).[42] How much more should pastor-theologians fear the prospect of speaking God's word in public! Perhaps that's why so many pastors do not even try, preferring rather to entertain, tell uplifting and funny stories, share their own experience, and offer vague moral and spiritual platitudes that are no more objectionable than the well-meaning sentiments of a Hallmark card.

Words are the most sophisticated medium of communication we have; through words we can share both simple experiences and complex ideas, not to mention everything that comes between these two extremes. Preaching, as a ministry of the word, is a form of verbal communication, one of the most challenging forms to master (and "mastery" may not even be an appropriate category to use when it comes to rightly handling God's Word). To communicate is to "make common," to share something with others. The important point is that communication involves both speakers and hearers. It takes at least two to communicate. If I speak without producing understanding, I am simply "speaking into the air" (1 Cor. 14:9).[43] Preachers must therefore be good listeners too, to the biblical text as well as to the questions the people have about the message. Still, even the most skilled of speakers cannot guarantee understanding. Only the Holy Spirit can open ears and hearts to receive the message. To deliver a sermon—to speak into the air, in public no less!—demands both courage and faith.

The challenge of preaching is even greater in the present day, when there is a systemic distrust of what authority figures tell us. The postmodern reflex

is to suspect that what a person says serves that person's interest first and
foremost. Moreover, saying how things are, speaking a truth claim, opens
oneself up to the charge of oppressing others with your point of view. Is it
only a coincidence that in our contemporary culture, the solitary television
newsman has given way to a news team, a team that typically reflects gender
and racial diversity? These days it is hard to imagine Walter Cronkite getting
away with his signature sign-off line, "And that's the way it is." But this is
precisely what pastor-theologians have to say week in and week out: and that's
the way it is *in Jesus Christ*.

Pastor-theologians speak forth what is in Christ because that is precisely
what Jesus did: "Jesus came . . . preaching the gospel of God" (Mark 1:14
RSV). Jesus came proclaiming the kingdom, and preachers today participate
in that dominical discourse: "Theological speech is possible therefore on the
grounds of Jesus bearing witness to himself through the Holy Spirit."[44] What
sets Christian preaching apart from every other form of human communication is its participation in what is ultimately a triune activity: preaching is
distinguished by its authoritative source (Scripture, the Word of God), unique
content (gospel, what is in Christ), and unique persuasive power (illumination,
the work of the Spirit). Preaching is a means of grace because it communicates
the one who is "full of grace and truth" (John 1:14).

This is not the place for a full-scale treatment of Christian preaching. My
immediate purpose is rather to highlight four functions that explain why the
sermon is the cutting edge of public theology, four reasons why the pulpit
"leads the world" as both prow of a ship (an ark?) and plough of a field.[45]

1. *Preaching fosters biblical literacy, biblical-theological competency, and
canon sense.* There is nothing like the disciplined exposition of Scripture to
help congregations learn to understand how the various parts of Scripture
(books; testaments) relate to the whole (canon) and to the person who stands
at the center of it all (Jesus Christ).[46] Every sermon should contribute in some
measure to a congregation's growing appreciation for the ways in which God's
work of redemption hangs together, both leading to and proceeding from the
cross of Christ.[47]

2. *Preaching fosters theological literacy, the ability to read (and, if necessary,
critique) our world—our history, our culture—in the light of God's presence
and activity.* While the primary task of preaching is to unfold God's Word,
throwing light on the church's contemporary situation is often an important by-
product. Though expositing Scripture unfolds the divine drama of redemption,

it is also important for local churches to know how and where they fit into that drama. It is not enough to understand the biblical story: we must also understand the present situation as caught up in that same story. Only then can the local church determine what it is to say and do in order to contribute to the ongoing action: renewing all things in Christ through the Spirit.[48]

Pastors have a unique privilege and responsibility in helping congregations to understand better both the Word of God and, thanks to this Word, the world we live in. The sermon, at its best, is the jewel in the crown of public theology. In expositing God's Word, pastor-theologians give their congregations a powerful means to discern, and then cast down, the idols of our time. Some of these idols, such as culturally conditioned models of "success," have made their way into the church.[49] Pastors do well to call their congregations' attention to the power of culture as a means of spiritual (de)formation. Indeed, pastors are never more prophetic than when they call people to stop pursuing false idols (e.g., fame, wealth, physical beauty, social status, popularity, career, self-actualization, etc.) and return to serving the living God.

The sermon, at its best, is the jewel in the crown of public theology.

Those who are unaware of culture are doomed to repeat it. Culture cultivates shapes of humanity. A materialist culture can turn us into materialists. Antonio Gramsci, an Italian sociologist, used a term for the process by which a dominant social class maintains its influence over people through noncoercive means (e.g., schools, media, marketing): "hegemony" (from Gk. *hēgemōn*, "ruler"). Hegemony works by getting people to think and feel for themselves that certain values and practices (e.g., same-sex marriage) are simply "common sense" or "natural" (even when they are not). An ideology has achieved hegemony when its way of looking at and behaving in the world pervades society. There is no need to fight a culture war if one side unknowingly acquiesces. It is precisely here that the notion of the pastor-theologian as organic intellectual comes into its own.

What Gramsci, a Marxist, originally had in mind in speaking of organic intellectuals were those who could represent the interests not of the ruling class but rather of the working class. My intent is to follow Augustine's example and plunder not the Egyptians but the Muscovites, effectively robbing Lenin to pay Paul. In the case of public theology, the "class" that pastor-theologians represent as organic intellectuals is the "poor *in spirit*" (Matt. 5:3), whose poverty includes low social status, the "class" of those whose citizenship is in heaven. The pastor-theologian is an organic intellectual who represents the interests of those who make up the body of Christ, and pastors organize the life of the body around the rule of Christ, not the rule of culture. In short, pastor-theologians help local churches to regain cultural agency—the ability to make one's own mark on culture rather than passively submitting to cultural programming—by "naming the [cultural] powers" and encouraging concrete practices of discipleship, ways in which church members present their bodies as living sacrifices (Rom. 12:1) to the Lord Jesus Christ rather than to the idols of our time.

3. *Preaching wakes up the local church, here and now, to the bracing reality of Jesus Christ, who is always and everywhere at hand yet beyond our grasp.* According to Aristotle's famous definition, "To say of what is that it is, and of what is not that it is not, is true" (*Metaphysics* 1011B.25). Similarly, preaching is a means of truth because, in saying "what is" *in Christ*, it says of what ultimately is that it is. Preaching is a means of grace because, in setting forth in speech *what is in Christ*, it also presents Christ.[50] The sermon is not a secondhand description of what is happening in a historical galaxy far, far away. On the contrary: gospel preaching speaks forth the true story of the world, acknowledging that all things "are from him and through him and to him"

> *The sermon is the gospel's Western Front, the cutting edge of the Word's forward progress as it conquers new territory, one heart at a time.*

(Rom. 11:36). The sermon is thus a word full of grace and truth that takes subevangelical thought captive, exposing the emptiness of other narratives and false gospels that seek to colonize our imaginations. The sermon is the heavy artillery in the pastor-theologian's arsenal and thus the best frontal assault on imaginations held captive by other stories, alleged gospels promising other ways to the good life. The sermon is the gospel's Western Front, as it were, the cutting edge of the word's forward progress as it conquers new territory, one heart at a time. In speaking forth *what is in Christ*, the sermon is not only a word of truth and means of grace but also a means of liberation (John 8:32).

A sermon must not only describe *what is in Christ* but also communicate its *excellence*. Preaching must not simply inform us but transport us. It must not only add to our stock of knowledge but move and delight us. To say *what is in Christ* is to enumerate and explore every spiritual blessing with which we have been blessed (Eph. 1:3; cf. Rom. 15:27). To say, on the basis of the Scriptures, *what is in Christ* is to stretch the limits of language. Perhaps that is why Scripture itself uses so many images and literary forms to describe salvation, and why pastors have to be "minor poets": those who are able to see, and express, the reality of things deeper than surface appearances.[51] Christ is real, and he is among us, but it takes the eschatological imagination, what Paul terms the "eyes of your heart" (Eph. 1:18), to discern his presence and activity. Yet, when our hearts are open to God's Word, we perceive in faith that Christ is indeed among us, ministering to us, for example, through the gifts with which the Spirit has equipped the church.

> *Preaching inscribes the gospel on listening hearts and inserts listeners into the story.*

Sermons are one of the principal means by which pastor-theologians minister understanding by waking people up to what is really happening in our world—to what God is doing in Christ. A sermon that tells us what is in Christ appeals to our imagination so that we can see reality as it truly is: not a mechanical universe in perpetual motion, but a divine creation in the midst of labor pains, where the new in Christ is coming forth from the old in Adam, in each of us as well as our Christian neighbors, near and far. All those who are in Christ are presently being transformed into his image. Christ is thus the meaning of the whole of history, the meaning of life itself, for Christ is the ultimate pattern of Deity (covenant lordship) and humanity (covenant servanthood).

4. *Preaching draws the local church, here and now, into relationship with the bracing reality of Jesus Christ, directing disciples to adopt beliefs, values, and practices that correspond to what is in Christ in order to get real.* The purpose of preaching is not merely to describe something external to the church, and only then to ask how it is to be "applied." Rather, preaching *inscribes* the gospel on listening hearts and *inserts* listeners into the story. Preaching is a practice "by which the church is taken into the very life of God."[52] When pastor-theologians proclaim the gospel, they participate in Christ's own prophetic office.

The word of God continues to increase and "prevail mightily," just as it did in the early church (Acts 6:7; 12:24; 19:20). It increases by building up the body of Christ, reminding disciples of their true identity hidden in Christ. It increases by helping individual disciples understand who they are in Christ and how to become who they are. It increases by helping local churches understand how bodily to behave so that their life together, here and now, becomes an enacted parable of the kingdom of God. The word of God increases each time congregations come to understand what is in Christ and begin to conform their hearts, wills, and minds to this reality.

Pastor-theologians have been given the dignity of communicative causality: through preaching God's Word, they minister reality to people, helping people to act in ways that correspond to what is in Christ, and hence to get real. The preacher is a "man on a wire," whose sermons must walk the tightrope between Scripture and the contemporary situation, bringing God's Word to bear on all of life and bringing all of life into conformity with God's Word. Preaching, speaking to confess and conform to what is in Christ, is the quintessential theological act of the church's organic intellectuals, charged with building up the body of Christ by cultivating understanding and obedience.

Sermons that minister God's Word cannot help but be edifying, though the result is neither automatic nor immediate. Ultimately it is the Spirit who unites and conforms us to Christ, in conjunction with the word that generates and strengthens faith. And indeed, faith is the operative term, for it takes faith and courage to speak God's Word into the air. And yet, out of the air, a body begins to materialize. The pastor is an artisan, a stonemason of God's house. In preparing to preach, it is important to remember what one is doing.

Two stonemasons were hard at work. When asked what they were doing, the first said, "I am cutting this stone in a perfectly square shape." The other answered: "I am building a cathedral." So it is with pastors. What are they doing? One pastor might say: "I am preparing well-crafted sermons, planning programs, and managing conflict." The pastor who is a public theologian (and minor poet) will answer differently: "I am building a temple." It takes faith, courage, and a biblically schooled imagination to see one's congregation as a living temple, but this is indeed the right answer. Pastor-theologians are chiseling, fitting, and polishing each living stone to join them with Christ, and with one another.

Catechist: Teaching What Is in Christ

There is nothing particularly valuable in learning complicated theological terms or formulas for their own sake. Greek and Latin terms like *homoousios* and *extra Calvinisticum* seem far removed from the everyday concerns of most local congregations. Why, then, did the early church insist that new believers undertake a one- to three-year period of catechesis (from the Gk. *katēcheō*, "to instruct orally") before their baptism and develop instruction manuals for this purpose?[53] The short answer: sacred *doctrina* ("teaching") exists for the purpose of building up disciples in their knowledge of what is in Christ.

The sober truth is that some kind of indoctrination is inevitable. During the course of our lives, we are all filled with various kinds of doctrines—economic, political, ideological, as well as theological. Doctrines—opinions, beliefs, and teachings—are ubiquitous: they are taught formally in schools but also informally in the home, neighborhood, athletic field, and workplace. Television educates or indoctrinates too. The various media are one means by which culture cultivates. Whatever doctrine we imbibe—communism, capitalism, consumerism, or something else—we live out what we believe to be true and right. To think wrongly about reality is likely to lead to foolish living. Theology—living to God—is the lifeblood of the body of Christ, and the present book aims both to stop the bleeding (i.e., theological illiteracy) that is draining the life out of the church when nonbiblical doctrines (e.g., selfism) lead us to live not to God but to oneself. Pastors need to inoculate the body of Christ against idolatrous toxins, ideological infections, and other forms of false teaching.

The Pastoral Epistles are filled with references to doctrine (Gk. *didaskalia*, "teaching"). Paul had to confront false teaching, and so do pastors today. Paul does not commend doctrine for the sake of doctrine, but he does urge Timothy and Titus to teach sound doctrine (*hygiainousē didaskalia*; 1 Tim. 1:10; 2 Tim. 4:3; Titus 1:9; 2:1). Sound doctrine is good for the health of the body of Christ; unsound doctrine (toxic teaching) leads to poor health, leaving the body of Christ unable to function rightly. Significantly, Paul uses "sound doctrine" as a contrast term not to ideas but to *practices*, like striking one's parents, lying, homosexual behavior, and kidnapping (1 Tim. 1:9–10). "Sound" doctrine, by way of contrast, is healthy in the sense of giving health. Doctrine is sound when it corresponds to what is in Christ.

In speaking of the various gifts the ascended Christ gives the church, Paul mentions prophets, evangelists, and, linked by a single definite article, "pastors and teachers" (Gk. *tous poimenas kai didaskalous*, Eph. 4:11).[54] This grammatical construction suggests that the two groups, while not necessarily identical, nevertheless have overlapping functions: "All pastors teach, . . . but not all teachers are also pastors."[55] The purpose of teaching is "to equip the saints for the work of ministry, for building up the body of Christ" (4:12). Pastor-theologians lead the church by teaching its members to become every-day ministers themselves. That way, everyone in the church, those with both extraordinary ministries (the aforementioned "gifts") and ordinary ministries, is involved in the activity of building the church, and hence of participating in Christ's own building project through the Spirit.[56] The goal of teaching is unity (of the faith and of the knowledge of the Son) and maturity in Christ (4:13). Those who are mature in Christ will no longer be "tossed to and fro by the waves and carried about by every wind of doctrine" (4:14).

Sound doctrine is vital for the health of the body. It is therefore fitting that theologians have been described as "doctors" of the church (from Lat. *docere*, "to teach"). Calvin is happy to call pastors "doctors" too, as long as we acknowledge another kind of doctor who superintends the education of pastors.[57] Doctors of the church preserve sound doctrine and correct false doctrine, especially by rightly interpreting the Bible. We are now able to see how pastor-theologians are organic intellectuals of a particular kind: they are doctors who both belong to the body and take care of it, not least by teaching what is and is to come *in Christ*.

Just as disciplined expository preaching, either book by book or following the lectionary, is the best way to foster biblical literacy, so disciplined expository teaching, either of creeds or confessions, is the best way for a pastor-theologian to foster theological literacy in the local church. In a particular place and time, local churches are instantiations of the catholic church and of the church in heaven; hence they do well to pursue "the unity of faith" (Eph. 4:12), and one way to do this is by learning Christian doctrine. The early church produced several treatises on the importance of catechisms, and in one of them Augustine encourages catechists to give not a list of doctrinal bullet points but rather a "full narration" of salvation history that starts with creation and unfolds the important turning points (e.g., fall, hope of restoration).[58] Augustine is right: rightly to say *what is in Christ* requires the catechist to teach all of the acts that make up the drama of redemption.

Calvin was a pastor, not a prophet, but the church today would do well to heed his claim on this issue: "The church of God will never preserve itself without a catechism."[59] Calvin's *Catechism of the Church of Geneva* (1541) consists of 373 questions and answers organized around the Ten Command-ments, the Apostles' Creed, the Lord's Prayer, and the sacraments; it touched on matters of faith, obedience, and church life.[60] This catechism was used in churches and homes, and public recitations of it took place four times a year. The first question set the stage for all the others: "What is the chief goal of human life?" Answer: "It is to know God."

Knowing God, and ourselves before God, is hardly theoretical if our vocation as human beings is to live to God. Perhaps that is why J. I. Packer, the author of *Knowing God*, thinks that the best way to describe himself is as "a latter-day catechist."[61] Packer defines catechesis as "the practically oriented imparting of the doctrine and ethics of discipleship. . . . [It] is Bible-based in method, Christocentric in perspective, declarative in style, and doxological in thrust."[62] Catechism is a response to the command to love God with all our minds. Yet most classical catechisms, in focusing our attention on the Lord's Prayer and the Ten Commandments, also take aim at our affections and actions, our devotion and duty.[63] Catechism is first and foremost learning the truth, goodness, and beauty of *what is in Christ.*[64]

> *A church body that is awake and alive to what is in Christ has doctrine coursing through its bloodstream.*

Every pastor must be a catechist. This fits well with what we said earlier about the theologian being a generalist.[65] Think of the pastor-theologian as a GP (general practitioner), whose responsibility is looking after the health of the body of Christ, in part by teaching sound doctrine. In many places on earth, the body of Christ is out of shape, perhaps obese or diseased. In that case, the church is an operating theater in which false teaching is surgically removed with the scalpel of the Spirit (viz., "the word of God"; Eph. 6:17), to be replaced by sound doctrine, perhaps by an intravenous catechetical drip. A church body that is awake and alive to what is in Christ has doctrine coursing through its bloodstream rather than idling in the mind.[66]

Liturgist: Celebrating What Is in Christ

The previous chapter highlighted the pastor-theologian as a personification and catalyst of the paradigmatic Christian mood: the joy of being-toward-resurrection. *What is in Christ* is indeed something to be taught, a way of loving God with our minds; yet it is also something to be celebrated, an expression of our love for God that flows from the heart. Many aspects of the gospel prompt rejoicing, but the one most closely related to catechism is baptism, which celebrates a person's incorporation into the body of Christ. In the early church, baptism was the culmination of one's course of instruction, a public demonstration of one's faith, and the beginning of one's life as a disciple. Baptism symbolizes dying and rising with Christ and thus marks a person's new birthday. Each new baptism celebrates another stone added to the living temple that is Christ's body on earth.

Pastor-theologians are responsible for leading congregations in celebrating what is in Christ—call it *orthodoxa* ("right praise, right glorifying"). Many pastors may not think of themselves as liturgists, but technically this is what rightly ordered corporate celebration of God is. Liturgy literally means "the work of the people" (from Gk. *leitourgia* = *leitos* ["public"] + *ergos* ["work"]). Those who order the church's corporate celebrations of God's work of salvation are engaged in public works administration. This too is public theology: working to order corporate expressions of Christian praise and worship.

Liturgies can be formal or informal. Examples of formal liturgies would be the Anglican Book of Common Prayer or the Church of Scotland's Book of Common Order. Many so-called nonliturgical services are actually informal liturgies, though some are so casual as to stretch the term "liturgical" to the breaking point. The question remains: how do pastors, as public theologians who work with people, lead their people in loving God not only with all their minds but also with all their hearts? How is the church rightly to order its celebrations of *what is in Christ*?

Gathering: What/Where/When Is a Worship Service?

Whereas doctrine sets forth in speech the truth of what is in Christ, worship sets forth this same truth in symbolic action in the church's corporate life, and does so in the form of a response or offering addressed to God. Pastors lose a valuable opportunity to build up the church when they simply turn over "worship" to others, usually musicians. This does not mean that pastor-theologians have to be musicians themselves, only that they misunderstand their vocation if they think they do not preside over this aspect of the gathering of God's people as well.[67] For *worship is the quintessential theological act*: an acknowledgment of the love that God offers the world and an offering of the love that the people return to God in the form of tithes, prayers, and obedience.[68] This is why the people of God gather together: to celebrate corporately the presence and activity of the Triune God in their midst.

The liturgy, and especially the liturgical calendar, is a kind of living *summa theologiae*, "a concise summary of the whole of Christian faith and experience."[69] It is a vivid way of drawing the body of Christ into the action of the drama of redemption. Baptism is only the port of entry: a church that observes the liturgical calendar, through Bible readings that are coordinated with events in Jesus's life (e.g., Advent, Christmas, Good Friday, Easter, Pentecost, and so forth), learns to experience its own life as caught up in that of Jesus, week after week and year after year.

Why is there church rather than nothing?[70] The church (Gk. *ekklēsia*) is a "gathering," a group of people who assemble at God's summons for some purpose, to do something together. The English term "worship" suggests that the purpose of this gathering is to ascribe supreme worth to the Supreme Being, and it is true that one work of the people is to praise God and the Lamb of God (Ps. 96:7–8; Rev. 5:11–12). It is an egregious error, however, to think (1) that worship is simply what humans do, (2) that it happens only during a Sunday morning church service, (3) that it happens only during the first half of the service and thus before the sermon, or (4) that worshiping in spirit and in truth is essentially "praise-induced ecstasy."[71]

In the first place, God is graciously active and present in worship, communicating Christ in Scripture, sermon, song, and sacrament. At the same time, the church's worship participates in Christ's prophetic, priestly, and kingly offices through preaching (truth-telling), praying (interceding), and praising (singing). How does praise correspond to and participate in Christ's kingly office?[72] By celebrating Christ's rule over creation and the coming of his kingdom on earth. The church's celebrating, like its hearing God's Word, is itself a Spirit-enabled work.

We can respond to errors 2–4 simultaneously by specifying what worship is and where/when it happens. The corporate gatherings of Christians in local churches today, like the earlier gatherings of the first Christians, involve activities such as praying, hearing the word of God expounded, taking up monetary offerings for God's work, observing the Lord's Supper, and offering sacrifices of praise. We know, of course, that God is not satisfied with people simply going through the external motions of devotion: God does "not delight in sacrifice" (Ps. 51:16) and actually "hates" religious ceremonies (Isa. 1:14) when they are not expressions of "a broken and contrite heart" (Ps. 51:17).

Worship goes wrong in one of two ways: either it is directed to something unworthy, such as an idol or false god, in which case it goes wrong objectively (so to speak); or it is directed to the right object in the wrong way, in which case it goes wrong subjectively.[73] Jesus's quotation of Hosea 6:6 indicates the way forward for those who would worship in spirit and in truth: "For I desire steadfast love and not sacrifice, the knowledge of God rather than burnt offerings" (cf. Matt. 9:13). Pastor-theologians lead worship rightly when they foster and direct the congregation's response to the one true God in the right way. Right worship, the kind that is pleasing to God, acknowledges the grace that is in Jesus Christ not only with our lips but also with our lives. Christ's own sacrifice makes possible the right kind of offering and proper worship: the sacrifice of the whole of our lives, a thanksgiving existence that proceeds from a mood of gratitude.

Worship (like theology) is ultimately a matter of *living to God*: "Contemporary Christians obscure the breadth and depth of the Bible's teaching in this subject when they persist in using the word 'worship' in the usual, limited fashion, applying it mainly to what goes on in Sunday services."[74] A less limited definition of worship might be "the celebrative response to what God has done, is doing, and promises to do."[75] This is Paul's understanding of worship, which is why he enjoins his readers in Rome "to present your bodies as a living sacrifice, holy and acceptable to God, which is your spiritual worship" (Rom. 12:1).[76] Worship, then, involves more than what happens in a church gathering, and church gatherings involve more than what we typically mean by the term *worship*.

We worship God when we offer our bodies—our whole selves—as living sacrifices for his service. One of the most important things we can do to serve God is to communicate the gospel. This is a task not only for clergy, who have a formal ministry of the word, but also for the laity, who minister the word informally, not least through "spiritual songs" (Eph. 5:19; Col. 3:16). What is worship? Worship is the offering of ourselves to God in love and praise for God's offering himself to us in love and mercy. Where and when does worship happen? Wherever and whenever the people of God offer themselves up to God. Even in ancient Israel, right service of God "demanded obedience and faithfulness in every sphere of life."[77]

According to Scripture, the primary purpose of the regular Sunday service is not what we commonly call "worship." What, then, is the purpose of local church gatherings? I have already suggested that the right answer is *celebrating what is in Christ*, but we can be more specific: the church gathers *to be built up into Christ*. Indeed, Paul typically uses the terminology of *edification* rather than *worship* when he speaks about the purpose of local church gatherings.[78] Edification is first and foremost something that God does. Church leaders participate in the work of the Triune God in building up the church by celebrating (which includes remembering, as we shall see below) and working together to make manifest what is in Christ. In brief: the people of God gather together to encourage one another to learn Christ, celebrate Christ, and to live out Christ's life in the body for the sake of the world. We gather together to manifest God's Son on earth as he is in heaven.[79]

Church liturgy (the order of corporate service) is thus training for the liturgy of life (the shape of one's individual service). Strictly speaking, there is no "ordinary" time for the saint. Each waking moment of every day presents us with opportunities to make our lives into offerings for God. This is why it is so important for pastor-theologians to be involved in all aspects of the Sunday service. Corporate worship in the context of the church is all about edifying a people who, individually and corporately, present their bodily lives as offerings set apart for God's service. There may be no greater example of public theology than that.

> *The people of God gather together to encourage one another to learn Christ, celebrate Christ, and to live out Christ's life in the body for the sake of the world.*

Why is there church rather than nothing? *The saints gather together as a local church to be built up in faith, hope, and love for the ultimate purpose of becoming the kind of people who can worship in spirit and truth anywhere and anytime.* Corporate worship is one of the primary means by which the saints are built up. Stated differently: the church gathers and worships in order to build up God's people, enabling them to serve God by offering themselves as living sacrifices on other days of the week, when they are not gathered together as a church. What we normally call the corporate worship service shows us, in concentrated form, what should always and everywhere be the case when Christians gather together: "For where two or three are gathered in my name, there am I among them" (Matt. 18:20).

Praying: Getting Real Out Loud

What is in Christ is nothing less than reality: the truth about God, the world, and ourselves. As we celebrate what is in Christ, we thereby reorder our ideas about and realign our hearts toward the real. Perhaps that is why Mark Labberton can write about *The Dangerous Act of Worship*.[80] Worship is dangerous because, in waking us up to the way things are in Christ (i.e., God's purpose for the world and for us), it threatens not only to overturn the tables of the money changers, but also to unsettle our cherished ideas and shatter our glittering self-images. We can say the same thing about prayer: it is dangerous because it reorders reality, lifting the fog of our idolatrous illusions.

Of all illusions, the one that confuses the creature with the Creator is the most dangerous and the most foolish. Few of us admit to feeling the attraction of this temptation, much less to claiming explicitly that we are like God. The temptation is nevertheless real, yet oh so subtle. We come close to this primal confusion when we begin to act, and pray, as if God is at our beck and call, a divine genie in the lamp to be rubbed—petitioned!—only when we want his help. When we learn to pray with Jesus, the psalms, and saints before us, however, we are quickly put into our rightful place: prostrate before the sovereign Lord, almighty God, Maker of heaven and earth. Prayer is not only living to but also speaking (and listening) to God. Indeed, prayer is a microcosm of a person's relationship to God.

> *Prayer is a microcosm of a person's relationship to God.*

If theology treats God's relation to the world, then prayer, like worship, can lay claim to being the quintessential theological act. In the words of St. Evagrius: "If you are a theologian you truly pray. If you truly pray you are a theologian."[81] Jesus was truly a theologian, then, because the disciples kept stumbling upon him in prayer. Luke's Gospel alone depicts Jesus at prayer at many points: 3:21; 5:16; 6:12; 9:18, 28–29; 10:21; 11:1; 22:41–45. Luke also records Jesus encouraging his disciples to pray (10:2; 18:1; 21:36; 22:40, 46) and teaching them how, both by negative examples (18:10–11; 19:46; 20:47) and positively by his own personal example (11:2–4). It is significant that Jesus's first concern was for the sanctity or set-apartness of God's name: "Father, hallowed be your name" (Luke 11:2).

The early Christians were theologians too: as they gathered together in the upper room in Jerusalem, they "were devoting themselves to prayer" (Acts 1:14). Pastors today lose a precious opportunity to do public theology if and when they forego the tradition of pastoral prayer.[82] Indeed, not to lead the gathered community in prayer is to miss one of the best opportunities not only to celebrate what is in Christ but also to teach people theology, for prayer enacts the good news that through Christ we have access to God not only as Maker of heaven and earth, nor even as Father, but also as Abba ("Daddy"). True prayer exhibits God's relationship to his people in a way that doctrinal theology struggles to articulate with its concepts of divine transcendence and immanence, namely, how the holy Creator God is also present to us as loving Father.

Pastor-theologians have a unique opportunity to minister reality in the pastoral prayer. The Western tradition has called pastoral prayers "collects," perhaps because they gathered the church together ("Let us pray") or perhaps because they gathered together the people's concerns and brought them, collectively in prayer, to God. In any case, a collect typically has five elements: the invocation ("O Lord"), an acknowledgment of a divine attribute (e.g., "who is rich in mercy"), a petition (e.g., "forgive us"), the reason for the request (e.g., "through the work of Jesus Christ"), and the conclusion (e.g., "in his name, Amen"). Liturgical churches often have books with "collects" for particular situations or special days, but pastors who serve in nonliturgical traditions do well to compose pastoral prayers too, even if they do not call them "collects." Indeed, pastor-theologians in churches that do not use something like the Book of Common Prayer have an even greater responsibility in leading public prayers.

Words matter, and pastors would do well to give careful consideration to the words with which they address God. Public prayer is a prime instance of public theology. As children learn how to address their parents by listening in to how Daddy speaks to Mommy, so pastor-theologians teach their congregations how to talk to God (Abba!) through the example of public prayer: "Pastors need to remember that prayers offered in public have a shaping effect on the entire prayer life of the congregation."[83] Pastors whose prayers never include confession of sin risk inadvertently communicating to the congregation that they need not do so either. Pastors whose prayers are always for the needs of the congregation, instead of for God's coming kingdom ("Thy kingdom come"), risk inadvertently communicating that God is at our beck and call rather than our being at his call.

Prayer celebrates what there is in Christ: not only the dialogue between Father and Son but also our adoption as children of God. When Christians pray, they participate in the Son's own fellowship with the Father ("Our Father . . ."). Furthermore, just as Jesus oriented his life on his God-given mission through prayer, so can we. It was through praying that Jesus got the strength to say, "Not my will, but yours, be done" (Luke 22:42). Similarly, it is through prayer that we are reminded about our own vocation and identity "in Christ." C. S. Lewis says, "Now the moment of prayer is for me . . . the awareness, the re-awakened awareness, that this 'real world' and 'real self' are very far from being rock-bottom realities."[84] To the extent that prayer reminds us who we are in Christ, it acts as a wake-up call, a bracing tonic of reality. Pastor, teach us to pray.

Communing: The Lord's Supper

For those keeping score, I have now used the phrase "quintessential theological act" three times to describe preaching, worship, and praying, respectively. Each is an act that engages God and shapes God's people, hence "public theology." We conclude our section on the pastor as liturgist (i.e., one who orders and coordinates the public work of gathering before God) with what is arguably the most appropriate use yet of our signature phrase: celebrating the Lord's Supper is a (the?) quintessential public theological act.

> The Lord's Supper is both a summary of Christ's story and a taste of his reality.

The Lord's Supper is all about *what is in Christ*, for what there is in the Lord's Supper is both a summary of Christ's story and a taste of his reality. Jesus himself instituted this practice at the Last Supper, when he told his disciples, "This is my body, which is given for you. Do this in remembrance of me. . . . This cup . . . is the new covenant in my blood" (Luke 22:19–20). When we celebrate the Lord's Supper, we "proclaim the Lord's death until he comes" (1 Cor. 11:26). When we remember Jesus's atoning death on the cross by sharing the bread and wine, thereby recalling Israel's Passover meal as well, we act out a verbal, visual, and altogether visceral summary of the whole drama of redemption. Celebrating the Lord's Supper is a present activity that looks back to a past saving event and to the future coming of the Lord.

To celebrate the Lord's Supper is consequently to obtain a precious taste of ultimate reality. For what is in Christ, what is ultimately real, is *communion*, with God and with one another. In celebrating the Lord's Supper, the church is not playing charades but participating in this reality, in both its vertical and horizontal dimensions. In celebrating the Lord's Supper, we participate bodily, in word and deed, in the fellowship (Gk. *koinōnia*) that Christ has established between God and the people of God and within the people itself. In a word: what there is in Christ is *peace* with God and our fellow Christians.

The occasion of Paul's teaching about the Lord's Supper was a problem in the church at Corinth: "I hear that there are divisions among you" (1 Cor. 11:18). Divisions among Christians are not only wounds in the body of Christ, but also a failure on the church's part to grasp what there is in Christ: "the communion of saints" (Apostles' Creed). Previously we saw that the church is a living temple, and that Christ's death has removed the "wall of hostility" (Eph. 2:14) that had previously kept the Gentiles from being incorporated into the people of God. In Christ there is reconciliation not only between sinners and God but also between various kinds of human beings: masters and slaves, men and women, Jew and Gentile. Pastors who celebrate the Lord's Supper engage in Christ's own "ministry of reconciliation" (2 Cor. 5:18).

The Lord's Supper is a dramatic exhibit of the unity that exists "in Christ." It is a powerful act of public theology that gets at the heart of what the gospel is all about. The good news is that the Spirit unites people of every color, class, and caste to Christ through faith. United with Christ, they are also united with one another. The Lord's Table is the place where this unity is on conspicuous display—or not. Paul was disturbed by the bad public theology being lived out at Corinth. Not only were there factions, but they also were eating the Lord's Supper unworthily: "When you come together, it is not the Lord's Supper that you eat. For in eating, each one goes ahead with his own meal. One goes hungry, another gets drunk" (1 Cor. 11:20–21). A few verses later Paul warns against eating and drinking "without discerning the body" (11:29).

Discerning the body means understanding how those from many tribes, nations, and classes have become one in Christ: "The cup of blessing that we bless, is it not a sharing [*koinōnia*] in the blood of Christ?" (1 Cor. 10:16 NRSV). Christian koinonia involves sharing something with, or sharing in something, with someone. What Christians share with one another is the reality of being in Christ, being "justified by his blood" (Rom. 5:9), and the joy of fellowship in Christ's resurrection through the Spirit. Pastors do an important work of public theology as they preside over a celebration that enacts, in a visible and tangible way, the gracious logic of the gospel itself, which is overturning the status logics of the world. Sharing the bread and wine with your neighbor on Sunday but not having anything to do with your neighbor the rest of the week—that is a performative contradiction of what is in Christ. The Lord's Supper is thus not only a celebration but also a kind of lived catechism through which the church comes to a deeper understanding and more authentic realization of communion in Christ.

We discern the body of Christ, then, when we celebrate the communion that we have with one another in Christ through the Spirit. This communion is real—more real than the superficial differences that appear to divide human beings (e.g., language, skin color). The horizontal aspect of discerning the body, then, involves grasping the real communion of the saints in Christ. Sharing Christ's body and blood with those with whom you would otherwise never have anything to do—that makes as provocative a "bodily" statement of public theology as there is. The church *is* public theology when it embodies the new humanity that exists in Christ, in whom there are no racial, social, or economic divisions.

There is also a vertical dimension to discerning the body, however.[85] Christ himself is *really present* at the Lord's Supper, not primarily on but rather *at* the table. It is the Lord's Supper, and he is both meal and host. He is alive and well; his resurrected body ascended into heaven: "the ascension changes not the fact and the reality of Christ's presence with the church, but its mode."[86] We commune with the living Christ as we partake of the Lord's Supper through the Spirit, who lifts our hearts up to the Lord, thus uniting guests to host. Again, it is not the elements per se but the whole action and event of the Lord's Supper that communicates Christ's real presence. The Lord's Supper reminds us that what there is in Christ is union with Christ and communion with God and with one another.

Celebrating the Lord's Supper is an act of public theology that is as sophisticated in meaning as it is simple in motion. Pastor-theologians do well to mine the theological riches of the Lord's Supper, perhaps by celebrating on a weekly basis, for it is an encapsulation of the gospel, a ministry of reality, and the enacted truth about the church.[87] In breaking bread together, the people of God acknowledge what they truly are in Christ through the Spirit. Indeed, regular celebration of the Supper counts as obedience not only to our Lord's command "Do this" (Luke 22:19) but also to his commission "Make disciples of all nations" (Matt. 28:19), for the Communion celebration is not only a profound teaching moment that includes, yet goes beyond, words but also a concrete way of building up the people of God in Christ: "The bread that we break, is it not a sharing [koinōnia] in the body of Christ?" (1 Cor. 10:16 NRSV).

Apologist: Demonstrating What Is in Christ

For more than a millennium, the best minds in Christendom have sought what we might call the "apologist's stone": a way of turning cosmological lead into theological gold, this-worldly evidence into conclusive proof of God's existence. Apologetics is the defense of Christian truth, and this is clearly one of the tasks of doctors of the church, where "Do no harm" translates into "Accept no error." Paul tells Titus that those who oversee the church must be able "to give instruction in sound doctrine and also to rebuke those who contradict it" (Titus 1:9). John Chrysostom applauds Paul's strong-mindedness: "Do you not see that Paul put to flight the whole world, that he was more powerful than Plato and all the rest? But it was by his miracles, you say. Not by miracles only, for if you peruse the Acts of the Apostles, you will find him often prevailing by his teaching."[88]

Pastors are apologists, charged with demonstrating the truth of the gospel and refuting false teaching. Stated differently: pastors are charged with maintaining a faithful and credible witness to the gospel and with helping members of their congregations to do the same. Does this mean that pastors, like Paul, must either work miracles or become academic intellectuals after all, purveyors in propositional syllogisms and particle physics, in order to refute not Plato but the New Atheists?[89] I believe there is an alternative way forward, which proceeds from an enlarged vision of what apologetics involves.

The truth pastors need to defend is not the existence of God but the wisdom of the cross: "For the word of the cross is folly to those who are perishing, but to us who are being saved it is the power of God" (1 Cor. 1:18). Paul explicitly says that he was "put here for the defense of the gospel" (Phil. 1:16). Does one need to be a genius, or to work miracles, to defend the truth of the gospel? In the introduction, I argued that the disciples were not geniuses, and pastors do not need to be geniuses either. For what needs to be defended is not theory but wisdom, and wisdom is lived knowledge. We "prove" wisdom by offering not theoretical proofs but practical demonstrations.

The gathered assembly of believers is the practical demonstration of the wisdom of the cross and of the risen Christ's lordship: "If the Holy Spirit does not witness to the Father and Son through the witnesses of Christians, then Christians have no arguments to make."[90] What pastors need is not a philosopher's stone but the theologian's cornerstone, namely, Jesus Christ, the one to whom all living stones are joined and in whom believers are growing together. This edifice—the people of God, the body of Christ, the fellowship of the Holy Spirit—is the embodied argument, the miracle that "puts to flight" the whole world (Chrysostom).

In point of fact, the existence of the church constitutes two arguments, two different demonstrations of the truth of *what is in Christ*. The first is the *argument from joyful endurance*. Christian faith "proves" true when the people of God willingly submit to every kind of critical testing, intellectual and existential, and endure to the end, rejoicing in the assurance that suffering produces endurance, character, and a hope that does not disappoint (Rom. 5:3–5). The author of Hebrews asks his readers to remember their previous endurance of sufferings, which included "being publicly exposed [*theatrizō*] to abuse and affliction" (Heb. 10:32–33). What is shown in the theater of faith is the truth that endures everything: critical testing, suffering, ridicule, and death. Christian martyrdom is a demonstration of Christ's life in us:

> *The gathered assembly of believers is the practical demonstration of the wisdom of the cross and of the risen Christ's lordship.*

"For everyone who has been born of God overcomes the world. And this is the victory that has overcome the world—our faith" (1 John 5:4). The proof that the church is Christ's building is the fact that "the gates of hell shall not prevail against it" (Matt. 16:18).

The church, second, is the embodiment of what we could call the *argument from expanding communion*. Again, the quality of the church's life together is a matter of the integrity of its gospel witness. When the church becomes what it is—a fellowship of the Holy Spirit—it becomes a lived plausibility structure. The philosopher Jacques Derrida would not be able to qualify forgiveness by the phrase "if such a thing exists" if Christians indeed forgave one another as Jesus commanded (Matt. 18:21–22). It is easier to dismiss abstract theological concepts or argue against what appear to be outmoded doctrines; it is something else altogether to ignore real-life scenes that enact the truth of the gospel through racial reconciliation, familial forgiveness, social justice, and sacrificial love. It is difficult to contradict the ministry of reconciliation.

The church cannot compel the world to taste and see the goodness of God. It is nevertheless responsible to communicate both the sense and the sweetness of *what is in Christ*. For this, there is perhaps no better public demonstration than celebrating the Lord's Supper—*being and doing communion*. Bonhoeffer states: "Christian community is not an ideal we have to realize, but rather a reality created by God in Christ in which we may participate."[91] The Lord's Supper is both *summa* and *apologia* of the gospel, for in celebrating the Supper the church not only proclaims but enacts in embodied fashion both union and communion, the reality of *what is in Christ*.

Jesus himself addressed the importance of this aspect of public theology: "By this all people will know that you are my disciples, if you have love for one another" (John 13:35). This final aspect of the pastor's vocation concerns equipping the church for its mission to the world: "The world will not believe and know that God sent Jesus because our theology is true, our doctrine correct, and our liturgy proper. The world will know and believe *when it sees Jesus in us*."[92] In the final analysis, the best apologetic is the people of God doing communion and performing works of love to the world, demonstrating the truth of what is, and what will be, in Christ.

> *The best apologetic is the people of God doing communion and performing works of love to the world, demonstrating the truth of what is, and what will be, in Christ.*

Why is there church rather than nothing? In order to exhibit the way things are in Christ. The people of God, living stones joined together to make a temple, the place of God's presence and activity, are to be a corporate demonstration of the truth, power, and reality of the gospel. It is the pastor's great privilege and responsibility to be an artisan in God's house and thus to construct and oversee such embodied arguments. The best apologetics is a lived public theology.

The Drama of Preaching

GUY A. DAVIES

As a pastor I find myself having to play several roles. I'm a preacher, counselor, church leader, chair of meetings, and so on. With many demands on my time, keeping up with my theological reading may not always seem like a priority. Spending precious moments with Augustine of Hippo, John Calvin, or Herman Bavinck may even seem like an indulgence. But it isn't. Without theology my ministry would barely be distinguishable from business management or social work. That is why I must aspire to be a public theologian for the sake of the people of God.

A pastor may serve as a public theologian in a number of ways. But it is above all in my work as preacher of the gospel that I bring theology into the public domain. This does not mean that my job is to serve up reconstituted dollops of systematic theology, however. Preaching is meant to be "theology on fire." No amount of pulpit histrionics would succeed in setting some of your typical works of systematics alight. We need, then, to give fresh thought to the relationship between theology and preaching.

In this regard I've found to be helpful Kevin Vanhoozer's proposal that theology is best viewed in terms of "theodrama":

> The gospel is "theo-dramatic"—a series of divine entrances and exits, especially as these pertain to what God has done for us in Jesus Christ. The gospel—both

177

the Christ event and the canon that communicates it—thus appears as the climactic moment in the Trinitarian economy of divine self-communicative action. Theology responds and corresponds to God's prior word and deed; accordingly theology itself is part of the theodramatic action.[1]

This insight has helped me to reflect on how theology should impact upon preaching. Theodramatic preaching is evangelistic. It is as we herald the good news of Jesus, calling for a response of repentance, faith, and obedience to the gospel, that people are incorporated into the drama of redeeming grace. Theodramatic preaching enables members of our churches to play their roles in the drama of redemption. It equips the people of God to stage the theodrama by acting out gospel in a way that is faithful to the authoritative biblical script and appropriate to the contemporary setting.

A theodramatic approach to preaching recognizes that the Bible gives us God's authoritative speech acts. We do things by speaking. With the exchange of words, a man and woman enter into a marriage relationship. With words we may insult people or encourage them. God's words in Scripture are the biblical *locutions*. These locutions (units of speech) have an *illocutionary* purpose. God does things by his words: he enters into a covenant relationship with his people, makes promises, issues warnings or commands. The Spirit gives *perlocutionary* power to these illocutions so that as we preach, promises are believed, warnings heeded, and commands obeyed. Theodramatic preaching seeks to discover and proclaim God's communicative action in Scripture. We can be confident that once proclaimed, God's Word will not return to him void, but will accomplish what he pleases (Isa. 55:11).

The redemptive-historical school of preaching locates particular biblical texts within the grand sweep of the drama of Scriptural revelation. This approach has value because individual texts are not understood in isolation from biblical metanarratives. But redemptive-historical preaching sometimes has difficulty with the exemplary and practical nature of biblical revelation. The effect of this is that preaching may become little more than an exercise in biblical theology. A more theodramatic approach has helped me bridge the gap between redemptive-historical metanarratives and the Bible's exemplary and practical teaching. In the light of what God has done in Christ as revealed in Scripture—the theodrama—we call believers to model their lives on the biblical examples and obey the Lord's commands. Theodramatic preaching gives weight to both the indicatives and the imperatives of the gospel.

Theodramatic preaching attempts to triangulate Scripture, the church, and the world. Yes, the Bible is our authoritative script, but we must not see the Scripture in isolation from the church. I don't want to interpret the Bible idiosyncratically, much less heretically. Bringing Scripture into conversation with the riches of the church's creedal inheritance is a helpful safeguard. In sermon preparation we engage with biblical commentators old and new to get to grips with the meaning of a text. But our job is only half done once we have prayerfully gained an understanding of the passage. We must then work out how to discriminatingly apply the truth to our people in their current cultural setting. Only then will the "gathered church" be equipped to live as the "scattered church," with believers living as whole-life disciples of Jesus on the world's stage.

The act of proclaiming the Word must itself be theodramatic. When preaching, my aim is not simply to give doctrinal instruction to the congregation I serve but also to enable the people of God to understand and feel the truth of Scripture in order to practice it. I need to think and feel my way into the text so that my ministry becomes a living performance of the message. This does not mean that I playact my sermons. But we must reflectively apply our message to ourselves before preaching them to others. I want my preaching to be nothing less than an enactment of the theodrama—a revelatory event where God's Christ-centered Word is proclaimed to his people, in the transforming power of the Spirit.

If my preaching is to accomplish anything, I need the Spirit of Christ to be at work in both me and the people to whom I proclaim God's Word. We must minister in conscious and prayerful dependence upon the Holy Spirit. The New Testament does not see preaching simply in terms of an accurate declaration of the truth, but a Spirit-empowered encounter with the God of the gospel (1 Thess. 1:5). That thought makes me pray for divine enabling every time I proclaim the Word of God to the people of God.

As a theodramatic preacher, I aspire to become a pastor-theologian for the sake of the people of God. When I began my current pastorate ten years ago, the churches I served were preoccupied with internal issues, and little attempt was being made to reach the lost for Christ. I believe it is now true to say that the believers have a deeper love for one another, and the churches are more orientated toward mission. It is as theology becomes "public property" in our preaching that the people of God whom we have been called to serve will be directed to play their parts in the great drama of God's redeeming grace. We have been privileged to witness the communicative action of God at work among us, slowly but surely making us more like Christ, through the presence of his Spirit in our midst. That is the drama of preaching.

The Pastor-Theologian as Pulpit Apologist

JASON B. HOOD

It's going to be a rough decade for Megan. She'll lose her job. She'll carry impossible expectations into a marriage before discovering that "Christian marriage" isn't nearly as rosy as she was taught: Christian romance novels didn't prepare her for a husband who spent his early twenties addicted to porn. A beloved aunt will be diagnosed with cancer. A favorite cousin will choose gender-reassignment surgery and hormone treatment. Her church will be a surprising mix of sinners and saints, equal parts threat and boon to her faith.

Megan is not equipped to meet these challenges. In her formative years she chased shots of Disney with deep draughts from the tap of American individualism. She learned that freedom and independence are the highest good a person can possess. She's flooded with hostile comments about Christian belief and practices on Facebook. Her coworkers proselytize for alternative allegiances with vigor and disdain.

This week real-life Megans will be attending a church near you. How can the church meet Megan's needs? Megan needs many things: a regular diet of the gospel; mature Christians who model faithful Christian living; a safe place to ask challenging questions; and the cultivation of a winsome, merciful posture to outsiders who are hostile to Christianity. Megan also needs a theologian in the pulpit who can do apologetics for her cultural context, not least by unmasking popular alternatives to Christianity, with their offers of false comfort. Apologetics is not just for unbelievers; it's for believers like Megan who are vexed by life, suffering, and a post-Christian culture.

Enter Tim Keller. Long before his *New York Times* best seller *The Reason for God*, Keller made a regular habit of addressing what he calls "defeater beliefs" in the pulpit. These barrier beliefs are culturally conditioned, foundational

commitments that make Christianity sound implausible if not altogether ir-
rational. In Cairo, every Muslim knows that Jesus didn't die on a cross and
that God has no offspring, hence Jesus is not the Son of God. In the West, no
one is troubled by Jesus's death on a cross, but the notion that one religion
possesses *the* way to God is simply unbelievable; conversely, this latter idea is
not a problem at all in Cairo.

Every passage in the Bible will touch at least one of six "barrier beliefs"
that make Christianity difficult to swallow in the post-Christian West:

1. There cannot be one true religion that falsifies all other views.
2. Evil and suffering make the powerful God of the Bible impossible.
3. Personal choice is sacred and cannot be violated by any religion or ideology that requires my submission to lordship.
4. The church's track record is too dismal.
5. God's anger or wrath is unpalatable, perhaps even criminal.
6. The Bible is untrustworthy and socially regressive.

These barriers to Christian belief are not found just in New York: they are
found everywhere, part of the cultural air. Again, they are hardly unique to
unbelievers, but they are so much a part of the cultural milieu that I hear
them raised by (surprisingly honest) students in Christian classrooms and by
parishioners who haven't fully extricated their worldview from the surrounding
culture. These barriers are so prominent that those who hold them have usually not critically tested them; yet such barriers are often surprisingly fragile.

As a test case, imagine a sermon on the well-known passage Matthew
28:16–20. I have heard many sermons on this passage, but I cannot recall
hearing one that addressed the objections of unbelievers in our current cultural ethos. The lordship of Jesus presented in Matthew 28:16–20 bumps up
against each of the first three barrier beliefs: the extent of his lordship is far
too sweeping (barrier belief 1) and the degree of suffering we see or experience leads us to question whether he really is reigning (2). Here I'll address
only barrier belief 3: Jesus's claim to lordship curtails the self-actualization
and self-definition prized above all else in our culture.

As I write, the pop music charts amply illustrate the third barrier belief.
Macklemore's "Same Love," a powerful and effective pro-gay marriage anthem,
strikes a much more sympathetic chord than Miley Cyrus's "We Can't Stop,"

a raunchy party anthem. But both songs function as contemporary narratives of unconstrained freedom. Both songs teach that my body is my own and I can't help my desires: I need to be free, autonomous, and affirmed.

Megan—and the friend she has brought with her from work—needs to hear Matthew 28 in context: the man who claims to rule over our life and the whole world only does so after he dies for us. The pulpit theologian points out that alternative "freedoms" are really alternative lords. Macklemore's chorus confesses, "I can't change, even if I tried, even if I wanted to." Miley also toes the line of fatalism cast as sexuality: "We can't stop." This freedom leads to the tyranny of self. Sexual radicals heralding the redefinition of marriage also bring us the end of all sexual constraints, which turns out to be slavery of a different sort. I am now required to let my six-year-old boy call himself a girl if he wishes, and our Christian counselor will lose his license if he encourages him to be comfortable with the skin and chromosomes God gave him. The "traditional" approach to gender is decried as slavery. But the child is then sold to the tyrant of his choice of gender. Radical sexual freedom very subtly begins to dominate our imagination, require our allegiance, compel our habits, and limit our liberty. As Dylan said, "You gotta serve somebody."

The quest for self-satisfaction and affirmation never ends; the god of self is never satisfied. The quest for that affirmation will dominate your desires, absorb your energy, and vacuum your money. Eventually the culture will find you too old or too boring. The culture will leave you. Your sex life will leave you. But King Jesus promises never to leave you, and he has secured a path truer than any you could blaze through the wilderness of cultural confusion. In his service we find true liberation, and in the arms of his father we find our identity as beloved children.

Conclusion

Fifty-Five Summary Theses on the
Pastor as Public Theologian

KEVIN J. VANHOOZER

Why does the church need pastor-theologians? What are pastor-theologians for? Our answer, in brief, is that pastor-theologians are gifts from the risen Christ, helps in building Christ's church, especially by leading people to confess, comprehend, celebrate, communicate, commend to others, and conform themselves to what is in Christ.

As suits a vision statement, in particular a book about reclaiming a vision, we conclude by summarizing our main theses, chapter by chapter. We believe these theses have implications for what ought to be happening today in churches and seminaries alike.

1. The church is in danger of exchanging its birthright for a mess of secular pottage in the place where one might least expect it: the pastorate (from the introduction).

2. Pastors, together with the churches they serve, are too often held captive by pictures of leadership (e.g., managers, therapists) drawn from contemporary culture rather than Scripture.

3. The location of theology in the academy, together with the disciplinary separation between biblical studies and doctrinal theology, serves neither pastors nor the church.

4. Pastors must exercise special vigilance in their ministries, taking care not to make the pulpit into a bully pulpit or to magnify their own names instead of, or even alongside, God's.

5. Pastors are theologians whose vocation is to seek, speak, and show understanding of what God is doing in Christ for the sake of the world, and to lead others to do the same.

6. Pastors are public theologians because they work for, with, and on *people*—the gathered assembly of the faithful—and lead them to live to God, bearing witness as a public spire in the public square.

7. Pastors are not unique in building others up into Christ (all Christians share this privilege and responsibility) but rather in being put into the position of overseeing this building project.

8. The pastor-theologian is an organic intellectual in the body of Christ, a person with evangelical intelligence who is wise unto salvation.

9. As an organic intellectual, the pastor-theologian articulates the faith, hope, and love of the believing community on the community's behalf and for its upbuilding.

10. The pastor-theologian is a particular kind of generalist: one who specializes in viewing all of life from the perspective of what God was doing, is doing, and will do in Jesus Christ.

11. The pastor-theologian's office is not a recent innovation but has its ancestry in the leadership offices of ancient Israel: prophet, priest, and king (from chap. 1).

12. The office of pastor-theologian was commissioned by Jesus, continues Jesus's ministry as good shepherd of the new covenant community, and participates in Jesus's threefold messianic office of prophet, priest, and king.

13. Pastor-theologians, like priests, represent God to human beings (especially regarding requirements for holiness, by directing the people to God's gracious provision in Christ Jesus for their ongoing sin) and human beings to God (especially by offering sacrifices of praise or thanksgiving and prayers of intercession).

14. Pastor-theologians, like prophets, exercise a ministry of truth-telling, primarily (but not exclusively) with words, communicating a God's-eye point of view, especially concerning the truth that is in Christ Jesus.

15. Pastor-theologians, like the good kings of ancient Israel, personify God's cruciform wisdom and righteousness through humble obedience to God's Word, thereby modeling what citizenship in heaven looks like on earth.

16. Pastors from previous eras of church history uniformly understood their vocation in theological terms, and most of the best theologians in the history of the church were also pastors (from chap. 2).

17. Pastor-theologians in the early church used the ancient Rule of Faith to provide the parameters for understanding the theological realities that are part and parcel of the gospel, and to identify the God of Israel with the Father of Jesus Christ, the Creator of all things with the Redeemer of the church.

18. At some point in the early church, bishops were not only pastors of local churches but also overseers of broader regions—"enlarged" pastor-theologians—responsible for representing the unity of the church, defending the true faith, and opposing error.

19. Pastor-theologians in the Protestant Reformation were viewed primarily as ministers of God's Word, whose discourse was thus more authoritative than any other earthly word.

20. Pastor-theologians in the Puritan tradition excelled in using right instruction for the purpose of transforming hearts and lives, deploying the doctrine of God for the sake of godliness.

21. Jonathan Edwards saw the pastorate as a "divine business," a participation in Christ's work of representing God to human beings (especially in preaching) and human beings to God (especially in prayer).

22. Nineteenth-century revivalists like Charles Finney were more concerned with moving the will to repentance and faith through fervent public speaking than with correct doctrine, effectively demoting theology in favor of "results."

23. Nineteenth-century theologians faced academic scrutiny from scientists and philosophers and turned their attention to the project of regaining intellectual respectability, thus distancing themselves from the concerns of pastors in the church.

24. Many modern pastors who came to see their vocation as a helping profession lost interest in theology since they were preoccupied with learning practical skills that would ensure success (i.e., results).

25. The 1940s saw the beginnings of an evangelical remnant that sought to recover the historic vision of the pastorate as a theological office.

26. The pastor-theologian, far from being a specialist, is rather a holy jack-of-all-existential-trades, charged with communicating Christ to everyone, everywhere, at all times (from chap. 3).

27. The pastor-theologian deals with death and dying, and the anxiety of being-toward-death in general, by administering a mood-altering dose of reality—the good news of the gospel—and by personally embodying, in contextually sensitive ways, the joyful mood of being-toward-resurrection.

28. Pastor-theologians embody an "evangelical mood"—an indicative declaration ("He is risen! He is Lord!") and a concomitant way of being that is attuned to the world as already but not yet made new in Jesus Christ.

29. The distinctive task of the pastor-theologian is to say, on the basis of the Scriptures, what was, is, and will be "in Christ."

30. Pastor-theologians who set forth in speech *what is in Christ* are ultimately engaged in a ministry of reality, that is, in administering the truth of *what is*: the truth about God, humankind, and the relationship between them.

31. To minister *what is in Christ* is to minister understanding, a grasp of how the parts—the persons, events, and things that comprise the gospel—relate to the whole, namely, their summation in Jesus Christ.

32. Pastor-theologians are public intellectuals because they address the big questions, and the big picture, through the filter and framework of the biblical story of God's work of redemption that culminates with Jesus's resurrection.

33. Pastor-theologians devote themselves to the privilege of studying, interpreting, and ministering understanding of God's Word to others; for Scripture alone is the divinely authorized account of what God is doing in Christ to reconcile humanity and renew creation.

34. Pastor-theologians endeavor to increase biblical literacy in their congregations, particularly by giving attention to biblical theology and the challenge of perceiving the unity of the biblical story of the Christ in the diversity of biblical books, persons, and events.

35. Pastor-theologians endeavor to increase cultural literacy in their congregations, knowing that culture is ultimately a means of spiritual formation that programs values and practices, beliefs and behaviors.

36. As public theologians who work with people to build them up into Christ, pastors would do well to read fiction with a view to understanding different kinds of people.

37. Pastor-theologians speak in the imperative as well as the indicative, exhorting their congregations not only to *say* but also to *conform* to the new eschatological reality that is available to us *in Christ* through Christ's Spirit.

38. Seminaries exist to foster biblical and theological literacy for the sake of understanding and living out what is in Christ.

39. Seminaries exist not to reinforce but rather to transcend the typical compartmentalization of "biblical," "systematic," and "practical" theology for the sake of interdisciplinary pastoral-theological wisdom.

40. Seminaries exist to foster a particular kind of generalist: one who understands all things in light of what is in Christ, keeps company with Christ, acts out the eschatological reality of being raised with Christ, and helps others to do the same.

41. The practices of the pastor-theologian are rooted in the pastor's own union with Christ and involve communicating what is in Christ (from chap. 4).

42. The Great Pastoral Commission is Christ's charge to pastors to be public theologians who work with people on God's behalf, workers who feed Christ's sheep and build God's house.

43. Jesus is the master builder who will build his church on the rock of confessors and confessions, though pastor-theologians play a special (i.e., set-apart) role in serving as authorized representatives of Jesus, charged with preserving the integrity of the church's confessions.

44. The pastor-theologian is a builder of God's house, a mason who works with living stones, joining them together with the cornerstone (Jesus Christ) in order to form a dwelling place on earth for God: a temple made of people.

45. As artisans in the house of God, pastor-theologians oversee a work not merely of urban but also of *cosmic* renewal as they, in the church's reconciling practices, anticipate the reconciliation of all things.

46. Pastor-theologians minister God's word of reconciliation and renewal in Christ through counseling and personal visitation as well as through teaching and preaching.

47. The sermon is a crucial instrument in the pastor-theologian's arsenal of grace and truth, fostering biblical literacy, biblical-theological competence, and a holistic appreciation for the excellency of Jesus Christ.

48. Sermons also serve as excellent means of fostering the congregation's ability to interpret culture, recognize cultural hegemony, and understand the way particular cultural texts and trends either contribute to or hinder the realization of God's rule on earth.

49. The sermon is one of the pastor-theologian's principal means of waking people up to the redemptive reality of what God is doing in Christ beneath, behind, alongside, and above the surface of sociocultural appearances.

50. Because indoctrination of one kind or another is inevitable, pastor-theologians must explicitly reclaim the role of catechist as set out in the Pastoral Epistles, teaching doctrine for the sake of enabling people better to understand and conform to reality, and thus to get real.

51. Pastor-theologians administer sound doctrine to the body of Christ for the sake of its health, flourishing, and growing up into maturity in Christ.

52. Pastor-theologians lead the gathered assembly, celebrating what is in Christ and using the time spent together to build up the congregation in faith, hope, and love so that disciples can worship both in and outside the corporate gathering by offering their bodies as living sacrifices throughout the week.

53. Pastors perform a quintessential public theological act in leading the congregation in prayer, itself a ministry of reality that acknowledges what sinners are before God and what saints are before God in Christ Jesus.

54. Pastors preside over the quintessential public theological act of celebrating the Lord's Supper, itself a ministry of the eschatological reality that, because of their common union with Christ in faith through the Spirit, believers enjoy as communion with the living God and with one another, despite penultimate differences of race, class, and gender.

55. Pastor-theologians function as apologists, defending the wisdom of the cross and the truth of the gospel, when they facilitate lived corporate demonstrations of faith's endurance and of the love, forgiveness, and communion that is in Christ.

Notes

Preface

1. The context was interpreting the Bible as God's Word. Here is the full quote: "The pastor-theologian should be evangelicalism's default public intellectual, with preaching the preferred public mode of theological interpretation of Scripture." Kevin J. Vanhoozer, "Interpreting Scripture between the Rock of Biblical Studies and the Hard Place of Systematic Theology: The State of the Evangelical (dis)Union," in *Renewing the Evangelical Mission*, ed. Richard Lints (Grand Rapids: Eerdmans, 2013), 224.

Introduction: Pastors, Theologians, and Other Public Figures

1. Terry Eagleton, *Culture and the Death of God* (New Haven: Yale University Press, 2014), 1.

2. We should not forget, however, that Paul lists "administrating" among the various gifts that God has given the church (1 Cor. 12:28). Yet, precisely because it is a spiritual gift (not an office), it should be used in all wisdom to build up the church.

3. See, for example, H. R. Niebuhr, James Gustafson, and Daniel Day Williams, eds., *The Purpose of the Church and Its Ministry: Reflections on the Aims of Theological Education* (New York: Harper & Row, 1956); and Edward Farley, *Theologia: The Fragmentation and Unity of Theological Education* (Philadelphia: Fortress, 1983).

4. All Christians have theological vocations: all are called to glorify God in whatever their life's calling may be (e.g., bank president, plumber, schoolteacher, nurse, etc.) and in all their roles (e.g., son/daughter, husband/wife, parent/grandparent, neighbor, citizen, etc.). The pastor's vocation to minister the gospel is not "higher" in the sense of more important, but it is "holier" in the strict sense of being "set apart."

5. David Tracy identifies these three publics in the course of providing a "social portrait" of the theologian. See the discussion in Tracy, *The Analogical Imagination: Christian Theology and the Culture of Pluralism* (New York: Crossroad, 1998), 3–31.

6. Ibid., 31. Gerald Hiestand proposes a similar threefold typology of the pastor-theologian, involving professor-theologians (academy), popular theologians (society), and ecclesial theologians (church) in his "Taxonomy of the Pastor-Theologian: Why PhD Students Should Consider the Pastorate as the Context for Their Theological Scholarship," *Expository Times* 124, no. 6 (March 2013): 261–71.

7. Cf. R. Albert Mohler Jr.: "The transformation of theology into an academic discipline more associated with the university than the church has been one of the most lamentable developments

of the last several centuries." Mohler, *The Pastor as Theologian* (Louisville: Southern Baptist Theological Seminary, 2006), 4. http://www.sbts.edu/resources/files/2010/09/the-pastor-as
-theologian.pdf.

8. For further treatment of this theme, see Gerald Hiestand, "Pastor-Scholar to Professor-Scholar: Exploring the Theological Disconnect between the Academy and the Church," *Westminster Theological Journal* 70 (2008): 355–69.

9. See chap. 2 for a fuller account of the historical background to the loss of vision for the pastor-theologian.

10. See further, David Kelsey, *To Understand God Truly: What's Theological about a Theological School?* (Louisville: Westminster John Knox, 1992).

11. For one who does, see Fred Sanders, *The Deep Things of God: How the Trinity Changes Everything* (Wheaton: Crossway, 2010).

12. For more on this unnatural divide, see Kevin Vanhoozer, "Interpreting Scripture between the Rock of Biblical Studies and the Hard Place of Systematic Theology: The State of the Evangelical (dis)Union," in *Renewing the Evangelical Mission*, ed. Richard Lints (Grand Rapids: Eerdmans, 2013), 201–25.

13. The situation may be changing, with more commentary series dedicated to reflecting on the theological message of the texts and the way the church has read them over the centuries, but the scholarly dust has not yet settled. For examples of new trends in commentary writing, see the Brazos Theological Commentary on the Bible and InterVarsity's Ancient Christian Commentary on Scripture series.

14. George Lakoff and Mark Johnson, *Metaphors We Live By* (Chicago: University of Chicago Press, 1980).

15. Elsewhere I argue something similar with regard to biblical commentaries. See Kevin Vanhoozer, "'Exegesis I Know, and Theology I Know, but Who Are You?': Acts 19 and the Theological Interpretation of Scripture," in the forthcoming *Theological Theology: Essays in Honor of John B. Webster*, ed. Darren Sarisky, R. David Nelson, and Justin Stratis (London: T&T Clark, 2015).

16. William H. Willimon, *Pastor: The Theology and Practice of Ordained Ministry* (Nashville: Abingdon, 2002), 55.

17. We do not want simply to swing the pendulum to the other extreme, exaggerate the intellect, and create a Rev. Frankenstein. We have an expansive view of the person and work of the pastor-theologian. We think emphasizing theology as wisdom strikes the right balance between knowing, doing, and being. As we argue below, pastors also need to know how to relate to people, because people are the "raw material," as it were, of public theology.

18. Joseph Hough and John Cobb, *Christian Identity and Theological Education* (Atlanta: Scholars Press, 1985).

19. Donald E. Messer focuses on five contemporary images: wounded healer, servant leader, political mystic, practical theologian, and enslaved liberator (*Contemporary Images of Christian Ministry* [Nashville: Abingdon, 1989]).

20. Each of these images is the focus of one or more chapters in Robert C. Dykstra, ed., *Images of Pastoral Care* (Danvers, MA: Chalice, 2005). Jonathan Edwards describes pastors as stewards, wise builders, architects, merchants, fishermen, and soldiers, giving biblical support for each image ("Some Thoughts concerning the Revival," in *The Great Awakening*, vol. 4 of *The Works of Jonathan Edwards* [New Haven: Yale University Press, 1972], 445).

21. Dykstra, *Images of Pastoral Care*, 3.

22. Karl Menninger, *Whatever Became of Sin?* (New York: Hawthorne Books, 1973), 17.

23. For a sobering history of how pastors have answered this question, see E. Brooks Holifield, *A History of Pastoral Care in America: From Salvation to Self-Realization* (Eugene, OR: Wipf & Stock, 2005). The subtitle signals the thesis: "The story proceeds from the ideal of self-denial to one of self-love, from self-love to self-culture, from self-culture to self-mastery, from self-mastery

to self-realization within a trustworthy culture, and finally to a later form of self-realization counterpoised against cultural mores and social institutions" (12).

24. John H. Leith, *The Reformed Imperative: What the Church Has to Say That No One Else Can Say* (Philadelphia: Westminster, 1988), 13.

25. Seward Hiltner wrote the book that launched a more secular understanding of pastoral theology. See his *Preface to Pastoral Theology* (Nashville: Abingdon, 1958). For a critique of Hiltner's need-based conception of the ministry, see Andrew Purves, *Reconstructing Pastoral Theology: A Christological Foundation* (Louisville: Westminster John Knox, 2004), xxxi–xxxiv.

26. Andrew Abbott, *The System of Professions: An Essay on the Division of Expert Labor* (Chicago: University of Chicago Press, 1988), 309.

27. Ibid., 308.

28. Cf. Andrew Purves: "Pastoral theology . . . has largely abandoned the responsibility to speak concerning God" (*Reconstructing Pastoral Theology*, xvii).

29. George Weigel, *Evangelical Catholicism: Deep Reform in the 21st-Century Church* (New York: Basic Books, 2013), 55.

30. Ibid., 79.

31. Eugene Peterson, *The Pastor: A Memoir* (New York: HarperOne, 2011), 4.

32. Eugene Peterson, *Under the Unpredictable Plant: An Exploration in Vocational Holiness* (Grand Rapids: Eerdmans, 1992), 20. Cf. William Willimon's gentle critique of Peterson's scorn for the institutional framework of ministry: "Eugene Peterson: American Pastor," in *Pastoral Work: Engagements with the Vision of Eugene Peterson*, ed. Jason Byasse and L. Roger Owens (Eugene, OR: Cascade, 2014), 53–62.

33. A point made by the authors of another valuable book that draws lessons about Christian ministry from masterpieces of world literature. See Leland Ryken, Philip Ryken, and Todd Wilson, *Pastors in the Classics: Timeless Lessons on Life and Ministry from World Literature* (Grand Rapids: Baker Books, 2012).

34. Ryken, Ryken, and Wilson encourage readers to ask four questions in particular: What roles does the pastor play in this book? What relationships are important for this pastor? What are this pastor's character traits? What is the pastor's place in the social context portrayed in the book? (ibid., 14).

35. David L. Larsen, *Oracles and Odysseys of the Clergy: Images of the Ministry in Western Literature* (Bloomington, IN: AuthorHouse, 2007), xi.

36. Wolff notes that what studies there are tend to focus on the Roman Catholic Church. See, for example, Les and Barbara Keyser, *Hollywood and the Catholic Church: The Image of Roman Catholicism in American Movies* (Chicago: Loyola University Press, 1984); and Colleen McDannell, ed., *Catholics in the Movies* (New York: Oxford University Press, 2008). Perhaps we should be grateful that no one has yet undertaken to write *Evangelicals in the Movies*.

37. Richard Wolff, *The Church on TV* (New York: Continuum, 2010).

38. Karl Barth, "The Word of God and the Task of the Ministry" (1922), in *The Word of God and the Word of Man* (Gloucester, MA: Peter Smith, 1978), 186, italics original.

39. The story was also staged as an opera in 2007. Lewis based his story on his observations of various pastors in Kansas City, where he did "research" by attending church twice on Sundays.

40. Ryken, Ryken, and Wilson, *Pastors in the Classics*, 44–45.

41. The pastor's paradox of being a public figure who points not to self but to God is best resolved in private, namely, in moments of solitude, study, and above all prayer, when pastors come before God and remember who they are (a point I owe to a comment by Paul Uyen). Prayer reorients and recalibrates not only priorities but also self-understanding. In short: it is in prayer that we remember who is the sovereign and who the servant.

42. I owe this point to a comment by Paul Maxwell.

43. Marilynne Robinson is another example of a public intellectual. See her collection of essays *When I Was a Child I Read Books: Essays* (New York: Farrar, Straus & Giroux, 2012).

44. Others have made helpful contributions as well. For example, see Derek Prime and Alister Begg, *On Being a Pastor: Understanding Our Calling and Work* (Chicago: Moody, 2013).

45. Theological intelligence, at least for pastors, includes relational and emotional intelligence, since the work of public theology, as we argue in later chapters, is precisely that of helping individuals and congregations to become mature in Christ. To anticipate: pastor-theologians need to understand people as well as God (which is also why we believe pastors should read fiction, as we suggest below).

46. Philip Clayton, *Transforming Christian Theology for Church and Society* (Minneapolis: Fortress, 2010), 19.

47. William Ames, *The Marrow of Theology* 1.1 (Latin, 1656; ET repr., Grand Rapids: Baker, 1968).

48. Max L. Stackhouse, "The Pastor as Public Theologian," in *The Pastor as Theologian*, ed. Earl E. Shelp and Ronald H. Sunderland (New York: Pilgrim, 1988), 111.

49. Ibid., 113–14. The situation is actually more complex; there are several types of political theology. See further Peter Scott and William T. Cavanaugh, eds., *The Blackwell Companion to Political Theology* (Oxford: Blackwell, 2004); and Elizabeth Phillips, *Political Theology: A Guide for the Perplexed* (London: T&T Clark, 2012). One issue that divides political theologians is whether Christians should or should not live as "resident aliens" within the broader society. Should Christians live apart from society or try to influence it in Christian directions?

50. Ibid., 114.

51. Ibid., 116.

52. Ibid., 120.

53. Ibid., 128.

54. Deirdre King Hainsworth and Scott R. Paeth, eds., *Public Theology for a Global Society: Essays in Honor of Max L. Stackhouse* (Grand Rapids: Eerdmans, 2010), ix.

55. See E. Harold Breitenberg Jr., "What Is Public Theology?," in ibid., 6.

56. Richard J. Mouw, "Foreword," in *Evangelicals on Public Policy Issues: Sustaining a Respectful Political Conversation*, ed. Harold Heie (Abilene, TX: Abilene Christian University Press, 2014), 9.

57. Richard Lints, "Introduction," in Lints, *Renewing the Evangelical Mission*, 4. For a broader account of this development, see Brian Steensland and Philip Goff, eds., *The New Evangelical Social Engagement* (Oxford: Oxford University Press, 2013).

58. See further the twelve case studies in Heie, *Evangelicals on Public Policy Issues*.

59. The classic statement is Walter Rauschenbusch, *A Theology for the Social Gospel* (New York: Macmillan, 1917).

60. Miroslav Volf, *A Public Faith: How Followers of Christ Should Serve the Common Good* (Grand Rapids: Brazos, 2011), xvi.

61. Rowan Williams, *Faith in the Public Square* (London: Bloomsbury, 2012), 2.

62. Ibid., 319.

63. J. G. Millar, "People of God," in *New Dictionary of Biblical Theology*, ed. T. D. Alexander and Brian S. Rosner (Downers Grove, IL: InterVarsity, 2000), 684.

64. Lesslie Newbigin, "The Congregation as Hermeneutic of the Gospel," in *The Gospel in a Pluralist Society* (Grand Rapids: Eerdmans, 1989), 222–33.

65. "A trinitarian understanding of God cannot become part of public truth except through the acknowledgement of the universal lordship and saviorhood of Jesus Christ" (Lesslie Newbigin, "The Trinity as Public Truth," in *The Trinity in a Pluralistic Age: Theological Essays on Culture and Religion*, ed. Kevin J. Vanhoozer [Grand Rapids: Eerdmans, 1997], 8).

66. Observant readers will have spotted the church spire just off Main Street in the picture on our book's cover.

67. Newbigin, "Trinity as Public Truth," 8.

68. Eugene Peterson, "Letter to a Young Pastor," in *Pastor*, 316.

69. Lesslie Newbigin, "Ministerial Leadership for a Missionary Congregation," in *The Gospel in a Pluralist Society* (Grand Rapids: Eerdmans, 1989), 234.

70. Thomas C. Oden, *Pastoral Theology: Essentials of Ministry* (New York: HarperOne, 1983), 50–52. See also Timothy Laniak, *Shepherds after My Own Heart: Pastoral Traditions and Leadership in the Bible* (Downers Grove, IL: InterVarsity, 2006). In contrast, Andrew Purves sees four problems that arise from the shepherding metaphor, including its tendency to encourage (1) a functional gap between "professional" shepherds and their sheep and (2) an imitative rather than participatory relationship to Jesus Christ (*Reconstructing Pastoral Theology*, xxvi–xxx).

71. Oden, *Pastoral Theology*, 51.

72. Newbigin, "Ministerial Leadership," 241.

73. King James Version. I take the term "organic intellectual" from Antonio Gramsci, a twentieth-century Italian social theorist and literary critic. See especially his *Selections from the Prison Notebooks*, ed. Quentin Hoare and Geoffrey Newell Smith (New York: International Publishers, 1971). See further Steven J. Jones, *Antonio Gramsci* (London: Routledge, 2006).

74. Gramsci distinguishes "traditional" intellectuals who reinforce existing social institutions and ideologies from "organic" intellectuals who represent the interests of "the people," by which Gramsci meant the working class. Gramsci himself associated "ecclesiastics" (i.e., theologians) with "traditional" intellectuals inasmuch as they enforce orthodoxy. In associating theologians with organic intellectuals, I am creatively appropriating Gramsci's ideas for my own purposes.

75. Gramsci, *Selections from the Prison Notebooks*, 10.

76. One Gramsci scholar designates Bishop Samuel Ruiz Garcia an organic intellectual because of his consciousness-raising efforts among peasants in Latin America. See Adam Morton, *Unravelling Gramsci: Hegemony and Passive Revolution in the Global Economy* (London: Pluto, 2007), 181–82.

77. For Gramsci, language is not an impersonal sign-system but the medium of social relations. This accords with the biblical emphasis on language as a medium of covenantal relations (i.e., interpersonal address) and with the pastor's task of ministering to people in, with, and through words.

78. David Wells, *The Courage to Be Protestant* (Grand Rapids: Eerdmans, 2008), 40.

79. More specifically: what the Father is doing in the Son through the Spirit is the overarching idea at the heart of the Scriptures, the concept that serves as the pastor-theologian's lens for viewing everything else. The fox/hedgehog contrast comes from Isaiah Berlin's gloss upon an ancient Greek aphorism. Berlin uses the saying to contrast thinkers whose thought is dominated by a single big idea and those whose worldview incorporates a host of experiences and notions that cannot be integrated into a single idea. See Isaiah Berlin, *The Hedgehog and the Fox* (London: Weidenfeld & Nicolson, 1953).

80. I am grateful for comments on earlier drafts of my chapters, from Wayne Johnson, Derek Rishmawy, Greg Strand, and especially Paul Maxwell, who disagreed the loudest (and most often).

Chapter 1: Of Prophets, Priests, and Kings: A Brief Biblical Theology of the Pastorate

1. Iain Murray, *D. Martyn Lloyd-Jones: The Fight of Faith, 1939–1981* (Edinburgh: Banner of Truth, 1990), 113–15.

2. This was no mean act of courage, whether spiritual or otherwise. Several days later, Murray reports, a high-ranking officer in the British army said to a fellow officer, "I have seen many things in the trenches in France, but I have never seen anything more remarkable than the way that man went on with his prayer as though nothing had happened" (115).

3. We could also treat judges and other OT figures but will limit ourselves to the three offices related here due to their prominence in the life of the nation.

4. For different perspectives on the covenant of grace that share a rich appreciation for its salvific nature, see O. Palmer Robertson, *The Christ of the Covenants* (Phillipsburg, NJ: P&R, 1980); Peter J. Gentry and Stephen J. Wellum, *Kingdom through Covenant: A Biblical-Theological Understanding of the Covenants* (Wheaton: Crossway, 2012).

5. For more on the priest, see William R. Millar, *Priesthood in Ancient Israel: Understanding Biblical Themes* (St. Louis: Chalice, 2001); Aelred Cody, *A History of the Old Testament Priesthood*, Analecta biblica (Rome: Pontifical Biblical Institute, 1969).

6. See Eugene Peterson, *Eat This Book: A Conversation in the Art of Spiritual Reading* (Grand Rapids: Eerdmans, 2006).

7. Ada Taggar-Cohen picks up the covenantal thread of this text by observing that it outlines "the special covenantal status" of the priests and Levites. As ministers of the covenant, priests and Levites ushered the Israelites into daily living before the Lord. The covenant, as we noted earlier, ordered reality. Taggar-Cohen, "Covenant Priesthood: Cross-Cultural Legal and Religious Aspects of Biblical and Hittite Priesthood," in *Levites and Priests in Biblical History and Tradition*, ed. Mark Leuchter and Jeremy M. Hutton, 11–24 (Atlanta: Society of Biblical Literature, 2011), 17.

8. One book that treats the law in this manner—and that fails adequately to treat promise and fulfillment as crucial biblical-theological categories—is A. J. Jacobs, *The Year of Living Biblically: One Man's Humble Quest to Follow the Bible as Literally as Possible* (New York: Simon & Schuster, 2007).

9. P. Ellingsworth, "Priests," in *New Dictionary of Biblical Theology*, ed. T. D. Alexander and B. S. Rosner (Downers Grove, IL: InterVarsity, 2000), 698.

10. James M. Hamilton Jr., *God's Glory in Salvation through Judgment: A Biblical Theology* (Wheaton: Crossway, 2010), 111.

11. Gordon Wenham, *The Book of Leviticus*, New International Commentary on the Old Testament (Grand Rapids: Eerdmans, 1979), 27. Wenham argues that the Levitical law drove the people to see that the "whole of man's life must be lived out in the presence of God" (17).

12. Walter Brueggemann, *Theology of the Old Testament: Testimony, Dispute, Advocacy* (Minneapolis: Fortress, 1997), 623.

13. Walter C. Kaiser Jr., *Toward an Old Testament Theology* (Grand Rapids: Zondervan, 1978), 228.

14. Paul House, *Old Testament Theology* (Downers Grove, IL: InterVarsity, 1998), 222.

15. W. A. Grudem, "Prophecy/Prophets," in *New Dictionary of Biblical Theology*, 704.

16. Abraham Heschel, *The Prophets* (San Francisco: HarperCollins, 2001), 73.

17. Graeme Goldsworthy, "Kingdom of God," in *New Dictionary of Biblical Theology*, 619.

18. Ibid., 637–38.

19. For more on the type and antitype of king and kingdom, see Graeme Goldsworthy, *Gospel and Kingdom*, in *The Goldsworthy Trilogy* (Cumbria, UK: Paternoster, 2000), 1–148.

20. C. G. Kruse, "Ministry," in *Dictionary of Paul and His Letters*, ed. Gerald F. Hawthorne, Ralph P. Martin, and Daniel G. Reid (Downers Grove, IL: InterVarsity, 1993), 605.

21. Eugene H. Peterson, *The Pastor: A Memoir* (New York: HarperOne, 2011), 308. For a helpful treatment of life in union with Christ and its implications for all of life, see J. Todd Billings, *Union with Christ: Reframing Theology and Ministry for the Church* (Grand Rapids: Baker Academic, 2011).

22. As Timothy Laniak has said, "The wide range of activities involved in shepherding is determined by the daily and seasonal needs of the animals. Consequently, attentive and careful shepherds become endeared to their flocks." Laniak, *Shepherds after My Own Heart: Pastoral Traditions and Leadership in the Bible*, New Studies in Biblical Theology (Downers Grove, IL: InterVarsity, 2006), 56–57.

23. We are reminded of the judgment of Samuel Wells on the centrality of Christ: "The Bible is about Jesus," for "Jesus was God's plan all along." Wells, *Speaking the Truth: Preaching in a Pluralistic Culture* (Nashville: Abingdon, 2008), 40.

24. For the text of the Heidelberg Disputation, which includes this commentary, see Gerhard Forde, *On Being a Theologian of the Cross: Reflections on Luther's Heidelberg Disputation, 1518* (Grand Rapids: Eerdmans, 1997); see also Alister McGrath, *Luther's Theology of the Cross: Martin Luther's Theological Breakthrough* (Oxford: Blackwell, 1985).

25. For an excellent treatment of this interlaced theme, see Jeremy R. Treat, *The Crucified King: Atonement and Kingdom in Biblical and Systematic Theology* (Grand Rapids: Zondervan, 2014).

26. J. R. R. Tolkien, "On Fairy-Stories," in *Essays Presented to Charles Williams*, ed. C. S. Lewis (Grand Rapids: Eerdmans, 1966), 81.

27. See also P. T. Forsyth, who spoke of the need of the preacher to unveil the unseen world: "The only business of the apostolic preacher is to make men practically realize a world unseen and spiritual." Forsyth, *Positive Preaching and the Modern Mind* (New York: Armstrong, 1907), 3–4; cited in Richard Lischer, ed., *The Company of Preachers: Wisdom on Preaching—Augustine to the Present* (Grand Rapids: Eerdmans, 2002), 99.

28. In relation to this text, Timothy Keller states: "Paul says he deliberately eschewed the typical forms of rhetoric and logic used by Greek orators." Instead, "he wanted the Spirit to work with power on the hearers, and therefore he was careful not to make his messages too much like a logical "lecture." Keller, "Preaching the Gospel in a Post-Modern World" (Jackson, MS: Christian Reformed Seminary, 2002), 15. https://simeon.org/cst/media/doc-tkeller-preaching syllabus.pdf.

29. See Kruse's words on Paul's ministry: "Through his apostolic preaching of the gospel he betrothed people to Christ. . . . Such devotion was under threat when their thoughts were led astray by false teaching, and so the apostle sought by all means to make plain to them the truth of the gospel" (Kruse, "Ministry," 606).

30. Paul was the preeminent pastor-theologian: "Paul's letters are a clear testimony to his pastoral heart. Indeed his letters are a product of his pastoral care, for through them Paul exercised a pastoral role in regard to the churches that he or his converts had founded. Paul was no academic theologian, far removed from the realities of church life; rather it was his concern for the churches which proved to be the springboard for his theology." P. Beasley-Murray, "Paul as Pastor," in *Dictionary of Paul and His Letters*, ed. Gerald F. Hawthorne, Ralph P. Martin, and Daniel G. Reid (Downers Grove, IL: InterVarsity, 1993), 654.

31. "The preacher who loves God with the mind and thinks with the heart will thoughtfully and lovingly ask, how, *theologically* speaking, shall this specific congregation be addressed?" John M. Stapleton, "Loving God with the Mind and Thinking with the Heart," in *The Power to Comprehend with All the Saints: The Formation and Practice of a Pastor-Theologian*, ed. Wallace M. Alston Jr. and Cynthia A. Jarvis (Grand Rapids: Eerdmans, 2009), 211.

32. Carl R. Trueman, "The Preacher as Prophet: Some Notes on the Nature of Preaching," in *The People's Theologian: Writings in Honour of Donald Macleod*, ed. Iain D. Campbell and Malcolm Maclean (Glasgow: Mentor, 2011), 205.

33. Without the personal dimension, preaching will be a lecture, a well-intended but insufficient intellectual exercise. We mark Lloyd-Jones's classic description of preaching: "logic on fire." See D. Martyn Lloyd-Jones, *Preaching and Preachers* (Grand Rapids: Zondervan, 1972), 97.

34. We are reminded of the words of R. Albert Mohler Jr. on the nature of the pastorate: "There is no more theological calling than this—guard the flock of God for the sake of God's truth." Mohler, *He Is Not Silent: Preaching in a Postmodern World* (Chicago: Moody, 2008), 107.

Notes to Pastoral Perspectives for Chapter 1

1. David J. Bosch, *Transforming Mission: Paradigm Shifts in Theology of Mission* (Maryknoll, NY: Orbis, 1991), 16.

2. This last remark is a close paraphrase of a comment by Ed Stetzer as reported in "Not Tweeting? Repent: Ed Stetzer on Why Ignoring Social Media Is No Longer an Option for Church Leaders," *Leadership Magazine* 34 (2013): 29.

3. I have, however, benefited from George Pattison, *Thinking about God in an Age of Technology* (Oxford: Oxford University Press, 2005); Jacques Ellul, *The Technological Bluff* (Grand

Rapids: Eerdmans, 1990); Quentin Schultze, *Habits of the High-Tech Heart* (Grand Rapids: Baker Books, 2002); John Dyer, *From the Garden to the City* (Grand Rapids: Kregel, 2011); and Arthur Boers, *Living into Focus* (Grand Rapids: Brazos, 2012).

4. Read Bain, "Technology and State Government," *American Sociological Review* 2 (December 1937): 860.

5. Money demonstrates these same two tendencies.

Chapter 2: Of Scholars and Saints: A Brief History of the Pastorate

1. Douglas Sweeney, *Jonathan Edwards and the Ministry of the Word* (Downers Grove, IL: InterVarsity, 2009), 199.

2. David Wells, *The Courage to Be Protestant* (Grand Rapids: Eerdmans, 2008), 40.

3. Irenaeus, *Against Heresies* 1.10.1; in *Apostolic Fathers with Justin Martyr and Irenaeus*, vol. 1 of *The Ante-Nicene Fathers*, ed. Philip Schaff (Edinburgh: T&T Clark, 1887), 330–31.

4. Fred Sanders, *The Deep Things of God: How the Trinity Changes Everything* (Wheaton: Crossway, 2012), cf. 8–12.

5. The *Shepherd of Hermas*, in *The Apostolic Fathers: The Shepherd of Hermas; The Martyrdom of Polycarp; The Epistle of Diognetus* (New York: Putnam, 1917), 39.

6. See the official documents at http://www.fordham.edu/halsall/basis/nicea1.txt. Valuable commentary on these developments is found in Chad Brand, Daniel L. Akin, and R. Stanton Norman, *Perspectives on Church Government: Five Views of Church Polity* (Nashville: B&H, 2004), 172–74.

7. See Alistair C. Stewart, *The Original Bishops: Office and Order in the First Christian Communities* (Grand Rapids: Baker Academic, 2014).

8. John Chrysostom, *On the Priesthood* 6.4.9; in *On the Priesthood, Ascetic Treatises, Select Homilies and Letters, Homilies on the Statues*, vol. 9 of *Nicene and Post-Nicene Fathers of the Christian Church*, ed. Philip Schaff (New York: Christian Literature Publishing Library, 1886), 69.

9. "For John Chrysostom, the ministry of the church is to be understood and practiced solely in terms of spiritual and theological criteria . . . that [pastoral] office also must be understood theologically first of all to be a sharing in Christ's own love for his people." Andrew Purves, *Pastoral Theology in the Classical Tradition* (Louisville: Westminster John Knox, 2001), 43.

10. Letter 73, Augustine to Jerome (AD 404), in *St. Augustine's Life and Work, Confessions, Letters*, vol. 1 of *Nicene and Post-Nicene Fathers of the Christian Church*, ed. Philip Schaff (New York: Christian Literature Publishing Library, 1886), 331.

11. Michael Pasquarello III, *Sacred Rhetoric: Preaching as a Theological and Pastoral Practice of the Church* (Grand Rapids: Eerdmans, 2005), 21.

12. I have referenced the classic trinity of *theologia*, *habitus*, and *sapientia* in offering this formulation. See ibid., 21. See also the stimulating discussion in Kevin J. Vanhoozer, *The Drama of Doctrine: A Canonical-Linguistic Approach to Christian Theology* (Louisville: Westminster John Knox, 2005), 252–56.

13. Augustine, *On Christian Doctrine* 4.4.6; in *St. Augustine: City of God and Christian Doctrine*, vol. 2 of *Nicene and Post-Nicene Fathers of the Christian Church*, ed. Philip Schaff (Buffalo: Christian Literature, 1887), 576.

14. Augustine, *Letters: Volume 1*, Fathers of the Church 12 (Washington, DC: Catholic University Press of America, 2008), 48.

15. "She . . . should not claim for herself any function proper to a man, especially the sacerdotal office [*nedum sacerdotalis officii*]." Tertullian, *De virginibus velandis* 9.1; in *Tertulliani Opera*, ed. E. Dekkers (Turnhout: Brepols, 1954).

16. Hippolytus, *The Apostolic Tradition*, in *The Treatise on the Apostolic Tradition of St. Hippolytus of Rome, Bishop and Martyr*, ed. Gregory Dix (London: Alban, 1992), 18.

17. Gregory, *The Book of Pastoral Rule: St. Gregory the Great*, Popular Patristics Series (Crestwood, NY: St. Vladimir's Seminary Press, 2007), 29.

18. Thomas Aquinas, *Summa Theologica* (Raleigh, NC: Hayes Barton, 1985), 2:4350.

19. See John Calvin, "Draft Ecclesiastical Ordinances" (1541), in *Calvin's Theological Treatises*, ed. J. K. S. Reid, Library of Christian Classics 22 (Philadelphia: Westminster, 1954), 58; idem, *Institutes of the Christian Religion*, ed. J. T. McNeill, trans. F. L. Battles, Library of Christian Classics 21 (Philadelphia: Westminster, 1960), 2:1068–69 (4.4.1).

20. Martin Luther, "Lectures on Galatians," in *Martin Luther's Basic Theological Writings*, ed. Timothy Lull (Minneapolis: Fortress, 2005), 23.

21. Calvin, *Institutes of the Christian Religion*, 2:1156–57 (4.8.9).

22. John Dillenberger, *John Calvin: Selections from His Writings* (Atlanta: Scholars Press, 1975), 35.

23. Scott M. Manetsch, *Calvin's Company of Pastors: Pastoral Care and the Emerging Reformed Church, 1536–1609*, Oxford Studies in Historical Theology (Oxford: Oxford University Press, 2013), 190.

24. Ibid., 188.

25. Ibid., 190.

26. Thomas Randolph to Sir William Cecil, September 24, 1561, cited in W. Stanford Reid, *Trumpeter of God: A Biography of John Knox* (New York: Charles Scribner's Sons, 1974), 216.

27. William Ames, *The Marrow of Theology* (Grand Rapids: Baker, 1997), 77.

28. Richard Sibbes, *The Bruised Reed*, Puritan Paperbacks (Carlisle, PA: Banner of Truth, 1998), 3–4.

29. Ibid., 34.

30. Richard Baxter, *The Reformed Pastor*, Puritan Paperbacks (Carlisle, PA: Banner of Truth, 1974), 177.

31. Purves, *Pastoral Theology in the Classical Tradition*, 113.

32. J. I. Packer, *A Quest for Godliness: The Puritan Vision of the Christian Life* (Wheaton: Crossway, 1994), 102.

33. Ibid., 103.

34. Jonathan Edwards, "Pastor and People Must Look to God," in *The Salvation of Souls: Nine Previously Unpublished Sermons on the Call of Ministry and the Gospel*, ed. Richard Bailey and Gregory Wills (Wheaton: Crossway, 2002), 142.

35. Robert Caldwell, "The Ministerial Ideal in the Ordination Sermons of Jonathan Edwards: Four Theological Portraits," *Themelios* 38, no. 3 (November 2013): 390–401, http://legacy.thegospelcoalition .org/themelios/article/the_ministerial_ideal_in_the_ordination_sermons_of_jonathan_edwards.

36. Jonathan Edwards, "The Excellency of Christ," in *Sermons and Discourses, 1734–38*, vol. 19 of *The Works of Jonathan Edwards*, ed. M. X. Lesser (New Haven: Yale University Press, 2001), 588.

37. Richard A. Bailey, "Driven by Passion: Jonathan Edwards and the Art of Preaching," in *The Legacy of Jonathan Edwards: American Religion and the Evangelical Tradition*, ed. D. G. Hart, Sean Michael Lucas, and Stephen Nichols (Grand Rapids: Baker Academic, 2007), 70.

38. E. Brooks Holifield, *God's Ambassadors: A History of the Christian Clergy in America* (Grand Rapids: Eerdmans, 2007), 78.

39. Nathan Hatch, *The Democratization of American Christianity* (New Haven: Yale University Press, 1991), 3.

40. Charles G. Finney, *Lectures on Systematic Theology* (London: William Tegg, 1851), 35.

41. Charles G. Finney, *Lectures on Revivals of Religion*, ed. William G. McLoughlin (Cambridge, MA: Harvard University Press, 1960), 13.

42. Randall Herbert Balmer and Lauren F. Winner, *Protestantism in America*, Columbia Contemporary American Religion Series (New York: Columbia University Press, 2005), 59.

43. Hatch, *Democratization of American Christianity*, 57.

44. George Marsden, *The Soul of the American University: From Protestant Establishment to Established Nonbelief* (Oxford: Oxford University Press, 1994), 105, 154–55.

45. Holifield, *God's Ambassadors*, 173–74.

46. See E. Brooks Holifield, *A History of Pastoral Care in America* (Nashville: Abingdon, 1983).

47. H. Richard Niebuhr, *The Purpose of the Church and Its Ministry* (New York: Harper & Brothers, 1956), 81.

48. George Marsden, *Fundamentalism and American Culture: The Shaping of Twentieth Century Evangelicalism, 1870–1925* (1980; repr., Oxford: Oxford University Press, 2006), 130.

49. Harold J. Ockenga, "Challenge to the Christian Civilization of the West" (Fuller Theological Seminary Convocation Address, Delivered on October 1, 1947, in Pasadena, CA, Ockenga Papers, Gordon-Conwell Theological Seminary, South Hamilton, MA), 9.

50. For more on the neoevangelical effort to catalyze the Christian intellect, see the forthcoming work by Owen Strachan, *The Reawakening of the Evangelical Mind* (Grand Rapids: Zondervan, 2015). See also Garth M. Rosell, *The Surprising Work of God: Harold John Ockenga, Billy Graham, and the Rebirth of Evangelicalism* (Grand Rapids: Baker Academic, 2008); Owen D. Strachan, "Reenchanting the Evangelical Mind: Park Street Church's Harold Ockenga, the Boston Scholars, and the Mid-century Intellectual Surge" (PhD diss., Trinity Evangelical Divinity School, 2011).

51. Cormac McCarthy, *The Road* (New York: Knopf, 2006), 70.

Notes to Pastoral Perspectives for Chapter 2

1. More fully, "What are the distinguishing qualifications of those that are in favor with God, and entitled to his eternal rewards? Or, which comes to the same thing, What is the nature of true religion? and wherein lie the distinguishing notes of that virtue which is acceptable in the sight of God?" Jonathan Edwards, *A Treatise concerning Religious Affections*, in *The Works of Jonathan Edwards* (Carlisle, PA: Banner of Truth, 1984), 1:234.

2. Ibid.

3. See Edwards, *A Faithful Narrative of the Surprising Work of God*, http://www.jonathan-edwards.org/Narrative.html.

4. All names have been changed.

5. Adapted from Charles Wesley's marvelous hymn: "Long my imprisoned spirit lay, fast bound in sin and nature's night. Thine eye diffused a quick'ning ray—I woke, the dungeon flamed with light. My chains fell off, my heart was free; I rose, went forth, and followed Thee."

Chapter 3: In the Evangelical Mood: The Purpose of the Pastor-Theologian

1. Cf. Paul W. Pruyser: "I have the growing conviction that people turn to pastors—correctly—because they want to have the opportunity *to look at themselves and their problems in the light of their faith and their religious tradition*, with the help of an expert in just this perspective." "The Diagnostic Process in Pastoral Care," in *Psychiatry, Ministry, and Pastoral Counseling*, ed. A. W. Richard Sipe and Clarence J. Rowe (Collegeville, MN: Liturgical Press, 1984), 109.

2. What of churches with several pastors? Do they all need to be public theologians? Must each be able to minister in exactly the same way, effectively ignoring their own gifts in a particular area? This is a complex question. The short answer is yes: they all need to be public theologians in the sense that, whatever their particular role or ministry, they are all working with people, and what they have to contribute theologically is the ability to view all of life, and to interpret every situation, in terms of the overall drama of redemption, that is, in terms of what the Triune God is doing to sum up all things in Christ.

3. Seneca, *On the Shortness of Life*, trans. C. D. N. Costa (London: Penguin, 2004), 1–33.

4. Paul Tillich, *The Courage to Be* (New Haven: Yale University Press, 1952), 46–50. "Age of Anxiety" is also the name of a 1948 Pulitzer prize–winning poem by W. H. Auden and of the symphony by Leonard Bernstein, which Auden's poem inspired. For his part, Tillich felt that every age of human history is prone to a certain kind of anxiety, be it ontic, moral, or spiritual (see *Courage to Be*, 57–63).

5. See Medco Health Solution's "America's State of Mind Report" on mental health medication trends from 2001–2010, http://apps.who.int/medicinedocs/documents/s19032en/s19032en.pdf.

6. The primary source for this material on Martin Heidegger is his *Being and Time*, trans. John Macquarrie and Edward Robinson (Oxford: Blackwell, 1980).

7. Søren Kierkegaard, *The Sickness unto Death: A Christian Psychological Exposition for Upbuilding and Awakening*, vol. 19 of *Kierkegaard's Writings* (Princeton: Princeton University Press, 2013), 5.

8. Sarah Bachelard, *Resurrection and Moral Imagination* (Farnham, Surrey, UK; Burlington, VT: Ashgate, 2014), 2. See also Oliver O'Donovan, *Resurrection and Moral Order: An Outline for Evangelical Ethics* (Grand Rapids: Eerdmans, 1986).

9. N. T. Wright, *The Resurrection of the Son of God* (Minneapolis: Fortress, 2003), 578.

10. See also Pope Francis, *The Joy of the Gospel: Evangelii Gaudium* (Frederick, MD: Word among Us, 2014).

11. For more on theological moods, see David F. Ford, *The Future of Christian Theology* (Oxford: Wiley-Blackwell, 2011), 71–83.

12. According to Rowan Williams, metaphysics—the philosophical study of *what is*—is best understood in terms of our underlying convictions about the ways things are implied by our most important practices. "Between Politics and Metaphysics: Reflections in the Wake of Gillian Rose," *Modern Theology* 11 (1995): 6.

13. See further Wright, *Resurrection of the Son of God*, 679–82.

14. In the next chapter we shall see that pastor-theologians serve the bread and the wine with a similar aim: to nourish and build up the body of Christ.

15. E. D. Hirsch, *Cultural Literacy* (New York: Vintage Books, 1988).

16. Ibid., xiii.

17. See Kevin J. Vanhoozer, "Scripture and Hermeneutics," in *Oxford Handbook of Evangelical Theology*, ed. Gerald McDermott (Oxford: Oxford University Press, 2010), 35–52; idem, "Ascending the Mountain, Singing the Rock: Biblical Interpretation Earthed, Typed, and Transfigured," *Modern Theology* 28, no. 4 (2012): 781–803; idem, "Interpreting Scripture between the Rock of Biblical Studies and the Hard Place of Systematic Theology: The State of the Evangelical (Dis)union," in *Renewing the Evangelical Mission*, ed. Richard Lints (Grand Rapids: Eerdmans, 2013), 201–25.

18. See the fine discussion in James M. Hamilton Jr., *What Is Biblical Theology? A Guide to the Bible's Story, Symbolism, and Patterns* (Wheaton: Crossway, 2014).

19. Jonathan Edwards, "The Church's Marriage to Her Sons, and to Her God," in *Sermons and Discourses, 1743–1758*, vol. 25 of *The Works of Jonathan Edwards* (New Haven: Yale University Press, 2006), 187.

20. American Standard Version. The reference is to Isaiah Berlin's distinction between two kinds of thinkers: foxes who draw upon a wide stock of different kinds of knowledge, and hedgehogs who tend to interpret everything through the lens of a single defining idea. Berlin bases his distinction on a line from ancient Greek poetry: "The fox knows many things, but the hedgehog knows one great thing" (Archilochus, fragment 103). See Isaiah Berlin, *The Hedgehog and the Fox: An Essay on Tolstoy's View of History* (London: Weidenfeld & Nicolson, 1953).

21. See further James K. A. Smith, *Desiring the Kingdom: Worship, Worldview, and Cultural Formation* (Grand Rapids: Baker Academic, 2009).

22. "Moralistic Therapeutic Deism" is how Christian Smith describes the theology of America's teenagers. See Christian Smith and Melinda Lundquist Denton, *Soul Searching: The Religious and Spiritual Lives of American Teenagers* (Oxford: Oxford University Press, 2005).

23. Carl F. H. Henry, *God Who Speaks and Shows: Preliminary Considerations*, vol. 1 of *God, Revelation, and Authority* (Waco: Word Books, 1976), 1.

24. For more on the particulars of interpreting culture theologically, see Kevin J. Vanhoozer, "What Is Everyday Theology: How and Why Christians Should Read Culture," in *Everyday*

Theology: How to Read Cultural Texts and Interpret Trends, ed. Kevin J. Vanhoozer, Charles A. Anderson, and Michael J. Sleasman (Grand Rapids: Baker Academic, 2007), 15–62.

25. For the role of imagination in understanding where we are, see Kevin J. Vanhoozer, "In Bright Shadow: C. S. Lewis on the Imagination for Theology and Discipleship," in *The Romantic Rationalist: God, Life, and Imagination in the Work of C. S. Lewis*, ed. John Piper and David Mathis (Wheaton: Crossway, 2014), 81–104.

26. Andrew Purves, *Pastoral Theology in the Classical Tradition* (Louisville: Westminster John Knox, 2001), 120.

27. The next chapter nevertheless commends the practice of pastoral visitation. Pastors must have firsthand personal knowledge of their congregants as well as being students of the human condition via literature.

28. C. S. Lewis, *An Experiment in Criticism* (Cambridge: Cambridge University Press, 1961), 141.

29. Lesslie Newbigin, *Foolishness to the Greeks: The Gospel and Western Culture* (Grand Rapids: Eerdmans, 1986).

30. Cornelius Plantinga, *Reading for Preaching: The Preacher in Conversation with Storytellers, Biographers, Poets, and Journalists* (Grand Rapids: Eerdmans, 2014), 42. See also his pastoral reflection elsewhere in the present book.

31. Similar shifts in mood from indicative to imperatival discourse occur in Eph. 4:1 and Phil. 2:12.

32. Richard B. Gaffin Jr., *By Faith, Not by Sight*, 2nd ed. (Phillipsburg, NJ: P&R, 2013), 82.

33. The Johannine Epistles similarly refer to "doing the truth" (1 John 1:6 KJV altered), and Paul can also speak of truth as something that is to be obeyed (Rom. 2:8).

34. See the excursus on "godliness" in Philip H. Towner, *The Letters to Timothy and Titus*, New International Commentary on the New Testament (Grand Rapids: Eerdmans, 2006), 171–74.

35. Oliver O'Donovan, *Resurrection and Moral Order: An Outline for Evangelical Ethics* (Grand Rapids: Eerdmans, 1986), 15.

36. Ibid., 25.

37. Ibid., 236.

38. C. S. Lewis, *Mere Christianity* (Glasgow: Collins, 1955), 171.

39. See further Jason B. Hood, *Imitating God in Christ: Recapturing a Biblical Pattern* (Downers Grove, IL: InterVarsity, 2013).

40. One of the most important things pastor-theologians can do is help the church understand the nature of this eschatological *is*.

41. Bonhoeffer, *Ethics*, vol. 6 of *Dietrich Bonhoeffer Works* (Minneapolis: Fortress, 2005), 49–50.

42. Christopher R. J. Holmes, *Ethics in the Presence of Christ* (London: T&T Clark, 2012), 12.

43. For more on the idea of putting on Christ, see Kevin J. Vanhoozer, *Faith Speaking Understanding*, chap. 5, "Learning (and Becoming) the Part: 'Little Christs.'"

44. Wallace M. Alston Jr., "The Education of a Pastor-Theologian: Toward a Learned Ministry," in *The Power to Comprehend with All the Saints: The Formation and Practice of a Pastor-Theologian*, ed. Wallace M. Alston Jr. and Cynthia A. Jarvis (Grand Rapids: Eerdmans, 2009), 68.

45. It is an open question whether wisdom can be taught but, if it can be, then perhaps the best way to do so is by apprenticing younger pastors to those who have more experience. Many seminaries require MDiv students to have an internship experience, but typically this is a practical thing that happens independently of the rest of the curriculum. Seminaries and local churches would do well to work together to create internship experiences that would expose students to a series of real-life case studies, which could provide helpful curricular capstone experiences as well as opportunities for learning in a mentoring relationship.

46. Ibid., 79.

47. Sarah Coakley suggests something similar in a 2012 interview, "Ministry Is Not Easier than Theology," http://www.faithandleadership.com/multimedia/sarah-coakley-ministry-not-easier-theology.

48. Purves, *Pastoral Theology in the Classical Tradition*, 121.

Notes to Pastoral Perspectives for Chapter 3

1. For a thought-provoking aesthetic of this kind of life, see N. D. Wilson, *Death by Living* (Nashville: Nelson, 2013).

2. Ernest Becker, *The Denial of Death* (New York: Free Press, 1973).

3. John Steinbeck, *East of Eden* (New York: Viking, 1952), chap. 24.

Chapter 4: Artisans in the House of God: The Practices of the Pastor-Theologian

1. Thomas C. Oden, *Pastoral Theology: Essentials of Ministry* (New York: HarperOne, 1983), 313.

2. Andrew Purves makes the point by paraphrasing Athanasius: "The ministry that is not assumed by Jesus Christ is the ministry that is not healed, but that languishes in the pride of our own attempts to storm heaven." Purves, *Reconstructing Pastoral Theology: A Christological Foundation* (Louisville: Westminster John Knox, 2004), ix.

3. Ibid., xxiii.

4. Purves unpacks what is in Christ in similar terms. He examines a fourfold ministry that stems from union with Christ: a ministry of the word, grace, presence, and reign of God (*Reconstructing Pastoral Theology*, part 2).

5. The New Testament categories for church leadership are somewhat fluid. It is the privilege and responsibility of all church elders, and not pastors only, to help church members grow in Christian maturity (Eph. 4:11–13). On church elders, see Jeramie Rinne, *Church Elders: How to Shepherd God's People Like Jesus* (Wheaton: Crossway, 2014).

6. Jonathan Leeman, *Church Membership: How the World Knows Who Represents Jesus* (Wheaton: Crossway, 2012), 27.

7. Grant Osborne, *Matthew*, Zondervan Exegetical Commentary on the New Testament (Grand Rapids: Zondervan, 2010), 627.

8. Ibid.

9. Robert H. Gundry, *Commentary on the New Testament: Verse-by-Verse Explanations with a Literal Translation* (Peabody, MA: Hendrickson, 2010), 72.

10. For a comprehensive defense of "this rock" as referring to the content of Peter's confession, see Chrys C. Caragounis, *Peter and the Rock* (Berlin: de Gruyter, 1989).

11. Jonathan Leeman makes the additional point that the keys of the kingdom mentioned in Matt. 16:19 concern the authority for deciding whose confessions are in line with the gospel and which confessors represent the kingdom of heaven. *Church Membership: How the World Knows Who Represents Jesus* (Wheaton: Crossway, 2012), 58–59.

12. Douglas Harink, *1 and 2 Peter*, Brazos Theological Commentary on the Bible (Grand Rapids: Brazos, 2009), 124.

13. Eugene H. Peterson, "Curing Souls: The Forgotten Art," *Leadership Journal* 4 (Summer 1983): 48–60.

14. This is the thesis of Boyd Taylor Coolman, *The Theology of Hugh of St. Victor: An Interpretation* (Cambridge: Cambridge University Press, 2010).

15. Ibid., 27.

16. Rhys S. Bezzant, *Jonathan Edwards and the Church* (Oxford: Oxford University Press, 2014), 107.

17. Matthew Levering, *Ezra and Nehemiah*, Brazos Theological Commentary on the Bible (Grand Rapids: Brazos, 2007), 20n2.

18. Mark A. Throntveit argues that the overriding theological concern of the book of Ezra is "to encourage the community to be the people of God within the political structures that presently obtain." *Ezra-Nehemiah*, Interpretation (Louisville: Westminster John Knox, 1992), 31.

19. Bede, *On Ezra and Nehemiah*, trans. Scott DeGregorio (Liverpool: Liverpool University Press, 2006), 1–2.

20. H. G. M. Williamson notes how the book of Ezra depicts the return of the exiles typologically, as a second exodus, and thus an act of divine grace. *Ezra, Nehemiah*, Word Biblical Commentary (Nashville: Nelson, 1985), 20, 111.

21. Ibid., 92. On Ezra as priest, see Throntveit, *Ezra-Nehemiah*, 40–41.

22. Derek Kidner, *Ezra and Nehemiah: An Introduction and Commentary*, Tyndale Old Testament Commentaries (Leicester, UK: Inter-Varsity, 1979), 62.

23. Bede, *On Ezra and Nehemiah*, 108.

24. It is significant that the New Testament explicitly rules out divorce in the case of believers married to unbelievers (see 1 Cor. 7:12–13).

25. So Williamson, *Ezra, Nehemiah*, 160.

26. Bede, *On Ezra and Nehemiah*, 139.

27. Throntveit, *Ezra-Nehemiah*, 78.

28. Bede, *On Ezra and Nehemiah*, 178.

29. Throntveit (*Ezra-Nehemiah*, 110) suggests that the text presents Ezra as a second Moses and the reading/response as a covenant-renewal ceremony.

30. Harink, *1 and 2 Peter*, 69.

31. Peter O'Brien, *The Letter to the Ephesians*, Pillar New Testament Commentary (Grand Rapids: Eerdmans, 1999), 219.

32. Ibid., 221.

33. G. K. Beale, *The Temple and the Church's Mission: A Biblical Theology of the Dwelling Place of God* (Downers Grove, IL: InterVarsity, 2004), 48.

34. Timothy G. Gombis, *The Drama of Ephesians: Participating in the Triumph of God* (Downers Grove, IL: InterVarsity, 2010), 182.

35. James M. Hamilton Jr., *What Is Biblical Theology?* (Wheaton: Crossway, 2014), 106.

36. Conversely, we ought not to put a happy face on the crucifixion. The tension for the pastor-theologian is to convey the life of Jesus in our mortal flesh, and to remember that the one who is risen is also the one who was crucified (see 2 Cor. 4:10–12).

37. John H. Leith, *Introduction to the Reformed Tradition: A Way of Being the Christian Community* (Atlanta: John Knox Press, 1981), 85.

38. William H. Willimon, *Pastor: The Theology and Practice of Ordained Ministry* (Nashville: Abingdon, 2002), 183.

39. James G. Samra, *Being Conformed to Christ in Community: A Study of Maturity, Maturation and the Local Church in the Undisputed Pauline Epistles* (London: T&T Clark, 2006), 167–68. To "have [Christ's] mind" (Phil. 2:5) refers primarily not to copying his cognitive content (i.e., information) but rather to imitating his attitude (i.e., orientation).

40. Oden, *Pastoral Theology*, 314.

41. Ibid., *Theology*, 127.

42. See http://www.psychologytoday.com/blog/communication-success/201311/5-tips-reduce-the-fear-public-speaking.

43. John Durham Peters defines communication as "the project of reconciling self and other." *Speaking into the Air: A History of the Idea of Communication* (Chicago: University of Chicago Press, 1999), 9.

44. Andrew Purves, *The Resurrection of Ministry: Serving in the Hope of the Risen Lord* (Downers Grove, IL: InterVarsity, 2010), 37.

45. Herman Melville likens the pulpit to a prow of a ship in *Moby Dick*, chap. 8. Cf. Oden's four dimensions of preaching: the evangelical, pastoral, doctrinal, and morally formative (*Pastoral*

Theology, 128–29); David L. Bartlett, "Sermon," in *Concise Encyclopedia of Preaching*, ed. William H. Willimon and Richard Lischer (Louisville: Westminster John Knox, 1995), 433–37.

46. Churches that use lectionaries provide weekly opportunities for the pastor to relate the Old and New Testaments and thus to address the oldest theological question the early church had to face, namely, is the Old Testament the church's book? Is the God of Israel the same as the Father of Jesus Christ?

47. See Graeme Goldsworthy, *Preaching the Whole Bible as Christian Scripture* (Grand Rapids: Eerdmans, 2000).

48. See the essay by Samra in this volume, which addresses the question "How should the church think theologically about technology?"

49. "There is no shortage of formulas for creating a successfully constructed pastorate being peddled in the professional religious market today. All of these formulas are based on the assumption that pastors need to meet the expectations of those who are already in the church and especially of those who are not there yet." Craig M. Barnes, *The Pastor as Minor Poet: Texts and Subtexts in the Ministerial Life* (Grand Rapids: Eerdmans, 2009), 12.

50. In Calvin's words: "Let those who want to do well in carrying out the task of the ministry of the Word learn not only to converse and to speak publicly, but especially to penetrate through into the conscience so that people can see the crucified Christ and his very blood as it flows. If the church has that kind of artists, it will need neither wood nor stone, that is to say dead representations, and will in fact not need any images any more at all." Cited in Herman J. Selderhuis, *John Calvin: A Pilgrim's Life* (Downers Grove, IL: InterVarsity, 2009), 115.

51. "Major" poets provide enduring expressions of life's deepest truths. (God is a major poet!) "Minor" poets have the lesser but nevertheless crucial task of "inculcating that truth to particular people in particular places" (Barnes, *Pastor as Minor Poet*, 17).

52. L. Roger Owens, *The Shape of Participation: A Theology of Church Practices* (Eugene, OR: Cascade, 2010), 67.

53. The best-known manuals include Hippolytus, *Apostolic Tradition*; Augustine, *On the Instruction of Beginners*; and Gregory of Nyssa, *Great Catechetical Oration*.

54. Stephen E. Fowl comments, "Pastors and teachers are *themselves* the gifts given by the ascended Christ through the Spirit." *Ephesians: A Commentary*, New Testament Library (Louisville: Westminster John Knox, 2012), 130, emphasis original.

55. O'Brien, *Letter to the Ephesians*, 300.

56. Notice how the combination of biological (organic) and architectural (inorganic) imagery in Eph. 4:12 parallels a similar juxtaposition in 2:20–21.

57. Calvin, *Commentary*, on Eph. 4:11. Scott Manetsch notes, with regard to doctors of the church, that in Calvin's Geneva "their mandate extended beyond the local congregation to the larger church . . . and included the responsibility to teach future pastors and protect the church from doctrinal error." *Calvin's Company of Pastors: Pastoral Care and the Emerging Reformed Church, 1536–1609* (Oxford University Press, 2013), 28.

58. *Catechizing the Uninstructed* 3.5. Augustine is quite realistic and devotes several chapters to dealing with "the various causes producing weariness in the catechumen."

59. Calvin, letter to Edward Seymour, October 22, 1548 (cited in Manetsch, *Calvin's Company of Pastors*, 266).

60. Calvin's catechism served a pastoral purpose, providing instruction in doctrine, duty, and devotion alike (http://www.reformed.org/documents/calvin/geneva_catachism/geneva_catachism.html).

61. J. I. Packer, "Reflection and Response," in *J. I. Packer and the Evangelical Future: The Impact of His Life and Thought*, ed. Timothy George (Grand Rapids: Baker Academic, 2009), 174.

62. J. I. Packer with Gary A. Parrett, "The Return to Catechesis: Lessons from the Great Tradition," in *Renewing the Evangelical Mission*, ed. Richard Lints (Grand Rapids: Eerdmans, 2013), 112.

63. Ibid., 129.

64. See further J. I. Packer and Gary A. Parrett, *Grounded in the Gospel: Building Believers the Old-Fashioned Way* (Grand Rapids: Baker Books, 2010).

65. Cf. Packer, who makes a similar point in his "Reflection and Response," 174.

66. Elsewhere I compare learning doctrine to theatrical direction: doctrine helps disciples act out what is in Christ and thereby to play their parts in the drama of redemption. See especially Kevin J. Vanhoozer, *Faith Speaking Understanding: Performing the Drama of Doctrine* (Louisville: Westminster John Knox, 2014).

67. "As liturgical leader of the congregation the pastor is responsible for organizing, interpreting, and presiding over the whole arena of worship, usually in consultation with laity through a church commission on worship" (Oden, *Pastoral Theology*, 90).

68. Cf. Martin Luther, who said the purpose of worship is so "our Lord himself may speak to us through his holy word, and that we in turn may speak to him through our prayers and hymns" (cited in ibid., 91).

69. Ibid., 93.

70. This may be the theological equivalent of an old philosophical chestnut: "Why is there something rather than nothing?"

71. Graham Kendrick, *Learning to Worship as a Way of Life* (Minneapolis: Bethany House, 1985), 32.

72. It is probably no coincidence that many of the psalms were written by kings.

73. See Daniel Block, *For the Glory of the Lord: Recovering a Biblical Theology of Worship* (Grand Rapids: Baker Academic, 2014), 23–24.

74. David Peterson, *Engaging with God: A Biblical Theology of Worship* (1993; repr., Downers Grove, IL: InterVarsity, 2002), 18.

75. John E. Burkhart, *Worship: A Searching Examination of the Liturgical Experience* (Philadelphia: Westminster, 1982), 17.

76. See D. Peterson's case for translating *logikēn latreian* (Rom. 12:1) as "understanding worship," in *Engaging with God*, 174. Paul's own living sacrifice took the form of his gospel ministry: "For I am already being poured out as a drink offering" (2 Tim. 4:6; cf. Phil. 2:17).

77. Ibid., 73.

78. See ibid., 206.

79. "Every Christian gathering may be regarded as an earthly expression of the heavenly church" (ibid., 205).

80. Mark Labberton, *The Dangerous Act of Worship: Living God's Call to Justice* (Downers Grove, IL: InterVarsity, 2007).

81. Evagrius Ponticus, *The Pratikos & Chapters on Prayer* (Piscataway, NJ: Gorgias, 2009), 65.

82. The late James Montgomery Boice lamented the "thinning" of evangelical worship, which includes the decreasing presence of traditional elements such as the public reading of God's Word and pastoral prayers (cited in Philip Ryken, Derek Thomas, and J. Ligon Duncan, eds., *Give Praise to God: A Vision for Reforming Worship; Celebrating the Legacy of James Montgomery Boice* [Phillipsburg, NJ: P&R, 2003], 18–20).

83. Scott Hoezee, "The Pastoral Prayer as a Theological Occasion," in Alston and Jarvis, *The Power to Comprehend with all the Saints*, 337.

84. C. S. Lewis, *Letters to Malcolm: Chiefly on Prayer* (New York: Harcourt, Brace & World, 1964), 81.

85. "The 'vertical' dimension of communal participation in the Lord's Supper . . . naturally spills over into the 'horizontal' dimensions of lifestyle." Anthony C. Thiselton, *The First Epistle to the Corinthians*, New International Greek Testament Commentary (Grand Rapids: Eerdmans, 2000), 770.

86. John Jefferson Davis, *Worship and the Reality of God: An Evangelical Theology of Real Presence* (Downers Grove, IL: InterVarsity, 2010), 162.

87. Cf. Davis's call for weekly celebration of the Lord's Supper as the climactic event of every weekly gathering of the church (ibid., 114).

88. John Chrysostom, *Homilies on Titus*, on Titus 1:9.

89. The New Atheists (e.g., Christopher Hitchens, Sam Harris, Richard Dawkins) contend that religion should not be tolerated but exposed as deficient in rational and scientific argumentation. For an (intellectual) rebuttal, see Tom Gilson and Carson Weitnauer, eds., *"True Reason": Confronting the Irrationality of the New Atheism* (Grand Rapids: Kregel, 2013).

90. Stanley Hauerwas, *With the Grain of the Universe: The Church's Witness and Natural Theology* (Grand Rapids: Brazos, 2001), 210.

91. Dietrich Bonhoeffer, *Life Together* (New York: Harper & Row, 1954), 30.

92. M. Robert Mulholland Jr. and Marjorie J. Thompson, *The Way of Scripture: A Small-Group Experience in Spiritual Formation* (Nashville: Upper Room Books, 2010).

Notes to Pastoral Perspectives for Chapter 4

1. Kevin J. Vanhoozer, *The Drama of Doctrine: A Canonical-Linguistic Approach to Christian Theology* (Louisville: Westminster John Knox, 2005), 31.

Contributors

GUY A. DAVIES trained for the ministry at the London Theological Seminary and obtained a BA (honors) in theology with Greenwich School of Theology. He is joint pastor of Providence Baptist Church (Westbury) and Ebenezer Baptist Church (West Lavington), both in Wiltshire, England. He is originally from Wales and is married to Sarah, and they have two teenage children.

KEVIN DEYOUNG is the senior pastor at University Reformed Church in East Lansing, Michigan. He studied at Hope College (BA) and Gordon-Conwell Theological Seminary (MDiv) and is currently enrolled as a PhD student through the University of Leicester. Kevin is the author of several books, including *Just Do Something*, *Crazy Busy*, and *Taking God at His Word*. Kevin and his wife, Trisha, have six children.

DAVID GIBSON (PhD, University of Aberdeen) is an ordained Presbyterian minister and serves at Trinity Church, Aberdeen, Scotland. His congregation and elders allow him furtive breaks to the library for various writing projects from time to time, currently on topics including baptism, Ecclesiastes, and the Synod of Dort. He and his wife, Angela, have four young children.

GERALD HIESTAND is the senior associate pastor of Calvary Memorial Church, in Oak Park, Illinois, and the executive director of the Center for Pastor Theologians. Gerald is a PhD candidate in classics at the University of Kent (Canterbury) and the coauthor (with Todd Wilson) of *The Pastor Theologian: Resurrecting an Ancient Vision* (Zondervan). He and his wife, Jill, have three children.

JASON B. HOOD studied at Reformed Theological Seminary and earned a PhD in New Testament from Highland Theological College and the University of Aberdeen. He and his wife, Emily, and four children live in Moshi, Tanzania, where Jason pastors an international congregation, St. Margaret's Anglican Church. His academic publications include articles in the *Journal of Biblical Literature* and *Bulletin for Biblical Research*, and his most recent book is *Imitating God in Christ: Recapturing a Biblical Pattern* (InterVarsity).

BILL KYNES received theological degrees from the University of Oxford (MA), Trinity Evangelical Divinity School (MDiv), and the University of Cambridge (PhD) before becoming the pastor of Cornerstone Evangelical Free Church in Annandale, Virginia, where he has served since 1986. His dissertation was published as *A Christology of Solidarity: Jesus as the Representative of His People* (University Press of America). He is married to Susan, and they have four sons, three daughters-in-law, and seven grandchildren.

JOSH MOODY (PhD, University of Cambridge) is senior pastor of College Church in Wheaton, Illinois. His books include *Journey to Joy: The Psalms of Ascent* (Crossway), *No Other Gospel* (Crossway), and *The God-Centered Life: Insights from Jonathan Edwards for Today* (Regent College Publishing). He grew up south of London in England and is married to Rochelle. He and his wife have four children. Josh blogs at GodCenteredLife.org, where he also posts his sermons.

WESLEY G. PASTOR is founding and senior pastor of Christ Memorial Church and founder and president of the NETS Institute for Church Planting, both in Williston, Vermont. After earning an MBA from Miami University in Ohio, Wes obtained an MAR in theology from Westminster Theological Seminary (Philadelphia) and an MTh in Scripture and theology for practice from the University of Wales. Wes and his wife, Sue, have five grown children and two grandchildren.

CORNELIUS ("NEAL") PLANTINGA JR. (PhD, Princeton Theological Seminary) is a theological educator, writer, and preacher who has cohosted seminars for preachers on "Reading for Preaching" for over a decade. The fruit of the seminars is in his *Reading for Preaching: The Preacher in Conversation with Storytellers, Biographers, Poets, and Journalists* (Eerdmans).

JIM SAMRA is senior pastor of Calvary Church in Grand Rapids, Michigan. Jim holds a BS in mechanical engineering from the University of Michigan, a ThM in New Testament and pastoral ministries from Dallas Theological Seminary, and a PhD in New Testament from the University of Oxford in England. He is the author of *God Told Me* (Baker Books), *The Gift of Church* (Zondervan), and *Being Conformed to Christ in Community* (T&T Clark). Jim and his wife, Lisa, have four children.

OWEN STRACHAN (PhD, Trinity Evangelical Divinity School) is assistant professor of Christian theology and church history at the Southern Baptist Theological Seminary and Boyce College. He is the president of the Council on Biblical Manhood and Womanhood and the director of the Carl F. H. Henry Institute for Evangelical Engagement at the seminary. The author of seven books, he is married to Bethany and is the father of three children.

MELVIN TINKER trained for the ministry at Wycliffe Hall, Oxford, and read for the Honor Schools of Theology at the University of Oxford (MA Oxon). He is the vicar of St. John, Newland, Kingston upon Hull, Yorkshire in England. He is married to Heather, and they have three grown-up sons and six grandchildren. His books include *Intended for Good: The Providence of God* (InterVarsity) and *What Do You Expect? Ecclesiastes for Today* (Evangelical Press).

KEVIN J. VANHOOZER (PhD, University of Cambridge) is research professor of systematic theology at Trinity Evangelical Divinity School. Previously he taught at New College, the faculty of divinity of Edinburgh University. He was ordained as an elder in his local Church of Scotland and at the national level served on the church's Panel of Doctrine. He is the author and editor of sixteen books, most recently *Faith Speaking Understanding: Performing the Drama of Doctrine* (Westminster John Knox). He is married to Sylvie, and they have two daughters and one son-in-law.

TODD WILSON is the senior pastor of Calvary Memorial Church, Oak Park, Illinois. He is a graduate of Wheaton College (BA, MA) and the University of Cambridge (PhD). He and his wife, Katie, are the parents of seven children, three biological, four adopted. Todd has authored several books, including *Galatians: Gospel-Rooted Living* (Crossway) and *Real Christian: Bearing the Marks of Authentic Faith* (Zondervan).

Scripture Index

Subject Index